Teaching / Discipline

TEACHING / DISCIPLINE

A Positive Approach For
Educational Development

Charles H. Madsen, Jr.
Clifford K. Madsen
The Florida State University
Tallahassee, Florida

EXPANDED SECOND EDITION
FOR PROFESSIONALS

ALLYN and BACON, Inc.
Boston • London • Sydney

Library of Congress Catalog Card Number: 74-7672

Printed in the United States of America

ISBN: 0-205-04413-1

Third printing . . . June, 1976

To our parents—lifelong teachers,
unwitting behaviorists,
wonderful people

CONTENTS

PREFACE

This edition of *Teaching/Discipline* expands considerably the original book and also includes revisions incorporated in *Parents/Children/Discipline: A Positive Approach*. It is written especially for the teacher and prospective teacher and is intended as a teacher's guide in the use of behavioral principles relating to classroom discipline and subject matter presentation.

This edition is presented in four parts. Part I is organized in question and answer schemata designed to help clarify the central issues that have arisen from the authors' interaction with children and teachers in the public schools. Part II represents a selected summary of scientific and professional practices deemed relevant, transferable, and directly applicable to classroom teaching. Part III treats the effect of teacher responses on student behavior. Part IV provides a learning and observational manual designed to augment class experiences. A Bibliography of Books and Articles and a Glossary are also provided for the convenience of the reader.

It has been the intent of the authors to present this material without excessive technical terminology. We assume that involved terminology is not warranted in an introductory text and initially offer only the Greek *apologia* to explain the manner by which we disregard, oversimplify, redefine, and generally abuse classical antecedents in order to effect communication with the teacher. A Glossary is included, however, with explanations especially written for those with little background in behavioral research, to serve as a transition from this volume to the published research found in scientific journals.

We are deeply indebted to the researchers whose studies are summarized as Scientific Applications in Part II and more specifically to their unnamed scientific progenitors. We are hopeful that this edition will not only stimulate the beginning of greater efficiency in the classroom but will also provide an impetus for teachers to take fuller advantage of the benefits being produced through scientific research.

PART I

TEACHING AND DISCIPLINE

CHAPTER 1

TEACHING

The Art of Discipline

A FIRST DAY?

As she approached the school, she wondered why all schools look the same. Why couldn't someone be imaginative enough to disguise the telltale landscape and those separate rows of windows that indicate the time-honored concept of individual classrooms? Why were all the buildings that didn't look as though they were designed by school boards called experimental? What about those experimental programs, anyway? Were there communities that really cared enough about education to pay for all that? It was obvious this wasn't one of them. Notice the dull color of the paint; that quonset hut must be new, but what a poor excuse for an education site. Oh yes, that must be a "portable classroom"—a nice euphemism for lack of planning or no money. Money—this job didn't pay that well. Why was she here? Parkside had a better program, or perhaps she should have stayed in school. The graduate assistantship could have come through, and why even teaching? But, then, why think about all that nonsense anyway? This is the day, the first day for the students. She felt her stomach skip and her throat tighten. Was it this bad for everyone? As she walked into the building she wondered why those other people looked so calm? She stopped at the restroom. Wasn't this the third time since getting up this morning? Her eye caught a limerick, and she wondered why students were not as creative in class as they were on bathroom walls. Why were all these wild thoughts so vivid this morning? "Okay, face it—you're scared. Just plain scared!"

Her mind wandered back to a discussion with her father. There was a teacher—fifty years in the public schools. She had gone home especially to talk to him those two weeks before the planning session. She remembered her father smiling as she asked him many questions. She remembered getting no answer day after day until the last evening before she was to leave. "But Dad, what makes a good teacher?" After a long silence his brow furrowed, and his bright eyes narrowed.

"Every teacher goes out with a golden apple of knowledge he wants to share, but some students don't want that knowledge, and their attitude becomes, 'Teach me if you can, but I'll make it as difficult as possible.' Remember two things. When it is as difficult as it can be, don't give up. You might think that it can't get worse, but it does when you give up. The second thing—*you can't even get started without discipline.*" As she looked in the mirror after washing her hands, she became suddenly angry with her father and that discussion. Clichés, clichés, that's all she needed now—two more clichés: "Don't give up. Discipline." She remembered her professors—more clichés. "Motivate the students, captivate their interests, recognize individual differences." Great, great, but how? No one ever says how. As she approached her room, she felt guilty about her thoughts concerning her father. Sure, he *was* a fine teacher—years of compliments, awards, letters, everything a teacher could want. Then she suddenly realized that even her father didn't know why. The art of teaching—is it really that elusive?

When she got to the door, she stopped for a long moment. "Please, please let me be a good teacher." Then it happened. The door knocked against her face as a student ran out. She watched the boy run down the hall as the students inside started laughing. She wondered quickly if she should go after him. "No, I'd better stay with the class." She had rehearsed an opening joke; that wouldn't work now. She felt her face flush as she tried to decide what to do. After a long pause she muttered, "Good morning," but instantly realized that it was a mistake when one boy softly mimicked her. Again, laughter. Why, oh why couldn't she start all over again? She looked over the sea of faces. Where was a friend? She quickly picked up a piece of chalk and began writing her name on the board. With her back turned, she tried frantically to think of some way to gain control. She heard some small noises, then a girl's louder voice, "Quit it." Was it this way everywhere? From kindergarten through twelfth grade, was this what teaching was all about? Finally she spoke. "Students, please take your seats so we can get started. As you notice on the board, my name is . . ." Two boys were standing in the back. "Would you please take a seat?" The class turned around to see. One boy shrugged "OK, OK, OK." The class burst out laughing again as he dropped into a chair. The other boy started to move, but then stopped as the class laughed louder. "Would you please sit down!" The class grew quiet. She felt her heart pounding and mustered the sternest look she could. Student and teacher were now staring at each other. The classoom became not only quiet but also electric as students looked from teacher to troublemaker and back again. After these thousand years of silence, she heard herself say angrily, "Now, you sit down this instant." Nausea came into her stomach as she watched the muscles tighten in his face, his lips curl sarcastically. "Are you goin' to make me?"

A first day?—A large majority of teachers who leave the teaching profession do so because of what they term "inability to discipline."

WHOM DO WE DISCIPLINE?

Many teachers and parents have drawn an artificial line between love and discipline. Some make a point for love; others for discipline. The wise think they solve the problem when they say it must be both, and all are perhaps equally naïve. The essential point is that we as teachers must understand precisely what we mean by love and/or discipline before we begin. The major thesis of this book is that we must be concerned with how people *act* in order to assess behavior or to define terms. How should one know that he is loved but by the way people act toward him: what they say, how they look, how they touch, in a word, what they *do?* Attention, praise, kind words, and physical contact have been demonstrations of love for years. Who cares if someone loves them if they never receive evidence through attention, contact, or by the spoken word? While it may be possible for love to exist in total abstraction, most people are not content with such little personal involvement, especially over an extended period of time. One often hears the phrase "I'll love you no matter what." This is a good example of a meaningless cliché.

Indeed very few, if any, really believe it. "No matter what" remains an abstraction that has little meaning until it is violated. That is, I'll love you until you desert me, find someone else, treat me cruelly, violate my trust, and so on. Most people do stress overt behaviors. A more fitting phrase would be, "I'll love you if you love me," or "I will act in certain ways with you if you reciprocate."

If such statements as "I will love you no matter what" were left to idle verbalizations, there would be little problem. When they are taken seriously, they pose a very serious problem, especially for the teacher. The teacher is led to believe that teachers should "love" everyone; and, if this were not damaging enough, the teacher actually may believe that one should continuously *act* as though one loves all students "no matter what."

One behavioral principle that we try to teach all youngsters is simple. "When you do nice things, nice things happen to you. When you do bad things, bad things happen to you." Even allowing for slight inconsistency, if we truly believed and taught in a manner conducive to this end, we would shortly have many "nice children." Yet we violate this principle regularly by teaching a child the exact opposite. This simple principle has several perversions: (1) when you do *bad* things, *nice* things happen to you; (2) when you do *nice* things, *bad* things happen to you; (3) no matter what you do, *bad* things happen to you; and (4) no matter what you do, *nice* things happen to you (i.e., I'll love you no matter what). Perhaps the saddest ramification of this last distortion is that while we treat the child, for a time, as though all behavior deserves nice consequences, we finally give up on the child at that precise point when he has finally learned exactly what we have taught him: No matter what he does, nice things happen to him. We often crown this educational achievement with statements such as: "I've tried everything with that child and nothing works," or "I just can't get through to that student."

Discipline is a process whereby certain relationships (associations) are established. It is a way of behaving, conducive to productive ends. First, it must be taught; secondly, it must be learned, i.e., internalized. Love, if it is to transcend mere rhetoric, is a way of feeling and acting conducive to productive ends. Most teachers enter the teaching profession because they truly love children (care about students) and desire to help each child achieve his greatest potential. Sometimes, people are paid to care about children, i.e., to teach.

The most difficult aspect of human interaction based upon love is to develop the ability to withhold overt acts of love (ignore or disapprove) to help the child learn appropriate ways to behave. When love responses have been previously established, we can then respond in similar kind to the child's behavior. Thus, when a child demonstrates inappropriate responses and we actively withdraw our overt responses of love, we teach the child that his behavior is not deserving of love responses from us. The most tragic mistakes of the teacher occur when the courage to act in this way is absent, and the teacher succumbs to "giving in." The child learns a perverted association: "When I do bad things, nice things happen to me." In the long run everyone suffers, but mostly the child. The authors call this teaching behavior "mistakes of love." More appropriately it might be classified as "naiveté" or "lack of courage." It is amazing, although apparent, that some people actually believe that all responses should be regarded with overt acts of love. The teacher who really loves a child will have the courage to teach him proper associations. We discipline only those people we care about; others we leave alone.

Whom do we discipline?—We discipline those we love.

WHY DO WE DISCIPLINE?

Discipline is necessary if a child is to function properly. All teachers have had the unfortunate experience of observing either children or adults who are "undisciplined." We usually refer to such people as lacking motivation, apathetic, rowdy, or even mean, spiteful, or deceitful. But why are children so classified? How do they become this way? If self-discipline is to be internalized, then how is the child to achieve this attribute? The answer is obvious—*it must be learned.* Teachers often "beg the question" by stating that it must come from *within* the child. Yet how does motivation or proper attitude get "in"? Even if some of it is "in," will it continue to serve in the future? These are questions with which the teacher must deal.

Particular patterns of responses are learned from the external world (external stimuli). If a student is "motivated," it is because he has leaned to associate certain behaviors with certain outcomes. Motivation does not exist in a vacuum; it is a way of behaving. If the teacher wants a student to behave in a certain way, the teacher must structure the student's external world (i.e., control his environment) to insure that the desired behavior will be learned. The disciplined child is a child who (1) has learned to behave socially in appropriate ways, and (2) evidences proper patterns of responses to academic work. If either one of these two general categories of behaviors is absent, we usually say the child "has a problem."

We must be very careful, however, not to designate many behaviors into one or two artificial categories and believe that we have solved the problem because we have arbitrarily classified it or given it a name. People react differently to various situations (stimuli). It is very interesting to take a pencil and paper and write down one's own responses in different situations. How do we act in the classroom, in church, at a football game, in faculty meetings, swimming, buying shoes, driving a car, getting out of an invitation, giving a speech, eating dinner, listening to beautiful music, listening to an argument? Yes, we act differently, we dress differently, we talk differently, we even smile differently in these diverse situations. If we were brave enough to list our most secret behaviors, we would probably shock those very people who believe they know us the best. It is unwise to classify behaviors into artificial categories that have to do with only a few situations. Perhaps some justification can be made for general attributes (e.g., apathetic, aggressive, boisterous, unmotivated), but such classification is extremely deceptive and at best provides only partial information.

When learning is defined as a change or modification of behavior, then three things are necessary: (1) experience, (2) discrimination, and (3) association. For instance, a child is presented with a color (*experience*). After a time the child *discriminates* the color from other colors or the absence of the color. Through repetition, an *association(s)* is made with the color, e.g., red. The child may then evidence in some behavior, most often previously learned, (e.g., pointing, matching, speaking, thinking) that he has learned the color. The preceding definition of learning based on reinforcement theory does not quarrel with mediational processes in learning or with the material to be learned. It proposes a method to promote or expedite this learning. In short, it asks, "How should we go about teaching the color red in the best possible manner to insure correct association?" If the child responds favorably to teaching, we assume the external stimuli are associated in a way that functions as a reward for the child. But what if the child does not respond? Then we must restructure the external environment so that the child does receive proper motivation.

How, then, are we to get the student to learn the many behaviors that will provide him with the necessary skills to achieve a productive life? Within the complexity of his many responses to his external environment, we must structure his external world to provide proper relationships to be learned. We should not sit back and hope that motivation will somehow "get inside." We must structure the environment to provide the student with proper associations. Discipline must first be external; it must come from *without* before it can be from *within*.

If learned relationships to external stimuli are conducive to productive ends, the child will have a repertoire of responses that will serve him well as he meets the constant challenges of life. If he is capable of following rules, acting enthusiastically regarding new learning experiences, staying on task during work periods, relating well with other children, knowing when to be assertive and when to acquiesce, indeed, if the student has learned to respond appropriately to many specific situations, then we say he is well disciplined.

Why do we discipline?—We discipline to provide for social order and individual productivity.

WHY DEVELOP TECHNIQUES FOR DISCIPLINE?

Mother has just finished teaching and expects her seventeen-year-old son to pick her up from school at approximately 4:00 P.M. Four arrives, no son; the woman begins to pace a little and thinks about a hectic afternoon and a ruined supper. At 4:15 she becomes a little angry and thinks about her inconsiderate offspring. Four-thirty P.M. arrives, and, in spite of trying to do something else, she begins to worry about his whereabouts. Between 5:45 and 6:00 (while many transportation invitations are turned down) he is imagined dead in a car wreck, attacked by someone, unconscious in the hospital, picked up by the police, drunk in an alley, and sundry other things, all of which are negative (she has even lost her concern for transportation). Is it not strange that during these times most people do not imagine that the son happened to get involved with a classmate and forgot the time while having a wonderful talk, enjoying a pleasant stroll, meditating by oneself while looking at flowers in the park, or perhaps shopping for a surprise gift for this mother.

What, in reality, is the problem in this case?—the mother who is "fretting and worrying" about possible catastrophic events or a seventeen-year-old son who is late. One real problem is the worry. When pick-up time arrived, if mother had waited a reasonable amount of time and then arranged other transportation, there would probably would have been much less of a problem.

Unfortunately, it happens frequently that many people reinforce in themselves (substitute husband for son and re-read the above example) and others the very worst. We often train ourselves to worry unnecessarily about terrible things that only might happen, such as potential loss of loved ones or inability to succeed in the future, for example. The problem is actually the worry itself, especially when nothing is done to change behavior. Many people manage systematically to increase their worrying and, in addition, convince themselves that it is being done because of sincere concern for themselves or others.

It would seem that every person should be trained explicitly to prepare for forseeable emergencies. We should teach ourselves and our students specific actions to deal with emergencies (what do you do when a stranger tries to pick you up; if the school is on fire and smoke is coming from somewhere; if you are hurt on the playground; if you are offered narcotics, and so forth). Potential situations should be handled by these procedures with extensive role playing. Correct responses may then be based on the values of teachers and should clarify just what "normal" routines ought to be in emergencies. When values *and* techniques are specified and practiced, then if worry occurs, it is definitely not conducive to happiness. When we are waiting for an errant progeny it is too late to do any teaching, and if some accident has occurred there is nothing to be done until we are notified.

Worry, or "depression," usually represents nothing more than statements to oneself or others indicating that we "feel sorry for ourselves" and as such are definitely unproductive. Frequently as we interact with each other and begin to spill our tale of "worry and woe" the "significant other" listens intently, nods his head, exhibits a "sad" face, and asks questions. Generally, as he performs for us this disservice, we pretend he "understands" and therefore reinforce our "depression." Teachers might tell friends, each other, and especially their students that if one wants to feel sorry for oneself and waste precious time instead of *deciding* what to do and then working on the problem, he had better find someone else with whom to talk. Often those students who "forget" or refuse responsibilities just want to spend time complaining. The only negative or similar comments we might allow are comments that honestly report the facts of a situation and are followed by an attempt to give a statement about what behaviors are being planned to alleviate the problem. "Tell me what you intend to do; do not give me your problem." It is astounding to find how fast "depression" and "worry" are relieved in children (and even adults) when no one pays attention and the negative verbal behavior is either punished or ignored while positive solutions are praised. "Is that what you will do next time? That's excellent. Let's pretend that I'm the other person and you show me what you will do."

Also, a teacher might be careful not to reinforce young children for crying following refusals and thereby reinforce the self-fulfilling prophecy that if only one could cry it out of his system, he would feel better. The teacher might focus on delineating the problem without reinforcing emotional responses and, at the same time, take the responsibility of planning a program with the student that will lead to behaviors incompatible with feeling sorry for one-self (doing something about the problem when possible or engaging a "fun" activity when it is not).

Worry, anger, and other responses are expected in human beings of all ages. These responses might be acknowledged immediately, and then followed by behavioral techniques to change the emotion. They should not be reinforced or worried about. Young people should be trained to deal with a problem immediately, rather than receiving reinforcement for extended periods of worry. Hence, the focus becomes one of solving the problems that have produced the worry, anger, or crying (depression) and thus of acting one's way into a new way of thinking.

Why develop techniques for discipline?—To stop worrying and start acting.

WHAT DOES DISCIPLINE TAKE?

In his book *Profiles in Courage*, the late President Kennedy stated the problems of the politician in facing the demands of continued popularity as opposed to having the courage to act on his convictions. Politicians are not alone in this dilemma. Few people realize the pressures placed on the teacher for conformity and popularity. This pressure comes not only from community, administration, and parents, but also from colleagues and students. It is much easier to go along, not to rock the boat, to reevaluate one's position, especially in relationship to touchy problems. It is difficult to discipline the principal's daughter, to face the disapproval of a colleague, or to face an irate parent who insists his child has been dealt with unfairly. It is difficult to explain a simple behavioral approach that rests on direct immediate consequences and not on intriguing deceptions. It is difficult to explain to a parent that *the question of discipline is not one of strictness or permissiveness but one of cause-and-effect relationships*. It is difficult to help a child when the behavioral interactions required may be different from those the teacher and the child are used to, or to show parents how they can help their child when the teacher's instructions to them require opposite parent/child interactions than those previously established. It is difficult to live through the first day of a new program in discipline without giving in. It is most difficult to lose, for a time, the favorable response of a child.

Every teacher is faced with the problem of wanting to be liked. In our society, being liked is an admirable goal. It is indeed easy to demand a little less, hoping to be liked. Some people's desire to be liked is so great that they will suffer mild contempt for the privilege. Furthermore, even though most adults do not hesitate to have a young child suffer momentarily for long-term gain (medical inoculations, drudgery of learning hard concepts), many teachers do not have the courage to initiate a program of discipline that, although it might cause temporary disruptions in classroom routines, would in the long run really benefit the child. In addition, most teachers come to realize that even the most sophisticated students often evaluate a teacher's worth in terms of entertainment: "Here I am; what do you have for me today?" The value of discipline is not likely to be cherished immediately. "Why didn't I have anything fun to do today?" Students may even respond negatively when entertainment is not forthcoming. Nevertheless, it should be remembered that the *teacher's approval* is probably more important to the student than vice versa. The teacher's personal approval is one of his most effective rewards. *It should not be given indiscriminately.* Indeed, one never does a person a favor by letting him get away with anything, especially anything he does not like about himself. If the teacher really knows in what he believes, then he is much less likely to succumb and give in to pressures.

What does discipline take?—It takes courage.

CHAPTER 2

DISCIPLINE
The Way to Learning

WHAT DO STUDENTS BRING?

At any time in the chronological development of a child, we are prone to look back into the child's history to explain his present behavior. Thus, we have a never-ending spiral that assesses blame backwards (behavioral antecedents). Colleges blame the public schools, public schools blame the home, and the parents blame each other or the child's progenitors *ad infinitum*. If we must stop somewhere, let us stop at birth, although some theoreticians would impute motives even before the child's first breath.

Let us consider three oversimplified, but rather characteristic, views of the child at birth: (1) the child is born good, (2) the child is born bad, and (3) the child is born neither good nor bad. If, as some believe, all children are born basically good, then the child's only impairment is the corruption of living. The teacher's goal would be not to corrupt his basic nature. This would not be difficult in a Utopian world. Perhaps it would not be difficult in the world in which we live, if all behavioral responses were predestined to be ideal. A problem arises, however, when "good" is specifically defined; each person's idea of the "good" does not always coincide with another's. A second problem arises for the teacher if the child has somehow been previously corrupted, for now the child evidences both "good" and "bad" behavior.

The second view proposes that children are born bad. In this case, the teacher's job would be to correct the basic "badness" so the child could be "good." Again we have a problem with definition of "bad," especially without reference to specific overt behaviors. It is curious that many people who believe in this "badness" theory assume quite readily that children's good behavior is *not* learned, while insisting that all bad behavior (usually referring to moral transgressions) must be eliminated. Regardless, if the child has learned any "goodness" at all, he will still present a mixture of both "good" and "bad."

The third position postulates neither good natures nor bad and, therefore, assumes that all behavior is learned. The teacher's job in this situation simply would be to teach the child correct responses. Nevertheless, in all probability the child will have picked up some "bad" behaviors. Therefore the same situation will be evidenced as with the other two positions. The important question regarding the foregoing is: What should the teacher do? Regardless of philosophical orientation, should the teacher's responses to the student be any different? Indeed, *is it possible to start teaching at any other place than where the student is?* Suzy, Sam, and Fred all cry out in class—Suzy because her sweet nature has become corrupted, Sam because he was born bad, and Fred because he learned some wrong associations. Does it really matter what their personal history or the teacher's philosophy has been? The important question seems to be: What does the teacher do? Even if we could solve the philosophical problem or know the particular individual reinforcement history of the individual children, they are still crying.

All too often, we pretend that we have solved a problem because we can find some explanation for the behavior (e.g., high score on "problem child tests," family depravity, "bad seed," terrible first-grade teacher). Unfortunately, the children will continue to cry out in class until we do something to change their behavior. During the very first processes of interacting with the child, the teacher should be able to find out just *where the students is both socially and academically* and assess the extent of any specific problems. These first encounters with the student provide all that is needed to determine where the student is. The teacher then can begin to do something concerning the student's behavior. A long involved analysis of the child's "personality" is generally both unproductive and unnecessary.

What do students bring?—Does it really matter?

WHO HAS THE RESPONSIBILITY?

Teacher X has a problem child. In almost every situation when he should be acting one way, he is acting another. His behavior gets constantly worse in the classroom until the teacher can take it no longer. The teacher passes the point of feeling frustrated and, if honest, may even admit dislike toward this source of constant irritation. The teacher decides to find out just what the student's problem is. The student is sent to the school counselor; and, after an extensive battery of tests, social reports, and time-consuming investigation, the teacher gets an answer: "Johnny is a problem child." On every one of the "problem child tests" (personality scales), he scored extremely high. Not only did all the tests indicate that he was indeed a problem child (exhibited deviant associations), but the report concerning his home life was even worse. Teacher X cannot help feeling pity when learning of his terrible home situation and begins to wonder how he survived as well as he did. Teacher X discusses his home situation with a close colleague, and both of them marvel anew how bad life for some children can actually be. Johnny continues to be a problem child, but now his teachers *"know why"* (high test scores—bad home). He may not even finish school; he will probably grow, continually harassing society, and end up in other more stigmatized institutions. "How tragic, but what can a teacher do with a home situation like that?" Obviously nothing—the end?

Man is a complex organism. Among his many attributes is an ability for exceptional discrimination. All of his empirical senses provide a basis for remarkable differentiation. At an early age (approximately six months) he can even discriminate between people. He learns what to touch, what not to touch; he learns a complex language system; he learns auditory and visual discriminations; he learns to yell at playtime and to sit quietly during individual study periods. He even learns to "put on" a teacher if he can get away with it.

Of course Johnny is a "problem child." That is precisely why he was sent to the counselor. And how unfortunate that there are many "diagnosticians" whose major purpose is merely to confirm the prognosis of the teacher—if their terminology can be understood. Johnny will continue to be a problem child until someone teaches him different responses. He has learned a repertoire of responses to deal with his world—the more antisocial his home environment, the more deviant his responses.

The truly pathetic situation is that no one will teach Johnny and change his behavior. The only place in which there is some hope for Johnny is the school. Yet many teachers quickly abdicate responsibility once his history is known. *Johnny can discriminate.* He can be taught new responses to deal with that other world outside the home. He can learn to read, write, spell; he can learn new rules of social interaction and thereby break the cycle of his past. If cooperation is possible, he can even learn these responses *in spite of a bad home.*

It is not easy to deal with the Johnnies. They take time, energy, and a disciplined teacher. All the Johnnies do not change for the better or even survive; yet for these children, *the school is their only hope.*

Who has the responsibility of discipline?—The teacher.

WHY DON'T THEY LEARN?

Many questions have been raised in relation to why Johnny does not learn. Too often criticism comes from proponents of these questions who do not support their queries with long-term constructive encouragement or positive alternatives. Instead, scathing indictments are directed toward those very teachers who spend a great deal more time worrying about why Johnny does not learn than do most of their critics. In every aspect of learning, continued educational research is needed to ascertain and remediate learning difficulties. Yet at present, the teacher must strive to do the best job possible.

Education is stressed in many ways in our culture. Quite naturally we often assume that everyone wants to learn. We even assume that they want to learn what we want them to learn. Some children do not want to learn. Others do not want to learn what we think they should learn. The reaction of the teacher should not be amazed bewilderment (the teacher's reinforcement history includes values established through sixteen years of learning) but a basic question: *Why should they want to learn?* Children must be taught to be motivated, curious, or interested, i.e., to establish their own goals. Some children are just too comfortable to learn. Why should one learn to speak, let alone properly, if all desires are met without this particular mode of verbal symbolization? Why should one learn a difficult mathematics system if gazing out the window passes the time better? Why should one practice spelling if one finds that more attention is received when one wanders around the room or writes a "special note" or plays at the pencil sharpener or does any number of things more fun than spelling?

The desire to learn must be taught. Appropriate learning behaviors, such as good study habits, paying attention, or working for long periods, must be established that provide some reward for the child. No thinking adult wastes time in idle pursuits that are difficult and meaningless. How can the teacher expect everyone automatically to want to learn, especially when it may represent work?

Why don't they learn?—Because the rewards of learning have not been established.

WHAT IF IT'S WORK?

Most people assume the responsibility of work. We speak often about work: working on a project, going to work, getting work, finishing our work, and so on. In education, we often speak about school work; yet we have a burgeoning conspiracy to turn work into play. Most teachers realize the importance of making work as palatable as possible. If students get excited about work they consider it play, and everyone is much happier. The ingenious teacher has striven for years to turn work tasks into play. The great teachers are those who are able to elicit a pleasurable response toward the most rigorous pursuits and make the most difficult task pleasant.

Unfortunately, our highly technological society has turned many work tasks into play without a corresponding discipline toward those tasks that entail "work-work" as opposed to "play-work." The young boy's delight in finally building his very own plane wanes appreciably when he is confronted with a common battery-propelled toy that flies instantly and can be purchased for a fraction of his allowance. Most adults will testify with pride to those endeavors that represented, for them, hard work and true discipline. Patience, repetition, and arduous industry are still required for long-term achievement and happiness in almost every activity of life. Yet we have more and more "instant avenues to success." The problem for today's teacher is not only in structuring "play-work" (technology is providing wonderful aids in this regard), but also in teaching the necessary discipline for *long-term* rewards as well (i.e., establishing maturity). If behaviors conducive to long-term goals are not acquired early, it is much less likely that they will be acquired at all. If a child does not learn early in life to work hard and long for specific goals, then he is not likely to change as he grows older.

Today's schools provide many extracurricular activities with almost as much turnover as there are activities. The possibilities for diverse activities become greater and greater for the growing child. Almost all his time can be spent changing from one activity to another. Consider specialized fields such as music, art, and creative writing. How many times have we said as adults, "I'd give anything to play like that, or to paint like that, or to write like that?" Of course, we would not. We know what it would take in time and effort. The irony is not that we do not often have such skills; it is that we do not have enough understanding concerning the importance of long-term skill acquisition to appreciate the skill evidenced in others and to insure that our students stay with an activity or task long enough to master it.

This should not indicate that the teacher ought to take pride in being a punishing taskmaster. It is extremely unlikely that students will want to continue learning, past formal experiences, if their true "reward" for learning (working) has been merely to have the gruesome experience stop. The secret for developing the capacity for work is to stretch the length of time between *rewards* so that the student will strive through some misery to seek long-term goals, e.g., a college degree, writing skills, continued reading of great literature, ongoing enjoyment in listening to music masterpieces, or an insatiable desire for scientific precision.

Thus, the problem for the teacher is not only to make work tasks pleasurable but also to develop the capacity for work. *This constitutes a process of teaching for delayed rewards over an ever-increasing temporal span.*

What if it's work?—Then work it must be and the capacity for work must be developed.

19

WHO DECIDES WHO DECIDES?

Power, by whatever name, is one of the most contingent of all behavioral interactions. When referring to physical objects in motion such as a moving automobile, few people question the power of the car to damage a person's body, only the intent, skill, or responsibility of the driv . Some people seem to assume power over other people; others manifest power that is thought to be given to them, such as the power of elected officials to enforce laws. Literary sources often portray individuals seeking power—others avoiding it. Most of us, however, choose either to relabel power (especially in this age of the euphemism) or to pretend that power actually does not exist. We prefer, instead, to talk about responsibility, duty, or rights, as in the discussion in the beginning of Chapter 2. Perhaps most of us would like to believe that no one has power over us and that anything we might say or do would be only by choice. Often it frightens us to realize the power that does exist—especially the power we, as teachers, have over our students. Not only are teachers often bigger, at least for a little while, but most of us also think faster than youngsters and, therefore, are able to "snow" them. We work through a problem quickly, we know many important facts, we answer a difficult question—*the awe and respect of students is very reinforcing.*

Often we use our sophistication to manipulate students into doing something that they do not think about: "Would you like to put your materials away before lunch?" We do not ask them, "Do you choose to be messy?" It seems that most often we do about "everything in our power" in order to impose our value systems on them: "Choose any story you wish . . . then we will take a vote on it . . . you must take turns . . . now we do want our room to be clean don't we . . . of course you don't take money from another student without asking . . . etc." It would appear that most of what we just assume to be the correct thing to do represents the imposition of our value system on the student. Probably almost all of our "acculturating process" actually represents the imposition of values, whether these values come from home, school, community, church, or elsewhere. Who decides a child should read, write, spell, not steal, or finish school? Teachers who have not thought about these activities as "imposition of their values" sometimes become extremely upset and state, "Well, how do you expect the child to live a happy life or get a decent job or anything else!" "I can't sit by and watch that child hurt himself." Do you expect me to be silent when I know she's ruining her life by quitting school now?" At the same time, teachers may say, "I do want my students to think for themselves and I want them to establish their own values. . . ."

Teachers who do not make clear differentiations in their own thinking about who decides who decides, probably will have many problems. Teachers are charged legally with the imposition of certain values concerning student's behavior; many would say that ethically teachers ought to be responsible for much of the student's behavior, and some would say, that is precisely what being a teacher is all about; to instill within each child the selected best from the cultural heritage in order that following school the young adult will function productively. Regardless, *who decides* is not nearly as difficult a question as *who decides who decides,* for most teachers truly want their students to be able to make decisions for themselves. Teachers therefore decide to allow their students to decide certain innocuous things; *When* do you choose to clean up your materials? *Where* can you be reached in case we need you? *Which* assignment do you choose to do? *Who* is it you will be leaving with? *Where* do you want to do your work?

Teachers who start early to teach students precise definitions and specific allocations of power will be better able to deal with apparent inequities as situations arise. Some teachers refer to this structuring as "defining limits" or specifying acceptable behavior regarding such aspects as social relationships, propriety, honesty, and so on. If a person is taught early that a teacher is not always right or an all-knowing genius; that teachers do not always evidence perfect taste, heal all wounds, or even "understand" some of the latter ones, then the child might not have to be so disenchanted when he discovers our feet of clay. If a teacher states precisely what power resides with the teacher and what decisions rest with the student, perhaps the student will continuously strive to earn more privileges rather than feel sorry for himself because he is not permitted to do something. Issues regarding power are not easy to think through nor are their behavioral contingencies easy to establish. Much like issues concerning "fairness," problems relating to power rest on the values of all individuals concerned. Even some adults have not established who decides who decides in regard to major issues concerning themselves and their employees or even spouses. Also, in the upper grades teachers and students must often decide to *agree to disagree* if harmony is to prevail. Anger is not reinforced in relation to those decisions that we definitely believe are not ours, only with those decisions that we believe ought to be within our own and not someone else's control.

Who decides who decides?—As far as the student is concerned, the teacher.

CHAPTER 3

LEARNING
The Modification of Behavior

WHAT IS BEHAVIOR MODIFICATION?

Behavior is a common word that is used casually in referring to many things. The term *behavior*, as used in this book, refers to *anything* a person does, says, or thinks that can be observed directly and/or indirectly. Besides referring to specific cause-and-effect relationships, behavior modification includes techniques for changing behavior. A well-behaved student is one who behaves in ways that the teacher and/or student thinks are appropriate to the situation.

Principles for teaching (shaping appropriate behaviors) should not be confused with other issues. It is important that techniques of behavior modification not be confused with the use of these same techniques to implement specific values. Many teachers regard the questions concerning *why*, *what*, and *for whom* as certainly more important that *how*. Therefore, after teachers have decided what is to be learned and why it is to be learned (i.e., chosen their values), a behavioral approach will help them go about teaching it. Also, we encourage teachers to involve their students in these decisions whenever possible. There is a simple rationale to explain the efficacy of behavioral approaches. Simply stated, *behavioral change must be based on a reason*: people work for things that bring pleasure, people work for approval of loved ones, people change behaviors to satisfy desires they have been taught, people avoid behaviors they associate with unpleasantness, and people act in similar ways to behaviors they have often repeated. The behavior modification approach

23

actually comes from science and represents nothing more than simple cause-and-effect relationships.

The scientific study of human behavior, or the study of cause-and-effect relationships, should not be confused with other value choices. It is generally useful to distinguish between values and techniques in this regard. For example, a positive value that many teachers hold is to teach youngsters to read (even if the desire to read is *not* present in the child). Once this value, and perhaps its imposition, has been determined, then the teacher may choose various techniques to effect the desired reading behavior. Application of a behavioral technique to establish this value would be concerned with the effects of academic feedback and/or other reinforcements to the youngster concerning shaping desired responses in relationship to the target goal (reading). It is important to realize that many values other than reading might be decided on by the teacher as well as other techniques to effect whatever values the teacher may choose to teach. Some teachers choose to have students raise hands for teacher attention, some do not. Some teachers specify "quiet time", others prefer the "hum of industry." Some teachers choose "communication" as a value and spend a great deal of time in verbal interaction, others spend more time helping students interact with subject matter. Behavioral techniques can be used to implement any or all of these values. Students may be taught (reinforced) to raise hands, not to raise hands, or any combination depending upon the situation. The "hum of industry" can be implemented or "quiet time" or again any combination depending on the circumstances and activity of the teacher. Students can be taught to communicate or to remain silent or to alternate during various time periods.

Techniques also can be used to implement what many teachers consider extremely negative values. Children can be effectively taught to cheat, lie, hit, steal, and even to "hate school." Of course, the selection of any technique represents a certain value choice; also, if one chooses a behavioral technique, then the determination of appropriate "reinforcers" represents an important value choice. However, basic social and academic values to be taught to students should not be confused with issues concerning techniques for implementation. It is assumed that Jesus, Socrates, and Moses were effective behaviorists. So was Hitler.

Some teachers might say, "Yes, but isn't that a cold approach?" Certainly not. Even though behavior modification is based on scientific principles verified in the laboratory, it is largely the nature of material to be learned that represents important value choices. Actually, because of its consistency and simplicity, behavior modification effected and applied by means of contingent reinforcement (approval-disapproval) represents a very kind and understandable system to students of all ages. The behavioral scientist who observes a classroom activity can behaviorally classify almost everything that goes on, regardless of how well the teacher may understand principles of reinforcement. Cause-and-effect behaviors are always present. For example, some teachers do not realize the effects of their own behavior on their students. Some do not understand the effects of their own approval or disapproval and do not realize when they are being sarcastic: "Why don't you just stand up and tell the *whole class*, Jimmy?" Whereupon Jimmy does. In such a situation teachers may unwittingly reinforce a wrong behavior, and problems are created because the student is not really sure of the teacher's meaning. Being taken literally is the price one pays for using sarcasm. The applied behavior analyst could demonstate how teachers might be more effective in the application of the teacher's own values through the judicious use of behavioral principles. Many teachers are actually surprised to learn how closely they approximate a fairly comprehensive behavioral approach. After being apprised of behavioral principles, many teachers exclaim, "Why, that's what I've been doing all the time!"

What is behavior modification?—Techniques for implementing values.

ARE VALUES IMPORTANT?

Techniques of reinforcement can be so effective that every teacher ought to choose the important values (ideas) to be implemented within the classroom. Yet even though many teachers believe in positive ideas, it becomes more difficult to specify the observable behaviors that students engage in when being in harmony with an ideal. It is therefore useful for teachers to structure commonly used words that represent "ideas" or abstractions into specific, overt, demonstrable behaviors. (It should be noted that even though all "words" may merely be symbolic representations, some words seem specific in their elicitations and, therefore, are preferred in describing empirical relationships. Thus, "verbalizes facts" appears more quantifiable than does "honest.") For example, most teachers believe students ought to be kind, communicative, cooperative, and sensitive. Yet for these ideas to be effectively taught, they must be described in greater specificity such that they can be counted, i.e., follows rules, helps others, talks with others, looks into eyes, shares materials, asks for help, and so on. Thus, we must define our values (ideas) so that the way a student acts provides some overt evidence as to whether the student is developing the particular patterns of responses that we desire. Every teacher usually demands this type of behavior in reference to academic responses (assessments, questioning, tests, etc.) yet does not specify as accurately concerning social behavior.

A specific behavior is anything a person does that can be observed and measured. Ideas are generally made more and more behavioral as behaviors are specified in observable and measurable terms. This is obviously the first step in structuring any learning sequence: to define values so that the behavior of the student provides some indication that learning is taking place.

Specificity is the key to behavioral analysis; the teacher must deal with each specific situation in order to teach proper associations. Differentiating in terms of one specific behavior that occurs in a particular situation is the key to effective teaching. In academic work, most teachers would not begin to classify children into all-inclusive categories. Because May is excellent in spelling does not mean that she is exceptional in geography. Similarly, because she does not constantly disrupt the class does not necessarily indicate that she is "well behaved." Is it not curious then that when referring to the many social skills necessary for any student we tend toward greater classification with much less justification considering the magnitude of individual responses to social stimuli? These classifications are even more undesirable if we consider that in our complex communication, we have developed a certain "shorthand" for descriptive purposes. Words such as "love," "motivation," and "discipline" are used as though these words had meaning apart from specific situations. Of course, it would be extremely difficult "to communicate" without using such a "short-word system." We should remember, however, that each situation is different. Every particular word refers to many different behaviors, and each association merits specific consideration. We must remember to deal individually with each behavior. When speaking of the "value of discipline," we should specify both the nature of each situation and the response. We must specify exactly *what* happens as well as *when* it happens. We must specify the nature of the situation (antecedent), the response, and the consequences that follow. When we use the word "discipline" as an abstraction referring to many separate behaviors, we must realize that definitions of discipline must be specific to certain behaviors if the teaching of proper associations is to take place. Disciplining a student, therefore, means something different in each situation if procedures are to be effective.

Are values important?—Important enough to be specified.

IS SUBJECT MATTER DISCIPLINE?

The recent impetus for behavioral theory, or reinforcement theory, or whatever one chooses to call behavioral principles, substantially grew from the works of B. F. Skinner. Programmed instruction is the best-known result of this initial work, as are many other "systems" relating to teaching, treating mental illness, behavioral research, and clinical psychology. Indeed, the entire rationale concerning behavior modification is that behavior is *learned*. What behavior? *All behavior, including knowledge of subject matter.* Behavior thusly defined includes emotional responses, attitudes, reading, listening, talking, looking into the mirror, liking a person, wanting to talk out a problem, hitting, being frustrated, staying "on-task," getting "off-task," responding appropriately to the desires of a teacher, not responding to the desires of a teacher, all "good" behavior, all "bad" behavior, disturbing the class, being well behaved, being excited about learning, hating to learn, and so on— and so on—and so on.

The most basic reductions of reinforcement theory as an explanation to assess a person's responses at any given time are: (1) a person has *not learned*, (2) he has learned correct associations, or

(3) he has learned *incorrect associations*. Exactly the same principles are used to teach subject matter as are used to teach appropriate social skills. If the teacher wishes that children have a real desire to learn a particular subject matter, then the teacher must structure the external environment so that children will seek the structured contingent rewards for their academic work tasks. After initial manipulation, the rewards for learning will often come from the reinforcement of the learning material itself. Incidentally, this is precisely what most teachers do when they initially make a "game out of learning." The children become enthused concerning the game *per se*, not realizing that it is a subtle hoax to stimulate effective learning. Curiously, some teachers who try desperately to make learning "fun" also say they reject any "manipulation techniques." The teacher's job is to structure learning experiences. This structuring process involves manipulating the environment conducive to effective learning, whether the goal be simple word associations, complex problem solving, or concept formation. It would seem that the teacher should structure as wisely as possible. One should know the subparts necessary to any complex academic task (e.g., English, reading, algebra, history) and structure the situation in order that each child have a "rewarding learning experience." It can be seen that even in reference to our most cherished clichés, we allude to behavioral manipulation. It appears paradoxical for the teacher to reject manipulation when this is indeed the essence of the teacher's work.

Behavioral research demonstrates that if subject matter can be: (1) geared to the student at his own level, (2) presented in logical sequences, with (3) appropriate feedback concerning correct/incorrect responses, and (4) contingent rewards given for successive approximations toward defined goals, then *learning will certainly take place*. Exactly the same principles apply to teaching subject matter as apply to teaching social skills.

Is subject matter discipline?—Yes.

ARE GOALS NECESSARY?

Traditionally, teachers have been instructed to prepare goals for the classroom. This usually represents at best a vague effort, often after the fact, to state formally what the learning experiences are aimed toward, i.e., what should be the learning outcome. The major problem regarding goals is that they are usually stated in euphonious clichés: "preparation for life in a democracy," "to develop language skills," "to understand the different cultures of the world," "to develop an appreciation for music." What do such statements tell us? How will we know if we have achieved our "goals"? Some educators try to solve the problem by proposing even greater hierarchies, including ideals, objectives, attitudes, and so on. The problem is easily solved, however, if the teacher states goals that represent overt behavioral changes. How else, incidentally, will we know that a student "understands" or has "learned"? The teacher must also decide whose goals are to be effected in the classroom: students', parents', administrators', and/or what combination.

Goals stated in behavioral terms are not only manageable, they are also clear in defining the behaviors to be learned: "to be able to verbalize the Constitution, giving dictionary definitions to all words found therein," "to recognize on a map the separate nations of the world," "to differentiate between ten musical compositions," "to have a reading, writing, and spelling vocabulary of three hundred selected words." If concepts such as appreciation, understanding, or attitudes are to have meaning, these meanings should be defined in ways conducive to assessment. It is very easy to hide behind such generalities. *If children are to learn, then we must know precisely what it is they are to learn, how to teach it to them, and also how to determine if they have learned it.*

Are goals necessary?—Certainly.

CAN BEHAVIOR BE MEASURED?

The most critical difference between a behavioral approach that pinpoints specific observable and measurable behaviors and other approaches to teaching is the keeping of behavioral records. Evaluation of any procedure instituted to induce learning (behavioral change) is virtually impossible without records. Formal and informal tests have always provided indications of academic behavioral change. Other indices of measurement, especially relating to social skills, have previously seemed to defy classification. It is possible, however, for the teacher to learn to assess social behaviors. Most individuals are not content to rely on a "feeling" concerning their bank balance, and the bank is even less likely to honor an overdrawn check because the depositor "feels" his balance is sufficient. Is it not then curious that when we deal with the social behavior of human beings (who are more important than bank balances) that we change rules, reinterpret contingencies, and fail to follow through because we "feel the behavior is really not that bad" or "feel" that the student *really* understands the regulations or perhaps "feel" that we may lose the student's respect? Measurement and specific records are crucial for accurate evaluation. The only difficulty regarding these classification procedures is that they take a little extra effort. Behavior *always* occurs in time intervals. If teachers are to know whether a particular social behavior is getting worse, better, or staying the same, the frequency of behavioral occurrences must be recorded *across time within specific time intervals*. Recording procedures are not difficult; one needs only paper, pencil, and some measure of time (clock).

For example, what if undesirable behavior in a particular classroom is defined as standing up? Instead of doing work at their desks, many students walk around the room. The first procedure would be to know precisely how much standing up is taking place (baseline). If this recording does not take place and the teacher first takes remedial steps, then it will not be known if the undesired behavior is getting better, worse, or staying the same. It may seem that this procedure is not necessary. "Why not just tell them to sit down and see what happens?" The problem, however, arises *in time*; i.e., some children will sit down immediately, but in the *long run*, more children may stand. Even if the standing students do sit immediately, the problem is not solved; it continues with the other students across time. To conduct this type of recording, the teacher might assign a work task and then sit so as to see every student and count the number of children standing in a number of time intervals. After a few days of recording the number of such behavioral occurrences on one individual or on many, the teacher has some idea of the *frequency of the behavior*. A checklist at the students' desks also can be very effective.

The same basic procedure may be used for speaking out, talking, playing at desk, looking out the window, cheating, hitting, sharpening pencils, disturbing others, crying, or any other conceivable behavior (adaptive or deviant). It is important for the teacher to have a record for *social behaviors* as well as for academic behaviors. A general "all right" or "satisfactory" will not accurately assess a student's academic progress over a period of time; neither will it accurately assess his social behavior. The time these behaviors take to record does not compare to the time a teacher spends repeating instructions (nagging). It is interesting that one of the author's experimental teachers who absolutely refused to "waste my time with all that book work" was recorded by experimental observers saying, "Now stop that talking," 143 times in one morning session. Checklists for assignments of any kind can be developed by the teacher with a minimum of effort. This process represents nothing more than extending principles of record keeping across time within a specific time interval (for example, twenty minutes, A.M., P.M., during rest time, one day, one week, playtime, lunchtime, ten seconds, ninety seconds, or any other time period).

Can behavior be measured?—Easily.

CHAPTER 4

BEHAVIOR
The Contingent Result of Life

WHO HAS THE PROBLEM?

Perhaps one of the most challenging tasks for today's teacher is to know what literature to believe and what to reject, which authority to respect and which to discount. In our multi-media world we seem to have experts by the score with almost as many admonitions as we have experts. Presumably many teachers are saying, "Why don't they get together; one says that what is right today was wrong five years ago; what we got when we were growing up was wrong, or another says right, depending on whom you read." The authors are sympathetic to this situation, especially since we are constantly dealing with children's problems. It is our strong belief, however, that many problems may be "caused" by reading and acting on some of the pronouncements of these articles. Teachers come to us constantly with "students' problems" that did not exist before an article was read. We are reminded of the man who worried for twenty years about latent fear until the day he decided he didn't have to worry about it as long as it was latent.

It would be less than honest for the authors to presume that we are not admonishing, we certainly are. Foremost, *severe problems should be referred to a professional*. It is our hope, however, that teachers will rely on their own honest assessments concerning most teaching. Honesty, we believe, is the key to behavioral assessment by teachers, even if students are being advised by professionals. If teachers are honest, they will not *give their problems away and absolve responsibility*. The attribute of giving a problem away is perhaps best illustrated by a graduate student in psychology who was presenting to a graduate seminar the case of his first interview with a client. He was apologizing to the other members of the seminar, "I guess I fouled up, about the only thing that I established was that the client had a studying problem." One of the older supervisory clinicians rose to his feet, smiled at the young man, picked a little at his pipe, and addressed the group, "As some of you know, I was an obstetrician before I changed to clinical work and I didn't learn much from my previous medical specialty that had immediate transfer. I did learn one thing, however, and that concerns *who's pregnant!* You know, the very first time a patient came to me, the one thing I tried to firmly establish was who's pregnant. 'No *we're* not going to have a baby, your *husband's* not going to have a baby, your *mother's* not going to have a baby, your *family's* not going to have a baby—you, *you're* the one who is going to have a baby.' It was always amusing to me to see some of the expectant mothers trying to give their problem away. Of course, it was they who had to eat properly, receive proper supplements when needed, go through the entire pregnancy, and so on. Son, if within that first session with your client you established *who* had the problem, you succeeded. If your client left realizing that her studying difficulty was not her roommate's problem or her professor's problem or her mother's problem or her counselor's problem, then you are well on your way."

Assessing who has the problem requires a teacher to decide if the problem really belongs to the student or to the teacher. Often both have a problem: the child, an inappropriate behavior that needs to be changed; the teacher, the responsibility to do something about changing it. Many times, however, problems are not real. The only problem extant is in the head of the teacher. After reading some article, the teacher begins to worry about a potential problem, sometimes to the extent that interaction with the student actually creates the very problem suspected. Certainly, these self-fulfilling prophesies should be avoided, especially when the suspected problem cannot be specified as a behavior(s), but refers only to an idea such as inferiority, lack of love, need for expression, need for individual achievement, or other non-specified ideas.

Even though the teacher is advised to be self-reliant in behavioral assessment of childrens' problems, the teacher also should be careful not to believe that deviant behavior is *just a stage* the youngster is going through. If by "stage" we mean precisely the length of time that a child exhibits incorrect responses until something is done to insure improved behavior or if by "stage" we mean those behaviors quite proper for one age but not for another, then there is no cause for concern—still no reason for alarm. If, however, we refer to "stage" in an attempt to *give away our problem* hoping that in some mysterious manner a day will come (perhaps next year) when the problem magically goes away, then perhaps we should re-evaluate. The very young child's occasional "disrobing" should not be equated with his occasional "lie." The social contingencies operating within his environment will probably modify his clothes wearing behavior, but probably not his lying. The student who occasionally "has severe temper tantrums" should not be equated with the student who occasionally "forgets to clean his desk." The younger who occasionally "refuses to share" is not comparable to one who "plots to put himself up by secretly bringing physical harm to another." Classifying problems into "normal stages of development" should be done with great care.

Teachers should realize that even seemingly innocuous behaviors probably change because something or someone in the student's environment interacts to modify specific responses—that is, some problems will extinguish when the older students' environment sets up different expectations; other problems will intensify. The extent to which these problem behaviors change is determined by the cause-and-effect relationships interacting within the student's world, not by magic or by just growing older. There are many old liars, adults who constantly lose their temper, and teachers who scheme in putting down other colleagues, workers, or even friends to get ahead. Being honest, there also are adults who are exhibitionists, extremely messy, and even stingy.

Who has the problem?—You decide.

WHAT IS THE PAYOFF?

A traditional viewpoint prevalent in education is to focus on many antecedent events (reinforcement history) leading toward a particular goal, rather than to focus on the manipulation and control of the present environment. This procedure of looking backward is both unproductive and unnecessary, especially when it absolves the responsibility of solving the current problem. When the teacher wants to change a specific inappropriate behavior, the teacher must first *find the payoff* and eliminate it if possible. *Behavior that goes unrewarded will extinguish.* The teacher must watch the student carefully to determine the payoff. The teacher must also recognize individual differences; the payoff is often different for each child. For example, students A, B, and C talk in class. After many warnings the teacher finally sends them to the principal's office. This is just exactly what student A wanted; he finally managed to goad the teacher into "punishing" him. Student B just liked to make the teacher angry. Every time she got stern it just "broke him up." He knew he was bothering her, and he enjoyed her distress: "Wow! She gave me such *stern* looks." Student C did not care about the teacher or the principal. He did care about students A and B. Everytime he talked, they listened. On the way to the principal's office, student A filled the others in. "Listen, the principal sits you down and comes on with all this 'You've got to be a good boy' stuff. Man, the last time I was in there I really had him snowed. Besides, he never checks to see if you go back to the class, so we're out for the day." When students A, B, and C return to class, they will continue to talk even more.

Teachers who have simple monolithic explanations for all maladaptive behaviors will be generally ineffective. "All those children need is a little love." "The thing they need is a good, hard paddling." "Get them out in the world; then you'll see how they do." "They need a decent place to live." "They need someone who truly understands them." The problem with this type of analysis is that it is neither differentiated nor individualized. There are some children who may fit one, none, or all of the above categories, plus countless others. The one thing that children exhibiting inappropriate responses *do* need is a teacher who can find the payoff. What is maintaining the problem, keeping the behavior alive? If the payoff can be found and completely eliminated, then the behavior will gradually extinguish—*if consistency is maintained.*

A word of caution is important. One significant result of eliminating the payoff is that the undesired behavior will get initially worse before it gets better. The teacher must remember that the student has learned a behavior to get what he wants. When the "reward" is abolished, he tries even harder (i.e., the inappropriate behavior increases) before he comes to realize that there is no payoff. After this initial surge the behavior will extinguish. The initial rise is extremely important to remember. Many people give up during the storm before the calm, "Oh, I've tried ignoring, but the baby cried even louder."—Of course.

Finding the payoff can be difficult, and sometimes the payoff comes from a source that the teacher cannot control (parents, peers, physiological reactions, internal imagery, etc.). Nevertheless, many problems can be solved by cutting out the "reward."

What is the payoff?—That which keeps the behavior alive.

P.S. Give student A a task much less desirable than talking in class, preferably where he cannot talk to anyone—isolation. Smile at student B when he is not talking; absolutely ignore him when he is. Move student C to the other side of the room away from students A and B, or make him apologize in front of the class, or perhaps even punish students A and B and tell them it's not their fault but student C's.

WHAT CONSTITUTES REWARD?

After a teacher determines the payoff for a particular behavior and eliminates it, the teacher will soon observe a decrease in undesirable behavior. Sometimes this alone is all that is needed. Yet more often other things in the students' environment (stimuli) must be controlled; that is, other contingencies must be structured in order to discipline. It is better to start with just one behavior and not try to eliminate everything simultaneously, unless the teacher has a great deal of help and can initially devote available time just to social behavioral problems. If many undesired behaviors are prevalent throughout the classroom, the teacher is advised to establish a priority and start with the inappropriate behavior that most interferes with learning. It is extremely important that teachers deal with overt behaviors, not ideas (for example, "getting to work on time" as opposed to "a bad attitude about math"). It is also advisable to make up a set of easily understood rules for each activity. In making up the contengencies (i.e., structuring the rewards) the new payoff for *desirable* behavior (following the rules) must be known, tangible, and close enough to the student's own behavioral responses to motivate the student to seek it. Initially it is far better to give too much reward than not enough. The idea is to get the student "winning" as soon as possible. For general control in the early elementary years, words, contact, and expressions are highly effective; group activities and peer group approval provide powerful rewards for the adolescent years (middle school, junior high, and high school); material things and individual activities for young adults (junior high, high school, college). Various "token systems" are generally effective at all age levels and come closest to representing our own monetary system. For young students correct responses can earn "tokens" that are exchanged for tangible goods (e.g., most young children enjoy things such as toys, trips, playthings, or food). Tokens may be chips, papers, check marks, or anything convenient. Rewards earned for tokens should have specified values (i.e., colored paper equals five points, a ruler equals eight points, a commercial game equals ten points) so that students can receive tangible credit for exhibiting appropriate behaviors, such as following specific rules (written on chalkboard). Each student could have a small notebook marked by teacher, students, or both. At appropriate intervals (after study, before lunch, following discussion, etc.) the teacher marks the students' points. The teacher may begin a program by displaying rewards and asking the students which one they are working toward. Then the teacher may go over the rules. The rules should be written down in a conspicuous place and explained daily—at a time other than when they have been violated: We sit quietly during individual study. We raise our hand before we interrupt to talk. We stay at our own desk during study time unless given permission to leave. We respect others' rights, and property, etc. At opportune times, the teacher circulates and writes down the points. The very act of recording may be used as an effective control. It is critical for the teacher to try very hard to *catch the child being good* and reward him with points paired with words and expressions of praise instantaneously.

In the initial stages of control it is important to have the student achieve success quickly, after which the time between behavior and reward can be stretched for longer periods while continuing to pair appropriate personal responses from the teacher (words of praise, expressions such as smiling, and closeness such as positive touching). In time the personal approval of the teacher, and later, the student's approval of himself will probably be all that is needed for proper motivation.

This is certainly what most teachers desire; but in order to achieve this level of sophistication, one must start where the child is. Some children enter school with response expectations amenable to smiling, pleasing teachers, being obedient, etc. Other have to learn appropriate responses through more tangible rewards. Token systems may be set up at all levels of sophistication in preparation for adult employment.

One extremely effective technique for small children is the use of food (candy, juice, flavored cereal) as contingent reinforcement. The teacher may start the very first day of the new program with a "goodie" party. The teacher gives the students a treat and while the students are eating the teacher says, "We will have another 'goodie' party if you are quiet while I count to ten." (The teacher then counts aloud quickly, making certain they win.) After giving the candy the teacher says, "If everyone is quiet for five minutes we will have another party, but if someone talks we will not get to have one." Now the teacher sits back and waits; in all probability someone will talk, whereupon the teacher says, "Oh, I'm *very sorry*. Mary talked before our time was up; now we will not get to have a party. Maybe tomorrow we may have one if everyone is quiet." (Some children will think this is not "fair"). *Because the teacher does not get angry at Mary, Mary cannot give her problem to the teacher*. Mary receives the disapproval of the group so there is no payoff from the other children. Instead of interacting directly with Mary, it may be better to use vicarious reinforcement and modeling. To use this technique the teacher chooses one of the most well-behaved children and says, "I surely like the way Sheila is sitting so quietly. If everyone behaved like Sheila, we could have our party." Sometimes the teacher may wish to give rewards to those children who were quiet and not give anything to those who were not. (Mary may not think this is fair.)

The use of group approval-disapproval is very effective, particularly with older students. When activities are given or denied contingent on the behavior of all concerned, the children themselves will take the responsibility for discipline, and discipline will start to evolve from within the group. *Peer approval* is extremely important to teenagers. This is precisely the reason for such high "esprit de corps" in many group organizations such as band, athletics, social clubs, and gangs.

When teachers as well as the other students are taught to cut out the payoff for a particular individual's inappropriate behavior, the undesirable behavior will generally decrease. Of course, students may indeed be embarrassed after receiving such responses from their peers—so be it. It is precisely this contingent embarrassment that solves the problem. If students do not care what others think of them, then withholding of approval or verbal disapproval is not effective. It is the teachers' value system that determines what contingencies are to be used. Contingencies, in both approving and disapproving ways, that the teacher *can* use include:

1. Words (spoken and written-rules)
2. Expressions (facial-bodily)
3. Closeness (nearness-touching)
4. Activities and privileges (social-individual)
5. Things (token, materials, food, playthings, money)

Other than the rewards of the activity itself (sometimes there are none), these categories constitute the *entire resources* that the teacher has for structuring. Teaching should develop them well. (Study the examples and lists in Parts II and III.)

What constitutes reward?—That which the student will work toward.

IS THE WORLD FAIR?

For years, teachers have been advocating the uniqueness of every student. "All children are not alike," they say. "Each child has had many different experiences." "Children come from many different backgrounds." "They need individual attention." One would assume from this dedication to individual difference that teachers would teach differentially and meet the discipline problems of each student in a unique manner; but this does not seem to be the case. Most teachers also seem preoccupied with an *undifferentiated* concept of "fairness."

Children do not have a problem with undifferentiated "fairness" until someone teaches it to them. Usually it is taught by their parents, who manifest the same thinking as some teachers. With little hesitation, parents will talk at length about how different their children are. Equally without hesitation, they try as hard as possible to be "fair." Fred and Jane are different in many, many ways. They like different things, they respond differently, and one child is almost always older. Yet, when Fred gets to go, Jane gets to go; when Jane gets candy, Fred must have candy. If Fred receives a toy, Jane must, also. Fred and Jane learn quickly "Why can't I stay up late?" "Why don't I get to go?" "How come I don't get a present?" "Why does she always get the biggest apple?" Thus Mother and Dad spend a great deal of time and energy trying to be "fair." They also create much anxiety for themselves by not admitting that they do treat the other children differently and from time to time may actually even like one child more than another. These are all unnecessary attempts designed to solve the problem of undifferentiated fairness they have created for themselves. "But Fred, your birthday will come next month." "Jane, you see Fred is older than you; that's why he stays up later." "OK, if you're going to fight over who gets the biggest apple, neither one of you can have one."

People *are* different. Some are extremely different, particularly if they have physical or mental handicaps. It would seem that the kindest teaching behavior would be to instruct students in this regard—let them know that the world is not always "fair." Prepare them for the suffering they will endure because of others' mistakes. Let them realize from the beginning that their efforts are not always evaluated fairly. Help them understand that in a democracy the group often suffers from the actions of a few. Let them realize that occasionally they will be punished for things that they do not do. Teach them to understand that justice is an ideal, less often a reality. *Yes, and also instruct them to be just in their own personal behaviors, but not always to expect it from others.* Some of the gravest problems encountered by students come from an undifferentiated concept of "fairness."

Fairness is not a simple matter. Men have labored for centuries to ascertain "what's fair" in relationship to many different situations (laws). Within the academic realm, the teacher also works hard at differential assessment. Grades are assigned differentially as are special projects, reports, reading groups, and so on. Thus, *the teacher* establishes rules of academic discriminations (fairness?). How naïve, then, to equip the students with one social response the teacher knows will cause him problems as he matures. The teacher also loses a most effective technique (group approval-disapproval) when refusing to use the group in "shaping up" individuals, for to punish the group because of the actions of one individual or vice versa does not seem "fair." Ideally, proper interaction patterns will eventually evolve from within the group. Students will help discipline each other, not by punishing, or tattling but by ignoring, attending to what is proper; not talking or listening to each other when they should not be, and generally *staying on-task*. Discipline, however, will not evolve from the group unless the teacher uses the group to bring particular individuals "in line."

No one wishes to be punished for another's actions. In cooperative societies, however, this goes on continuously. If elected officials in a representative government decide to enter a war they do not ask the individual student. If a student in the bud of maturity is drafted, fights, and subsequently dies in battle, then who suffers? Why not prepare students for the world in which they live, where everyone's life is affected by the acts of others? Let them realize early that if we are to function socially then we must take the responsibility and the results of interacting with others—we do not stand alone. Help students understand that "what's fair" is a big question relating differentially to almost all aspects of life. Do not prepare them for certain disillusionment with one undifferentiated response. Help them discriminate between the many issues of fairness and be prepared to deal realistically with these discernments. Students may then come to accept life's inequities while doing something to change many of them, rather than feeling sorry for themselves because they find some aspects of interaction "unfair." When the teacher deals with fairness, optimism need not suffer—only naïveté.

Is the world fair?—Sometimes.

CAN CONTINGENCIES BE STRUCTURED?

The basic premise of reinforcement teaching is to arrange the stimuli of the external world to shape the behavior of the students—to structure the environment so that the student receives approval-disapproval reinforcements contingent on appropriate/inappropriate behavior. Therefore, *reinforcement teaching is the structure of approval and disapproval reinforcers, across time in precise intervals, to shape desired behavior toward specific goals.* Experimentation in learning demonstrates that: (a) If a student knows specifically what is expected of him and (b) he wants to do it, then (c) he probably will. The necessity for specific measurable goals (expectations for students) has already been mentioned. The crux of the problem rests with (b): arranging the contingencies of reinforcement so that a student will want to do what the teacher expects.

Five techniques used in structuring contingencies are:

1. *Approval* (rewards)
2. *Withholding of approval* (withholding rewards—hope)
3. *Disapproval* (punishment)
4. *Threat of disapproval* (fear)
5. *Ignoring* (not attending in any manner, verbal or non-verbal)

Approval is easily understood. Approval is anything that is generally thought to be related with "happiness": *Words* used as praise; *expressions*, such as smiling; *closeness*, such as embracing or touching; *activities* that are enjoyable; *things*, such as games, badges, food, trinkets, etc. Teachers must be sure, however, that what they believe is functioning as positive reinforcement is truly positive (some children don't like ice cream).

Withholding of approval (withholding rewards) is used when the positive reinforcer functions to produce "hope" for the attainment of a reward the next time when the behavior is improved. In a way, this procedure functions as "punishment" (disapproval), although with potentially greater effect for improvement and less wear and tear on everyone concerned. Teachers may also place the responsibility for improvement on the student and perhaps avoid negative emotional reactions directed toward themselves following punishment. "I'm sorry you didn't finish on time. Now you cannot go out to play. Perhaps tomorrow you will finish on time. Then you may play."

Disapproval is also easily understood. Disapproval is generally synonymous with what most persons term *unhappiness*. Disapproval comes in such forms as *words* when one is getting yelled at; *expressions* such as frowning; *closeness* when one is being hit or placed in isolation; *activities*, as when one is deprived of something he wants or made to do an unpleasant task; and *things*, such as feared objects.

The teacher must also be careful not to conclude too easily what constitutes disapproval. Students may often exhibit many inappropriate, maladaptive, and perverted associations. "I like to get spanked." "I enjoy making my teacher angry." Extreme disapproval (corporal punishment) should be used very sparingly, if at all. Perhaps the most important thing to be remembered about physical punishment is that if teachers decide to use it, *it should be strong enough to stop the behavior immediately and eliminate the problem at once,* otherwise teachers may only insure that the student will engage in similar behavior in the future and, therefore, punishment will probably intensify, especially if teachers become angry and do not realize that they themselves are contributing to the problem. Many children have been gradually conditioned to endure severe beatings, usually *without* a decrease in maladaptive responses.

Threat of disapproval (fear) should be used rarely, yet it is profoundly effective once the knowledge of disapproval is established. Individuals learn how to behave in order to avoid disapproval (unpleasant consequences): "I am careful when crossing the road to avoid getting killed." "I don't play with guns because I could get shot." "I study so I won't fail." Even though fear is an extremely effective suppressant of much inappropriate behavior, it does little to establish the joy of learning and living. Children (or adults) who are completely negatively motivated are usually tense, unenthusiastic, quiet, shy, passive, and generally fearful. Some of these children do eventually succeed, although this negatively motivated "success" usually comes at the high price of guilt, compulsiveness, generalized anxiety, and perhaps later, even ulcers.

Ignore—just that—Ignore.

The formula in Table 4-1 represents interactions for behavioral shaping.

Table 4-1

		Teacher Behavior				
		Approval	Withholding of Approval	Disapproval	Threat of Disapproval	Ignore
Student Behavior	Appropriate	Yes	No	No	No	No
	Inappropriate	No	Yes	Yes*	Yes	Yes**

* Unless payoff   ** Unless dangerous

43

The teacher is advised, if at all possible, to use primarily approval, withholding of approval, and ignoring in controlling behavior. There is some indication that these "positive approaches" can be more effective, but, more important, *much less damage can be done than through the use of extreme disapproval (punishment)*. This does not mean the teacher should be permissive. It indicates that as teachers structure the students' environment contingent on appropriate behaviors (that is, produce appropriate cause-and-effect relationships), they should diligently try to do so through the use of "positive" techniques and structuring incompatible responses. Withholding an overt love response seems much more kind than corporal punishment. Alternately, there are times when disapproval (punishment) might need to be used. Some maladaptive behaviors of children are much worse than the punishment it could take to eliminate them.

Can contingencies be structured?—They must.

CHAPTER 5

LIFE

The Structure of Activities in Time

IS TIME IMPORTANT?

Thank you, reader. Thank you for what? Thank you for reading the next paragraph. You have not read it yet? Oh.

Why is the preceding rather absurd? It is because the "thank you" comes before the fact. Therefore, it has little meaning and even less significance in modifying your behavior (except perhaps in creating confusion). In all research concerned with behavior, no one has ever been able to teach anything through the use of antecedent rewards. *Rewards must come after the fact.* Thus, we enter the most elusive aspect of teaching—time. All events take place in time. Benjamin Franklin has this maxim: "Dost thou love life? Then do not squander time, for that is the stuff life is made of."

One of the most basic differentiations of the growing child comes in his progressive sophistication regarding time. Even adults cannot really tell time, as evidenced by the chronoscopes we strap to our arms. Man's temporal span is exceedingly short, and our assessment of ongoing time becomes humorous (try to estimate a minute without counting to yourself)! Even with a minute you must "fill it up with something" in order to approximate the passage of time. Now consider these foolish temporal contingencies: One-year-old: "Baby knows I'll pick her up after I finish my work." Three-year-old: "Tomorrow we will go out to play." Six-year-old: "Be good, next week is party time." Nine-year-old: "When you get to eleven, you may join the scouts." Thirteen-year-old: "If you pass all your classes, you may have a car when you're sixteen." Sixteen-year-old: "You must graduate from high school if you expect to have a good life." College freshman: "Study diligently and you will be a good teacher." If these sequences sound long, try a few out on yourself just to see how close a contingent reward or punishment must be in time to motivate you. "One more drink and tomorrow morning, wow!" "You don't have the money—why not just charge it?" "Better stop this late discussion—8:00 A.M. comes early." "Better start studying—final exams in just two weeks." As you can see, your temporal motivation is not long at all. Of course you realize the necessity of working toward or avoiding all those things, but they are up there in time somewhere—not now—not close enough in time really to motivate *you*.

If contingent rewards/punishment for behavior are to be most effective, they should take place immediately; and *the teacher must always know, before the fact, just what the contingencies are to be*. With small children this is tremendously important. "Daddy's going to spank you when he gets home" is a typical example of a ridiculous contingency.

It is also important to correct any inappropriate behavior before it becomes full-blown—to nip it in the bud. The teacher who believes that a small disturbance "will get better" is right. It will get better and better and *better* and BETTER! Full-blown disorder is usually encouraged by hesitation and caused by self-deception. *Initial stages of control are the most important*. As the child matures, his temporal span will increase if he is taught proper behaviors while progressively lengthening the time between action and consequence. If the bag of oats is too close to the horse, he eats the oats; if the bag is too far away, he does not move. Time and the control of reinforcement schedules across time is imperative. Reinforcers can be delivered on many different schedules depending on the circumstances (fixed time, fixed interval, variable time, variable interval, or mixed). The job of the teacher is to meet the student where he is and then progressively take him to the point where he will be content to wait for longer and longer rewards while still exhibiting proper behavior (e.g., structuring progressive work tasks toward final grades). Actually, many people guard time more jealously than anything over which they have control. *The art of living evolves from the structure of meaningful activities in time.*

Is time important?—Time is life.

IS CONSISTENCY DIFFICULT?

If one were to take the principle *"Behavior that is partially reinforced is the most difficult to extinguish"* and asked to devise a system whereby he could make a million dollars through its use, one might come up with gambling. Gambling is an activity that represents partial reinforcement at its best. If a gambler knows he will always lose, he will not gamble. Obviously he cannot always win, so the trick is to structure the environment (e.g., set the odds in a machine or roulette wheel) so that he *wins* often enough to *lose* his money in the long run.

Such is the case with other behavior. The child does not remember the 1,321 times he went to bed at 8:00 P.M. He remembers the two times he got to stay up. The third grader does not really believe that the teacher will send him to "the time-out room (isolation) for ten minutes." This is already the sixth time the teacher has threatened and nothing has happened yet. The ninth grader cheated before and didn't get caught; why should he get caught this time? The college student has turned in late papers before; why should this professor be such a "hard nose?"

Inconsistency teaches just that—inconsistency. At best it produces gambling children, at worst large-scale mental illness. *The most difficult task for a teacher is consistency!* The teacher should plan how the contingencies are to be structured, make the rules, and *follow through.* The only thing that you teach a child when you break the rules is just that—to break the rules. How pathetic it is to observe children who have many severe maladaptive behaviors that have paid off and therefore allowed to fester for longer and longer periods because of partial reinforcement. It is much like *favorable* responses; we stretch the temporal spans between reinforcement to provide longer periods of productive activity. The reinforcement history of some childrens' maladaptive responses contains so much partial reinforcement that they will fight for weeks and months before giving up their learned behaviors.

Is consistency difficult?—It is the most difficult aspect of discipline.

IF AT FIRST YOU DON'T SUCCEED?

If behaviors can be learned, they can also be unlearned or relearned. Sometimes in our zeal to get through to our students, we make mistakes. Sometimes regardless of zeal, we make mistakes. The effectiveness of behavioral techniques with severe problem behaviors within mental hospitals and institutions for the retarded and handicapped should give us the courage to move forward. Behavioral techniques have demonstrated that even severely handicapped children can learn much faster and a great deal more than we previously believed possible.

Since it is impossible for the student to maintain two contradictory responses at the same time, the skillful teacher will program to elicit responses *incompatible* with inappropriate behavior. "Count to ten before you get angry; think before you begin your work; raise your hand before you talk; take three big breaths before you cry; speak softly so we can have a soft argument; now we are practicing good grammar; let's take a break so we can begin with freshness; I'll close the curtain so the outside will not distract us; let's put our other materials away before we begin the new activity," and so on. Severe disapproval (punishment) alone may stop inappropriate behavior, but it will not necessarily teach a correct association. The child who is hit with his spoon because he cannot use it properly will not necessarily learn proper etiquette. Similarly, the student who is punished for his faulty reading will not necessarily learn to read efficiently. The one child might shun the spoon; the other student may stop reading. Teaching the incompatible responses is perhaps the most effective behavioral technique because it constitutes a double-edged approach. Not only is the inappropriate behavior eliminated, but it is replaced by a correct response as well. Thus the student unlearns and relearns at the same time. It should be obvious that in this case appropriate responses are directly proportional to decreases in inappropriate responses. This procedure eliminates the need for much disapproval (punishment) and at the same time teaches correct associations. However, the teacher must deal with overt behaviors. *It is much easier to act your way into a new way of thinking than to think your way into a new way of acting.*

Four principles* for the teacher are:

1. *Pinpoint:* It is necessary to pinpoint explicitly the behavior that is to be eliminated or established. This takes place at many different levels relating to many differentiated behaviors. It leads to

* These principles were adapted from the work of O. R. Lindsley, "Teaching Teachers to Teach," a paper presented at the American Psychological Association Convention, New York, September, 1966.

a hierarchical arrangement of skills and behaviors based on expected specific behavioral goals. Do not deal with intangibles or ideas. If the behavior cannot in some way be both *observed* and *measured*, then you can never know if it has been either established or unlearned.

2. *Record*: List the specified behaviors in time intervals (seconds, minutes, hours, A.M., etc.) and thereby establish a precise record from which to proceed. Keep the record accurate. Do not guess; be scientific. As maladaptive responses are eliminated, or decreased, more time can be devoted to more productive learning.

3. *Consequate*: Set up the external environmental contingencies (including primarily your own personal responses) and proceed with the program. Contingencies include: approval, withdrawal of approval, disapproval, threat of disapproval, and ignoring. Reinforcement techniques can be: words (spoken or written), expressions (facial or bodily), closeness (nearness or touching), activities (social or individual), and things (materials, food, playthings, awards). Remember that when you ignore, behaviors often initially increase (sometimes for long periods) before they are eliminated.

4. *Evaluate*: Be prepared to stay with a program long enough to ascertain its effectiveness. Compare records after consequating with records taken before. Is the behavior increasing, decreasing, or remaining the same? Learn from your mistakes. And:
   "If at first you don't succeed . . ."—Well, you know.

WHEN WILL STRUCTURE END?

It is clear that the final goal of the education process is to provide the student with behaviors necessary for self-discipline. Indeed, persons whom we as teachers have the privilege to instruct and teach at some future time must be able to be independent. This is, perhaps, the end for which the beginning was made. The goal is achieved less often than most teachers would desire. Students sometimes graduate in ignorance, because of age, to find a job, go to war, but generally not because they have developed sufficient "love" for themselves and others to achieve a state of "independence." We hope that when they must leave for other reasons that then they will be independent. It seems important to insure that this goal is achieved, for when other conditions impinge on the youngsters' environment they must be prepared.

When an individual has learned from his past reinforcement history to arrange his values hierarchically, when he is able to work productively over long periods of time, when he is able to delay gratification, when he is able to be content with his own company and refrain from haphazardly seeking other individuals, when he is able to modify and control the environment that, in turn, controls him, then perhaps he has achieved an appropriate level of independence. Many problems arise in interpersonal relationships because one or more of the individuals are unable to exhibit any independent behavior. Additionally, some teachers are concerned with vague concepts of "togetherness" that somehow are supposed to develop positive values automatically. Like many ideas (as opposed to overt behaviors), these concepts are highly elusive. When teachers sincerely believe that children will turn out all right if only the child graduates or spends time with "good" companions this can be devastating.

It is necessary to specify both the overt behaviors that the individuals value in terms of "independence" and the precise amount of time necessary to effect goals (e.g., honesty, kindness, creativity, sensitivity, communication, spontaneity). Before structuring training for independence, teachers should: (1) assess specific values that they cherish and arrange these values in a hierarchical order from the most to the least important. The next step is to (2) define specific behaviors that relate to each of the abstract values, and then (3) teach these behaviors (values) following the behavioral model. The amount of time to be devoted to teaching as well as the time important to spend with certain individuals (alone or in groups) should be outlined.

"Independence," or lack of it, becomes a problem when individuals are unable to be happy when alone or sometimes even when with others. It would seem that everyone should learn to be happy under each condition, as both situations are considered important. Therefore, structuring specified temporal intervals is important. Individual students should be helped with programs that increase both independent activity and joint activity. Truly happy people seem to be those who are happy to be alone, perhaps even for extended periods of time when necessary (vacations, military service, etc.) and also very happy when with others. This condition is not accomplished by students becoming dependent on others to provide a little more life into an otherwise dull existence. Regular routines to occupy one's time can be developed in advance and be readily available when a person needs to be self-reliant. *When will structure end?—With independence.*

TEACHING—ART OR SCIENCE?

The question will continue to be asked: "What makes a good teacher?" We have all known some great teachers as well as others who wane by comparison. Analyzing teaching behavior is really no different from analyzing student behavior. Earlier it was stated that students must know what is expected of them and want to do it. Most teachers have at least a general idea of what is expected of them and also want to be good teachers. However, if they do not structure the behaviors to be learned, practice techniques of effective classroom control and subject-matter presentation, and maintain consistency, then they fail. Every principle relating to student behavior throughout the preceding chapters also applies to the teacher. It is more important, however, for the teacher to realize that *it is the teacher's responsibility* to insure that proper learning actually takes place—not the student's. How easy it is for some teachers to give *their* problem to the students. "They don't want to learn." "I can't wait to get out of this chalkboard jungle." "Why should I care if the students don't?" Perhaps the extreme of this attitude is manifested by some college teachers who judge their academic prowess by how many students they fail. The teacher who really cares will persevere. Through trial and error, the teacher will find better ways to stimulate students toward their optimum potentials. With or without a full understanding of behavioral principles, the teacher will come to find better methods of behavioral control and subject-matter presentation.

The ability to recognize individual differences and to structure a class environment with meaningful contingencies relevant to specific situations represents an outstanding accomplishment. However, good taste is also of major importance. The authors know of one seventh-grade teacher who controlled her class by having the most deviant children "participate in a mock wedding ceremony if they were very bad." When the children evidenced proper behaviors, they were then allowed to "get divorced." This disciplinary procedure was tremendously effective and used behavioral principles. However, it raises serious questions regarding the teaching of other associations.

Another teacher told of a technique she used with second-grade boys. "When a boy misbehaves, I make him wear a girl's ribbon in his hair." Does it work? Very well, but again we question the advisability of such insensitivity. It is ironic that this same teacher thought it "terrible" that parents were asked to send some children to school without breakfast occasionally in order to effect proper behaviors through *rewards* of cookies, cereal, and milk.

It is readily apparent that regardless of how many "behavioral recipes" are available, the insensitive teacher will still be found wanting. The art of being a good teacher seems directly contingent on the behaviors of the teacher as a person. Modeling effects assimilated through the influence of an outstanding individual are still some of the most powerful and far-reaching. Most teachers will allude to a special teacher in their past who influenced them tremendously, even to the point of going into the profession. The truly effective teacher will combine the science of behavior with the art of living to create that exceptionally rare atmosphere—an environment in which children not only take excitement from discovery but also learn to be nice people.

Teaching—Art or science?

SUMMARY

Teaching—The art of Discipline

Many teachers leave the teaching profession because they have not developed effective techniques of classroom control and subject-matter presentation. Even though some teachers believe that discipline refers to a continuum from permissiveness through strictness, it is easily observed that this is not the case. Effective discipline ensues from direct cause-and-effect relationships. Therefore, concepts such as spanking vs. loving, classroom freedom vs. dictatorship, expression vs. subjugation are extremely deceptive. Indeed, we discipline only those we love; social freedom can exist only within defined parameters; and self-expression, much like everything else, must be *learned*. The reason we discipline is to provide each child with behaviors necessary for individual productivity. Realizing that decisions determining what constitutes these basic behaviors (curriculum) are our responsibility, we should structure wisely and not deceive ourselves by stating that children are deciding all things for themselves. When we teach children to think (i.e., establish values, decide), we should do so with the express purpose of insuring logical mediational sequencing and not use the euphemism "thinking" as a rationalization to eschew the responsibility of our job. Every teacher should initially realize that the teacher's primary responsibility is to acculturate the child. Teaching a child to spell, read, write, as well as to be well behaved, represents the *imposition* of social and educational values that do not originate with the student. The teacher who states, "Oh, but that's not what I mean," obviously needs some personal remediation in thought processes to differentiate between those aspects of life that are definitely mutually exclusive and those that are not. Every teacher should know precisely what decisions are to be the student's and what decisions are to be the teacher's. If a teacher accepts this responsibility and does not try to "give the problem away," then children will acquire the basic learnings necessary to develop their own values. Regardless, one should realize that it takes a tremendous amount of courage to act on the basis of one's value orientation, whether he be student or teacher.

Discipline—The way to Learning

Learning necessitates experience, discrimination, and association. The first aspect of learning both socially and academically is to determine just *where the student is*. That is, to determine what behaviors currently are present and, therefore, to know precisely where to start. *Academic learning* involves structuring subject matter in easily attainable sequential steps beginning at the student's own level. In assessing *maladaptive responses*, the deviant behavior itself is the foremost concern. An involved history of how the student got that way is both unproductive and unnecessary. Academic assessment should take several days, social assessment several minutes. All too often, knowledge concerning a terrible home life, bizarre past experiences, or personality test scores provides the opportunity for some teachers to give up on the child because the teacher discovers a "reason" for the deviant behavior. If students are not "motivated to learn," then motivation must be taught before the teacher should expect it to be internalized; it must come from without before it can be from within. Desire for learning (motivation) is taught by establishing *rewards* for learning, first extrinsically, later intrinsically. Realizing that at some point learning usually represents work, the teacher must stretch the ratio of previously established rewards to motivate students through the difficult times. This represents a process of partial reinforcement to teach for long-term goals, i.e., establish maturity. The teacher also defines limits of acceptable behavior by initially deciding which decisions are to rest with the student and which with the teacher.

Learning—The modification of Behavior

Behavior modification is a process for structuring learning experiences to provide both fine discriminations and correct associations. However, the teacher must deal with specified overtly demonstrable behaviors if the teacher expects to know what has been learned. It has been demonstrated that if a student knows precisely what is expected of him and if he wants to do it, he probably will. Preparing expectancies for students necessitates the structure of goals. Instructional goals should represent definable overt responses that are realistic, manageable, and, above all, measurable. All behaviors, both social and academic, must be measured *in time intervals*. Precise and accurate records must be kept.

Behavior—The contingent result of Life

Behaviors are learned in time through contingent reinforcement. Therefore the teacher must structure the student's life experiences if effective learning is to take place. How much control is to be exercised depends on the values of the teacher (deciding who has the problem). *Reinforcement teaching is the structure of approval and disapproval responses, in time, to shape desired behavior toward specific goals.* Deviant behavior is often eliminated by cutting out the payoff; wholesome learning is established by instituting a payoff. The teacher must observe the student closely—paying particular attention to what happens immediately before and after a specified behavior—to become proficient in behavioral analysis. It should be remembered that when the teacher begins to structure or restructure environmental contingencies, problems of "fairness" arise. The teacher then must discriminate between many separate and related social and/or academic issues to decide what is to be done, i.e., what's fair. Approval-disapproval techniques for shaping desired behavior include every available personal response as well as all objects at the teacher's disposal: subject matter, words, expressions, closeness, activities, and things. Personal responses should be overtly practiced. Merely reading, discussing, and thinking about responses is not enough to develop these tools effectively.

Life—The structure of activities in Time

Everything happens in time; indeed, *life is time.* Temporal aspects of life are not only extremely important but highly elusive as well. Therefore, precise timing in delivering responses cannot be overemphasized. While temporal consistency is the single most important aspect of discipline, it is also the most difficult. In order to discipline effectively, the teacher must structure everything *in time.* Structural manipulation of the external environment is based on these steps: (1) *Pinpoint*—defining the *problem* behavior to be eliminated, the *new behavior* to be learned, or both (teaching incompatible responses). Pinpointing regarding *subject matter* is accomplished by structuring specific measurable goals; pinpointing *maladaptive social responses* necessitates defining deviant responses specifically in overt categories and observing the child carefully. These observations not only establish what stimuli are presently reinforcing undesired behavior but also provide clues for selecting effective reinforcers that can be used to establish other responses. (2) *Record*—assessing behavior quantitatively. It is imperative that accurate records be kept. Otherwise the teacher can never ascertain the relationship between the frequency and magnitude of the *old* social/academic, adaptive/deviant behaviors and the new. Records must be precise and recordings must be done *in time intervals*. (3) *Consequate*—controlling the external environment through the use of approval-disapproval reinforcers delivered contingently on time schedules to teach desired behaviors. (4) *Evaluate*—measuring the frequency of behavior to see if the behavior gets better or worse. Most often, thoughtfully prescribed contingencies decrease objectional behaviors from the original recorded level and/or increase desirable responses. If selected reinforcers are not effective, a new structure may be required and other contingencies established. Indeed, restructuring regarding all aspects of instruction should represent a continuous process toward greater refinement and increased teaching effectiveness aimed toward student independence.

Effective teaching takes much practice. Similar to other pursuits in life, the rewards of teaching seem both proportional to, and contingent on, thoughtful involvement, structured action, and continuous learning and evaluation. Hopefully, the end product of this teaching will be a person who is informed, who is individually productive and socially responsible, who has the ability to analyze, criticize, and choose alternatives, and who has a compelling system of values whereby he may actualize his life in a manner consistent with ever-increasing knowledge—in a word, a person who evidences discipline.

PART II

BEHAVIORAL PRINCIPLES APPLIED

CHAPTER 6

CHANGING WRONG
ASSOCIATIONS

The preceding essays comprising Part I were not presented to express maverick points of view. These issues were developed to prepare the teacher to deal with human behavior more objectively. It is extremely easy to make-believe, to pretend that behavior is mystical and that somehow children will learn the opposite of what they are taught. Are the fine, gifted students direct products of our inspired teaching, whereas the slow, mischievous, or dull students products of someone else? If we are honest, we must take our share of the grief as well as the joy. Perhaps the most frightening aspect of teaching is that behavior is most certainly learned, and, for this, we as teachers must take full responsibility. Pretending is easier, for discipline is an awesome challenge. We prefer to believe that the deviant child will somehow change—that his bad behavior is just a stage, or if only he could work it out of his system everything would be all right. We hope, but hope wears thin without positive signs of improvement. We struggle, we wait, we often become discouraged, and finally we realize that it is indeed a cause-and-effect world—in the long run we do "reap what we sow." After myths are laid aside; after the teacher stops worrying and starts acting; after personal beliefs, consistency, and individual responsibility are all in harmony—the teacher begins to teach. Subsequently, behavior becomes more predictable and effects of specific actions assured. As behavioral principles are practiced and applied, the teacher becomes confident that *wrong associations can indeed be changed.*

The following examples represent selected scientific and professional applications of behavioral changing. These excerpts are presented in a form that should be easily understood by teachers. *Scientific Applications* are summaries of scientific studies that have been published in journals or presented by researchers at scientific conventions. Sources for these reports are noted in the selected bibliography, with the example number following the reference. *Professional Applications* represent the attempts of "ordinary" teachers, parents, counselors, and others to deal with specific problems systematically. These examples are selected from the authors' files.

This format does not begin to do justice to the original reports. The thoughtful reader will not only seek other professional examples directly applicable to his own teaching situation but will also begin to read original scientific literature while trying to study carefully the cause-and-effect relationships obviously evidenced in behavioral research and writing. The Glossary of Behavioral Terminology (pp. 195–214) is designed to help in this transition. It is important for the teacher to understand the principles underlying discipline before choosing specific techniques. Processes and principles are of much greater consequence than is the choice of reinforcers. When processes of education are fully understood, fanciful gimmicks become sound pedagogy.

The following examples are structured to start with simple applications and progress to more difficult and complex issues with some deviation for variety. The following is a list of examples by pinpointed problems.

Example Number	Pinpoint	Example Number	Pinpoint
1	Bothering teacher at desk	7	Fighting over toys
2	Teasing other children	8	Simple arithmetic reasoning
3	Inappropriate pencil sharpening	9	Talking, standing, blurting out, noisy inattention, turning around
4	Overactivity		
5	Homework study time	10	Vandalism
6	Littering	11	"Love note" passing —boy-girl talking

Example Number	Pinpoint	Example Number	Pinpoint
12	Increases in speaking about oneself	38	Increasing math responses
13	Disruptive classroom behavior	39	Striking other children with objects
14	Chewing-gum problems	40	Discriminating "courage" behavior
15	Disruptive noise	41	Arithmetic achievement
16	Boredom		
17	Show-off	42	Excessive dawdling
18	Off-task individual study	43	Isolate behavior
		44	High noise level— lunchroom
19	Reading "bad" literature	45	Inappropriate behaviors
20	School failure		
21	Nail biting	46	Stuttering
22	Guffaw laughing	47	Constant talking and disturbing others during study time
23	Fear in young children		
24	Fear of going to school	48	Teaching lying behavior
25	Repeated crying	49	Standing up, walking around
26	Writing vulgar words	50	Disruptive social talking
27	Asking about sex	51	Rest time disruptions
28	Low-level skill achievement	52	Fear of failure, worrying
29	Noisy transition changing classes	53	Teaching contractual agreements
30	Rowdiness	54	Hyperactivity
31	Low frequency talking	55	Positive verbalizations about oneself and positive social interactions
32	Off-task during individual seatwork		
33	Crawling during school	56	Teaching beginning reading
34	Homework study	57	Sex-role behavior
35	Discriminating rules for visiting children	58	Noncooperation
		59	Use of illegal drugs
36	Physical aggression	60	"Bad attitude"
37	Aggressive hitting	61	Temper outbursts

Example Number	Pinpoint	Example Number	Pinpoint
62	Academic failure	73	Walking in street
63	Thumb-sucking	74	Talking out, standing
64	Classroom "out-of-control"	75	Embarrassment
65	Volunteering answers	76	Arithmetic problem-solving
66	Rehearsal effectiveness	77	Lawbreaking
67	Fighting during recess	78	Low level English achievement
68	Rebelliousness, disagreements, and refusal to talk to parents	79	Tardiness following recess
69	Using adoption to control adults	80	Children manipulating parents
70	Disruptive behaviors —talking, fighting, out of seat, throwing objects, noisy	81	Academic underachievement
		82	Academic "apathy"
		83	Physical abuse of mother
71	Unfinished assignments, bothering neighbors, playing	84	On-task attention, academic accuracy
		85	Off-task, low achieving students
72	Following instructions	86	Developing a study routine
		87	Dishonesty

Example 1

Pinpoint: Bothering teacher at desk (4th grade)

Record: Students unnecessarily at teacher's desk (twenty-eight occurrences—one week)

Consequate: Teacher *ignored* all children who came to desk—made no eye contact, said nothing. Teacher recognized only those children who raised hands at seats.

Evaluate: Occurrences of students at teacher's desk steadily decreased. After two weeks, daily average between zero and one.

Professional Application

Example 2

Pinpoint: Teasing other children (Individual student, 4th grade)

Record: Disruptive behavior 83°₀ (teacher's observation—two days)

Consequate: *Isolation.* A coatrack and bookcase rearranged in back of classroom, making small isolation cubicle for child. Child sent to this "time-out place" for ten minutes every time he disrupted class.

Evaluate: Disruptive behavior steadily *decreased.* After nine isolations (four during first day) disruptive behavior dropped to 10%.

Note: This child's teasing behavior was probably producing "payoff" from class (laughing, complaining, attending).

Professional Application

Example 3

Pinpoint: Inappropriate pencil sharpening (3rd grade)

Record: Substitute teacher noticed two children going to pencil sharpener, then five, then entire class.

Consequate: Substitute got up from desk, gently removed sharpener bin, told children she would read a story if they completed work during next twenty minutes. They did—she did.

Evaluate: A pleasant day.

Note: Any teacher, especially a substitute, must catch a problem immediately.

Professional Application

Example 4

Pinpoint: Overactivity (Six boys, 9 to 13 years, low-level intelligence)

Record: Boys observed in playroom for eight days

Consequate: Rewarded following thirty seconds of "quiet time" (tokens exchangeable for candy). Procedure continued thirty days; during last four days token given after forty-five seconds.

Evaluate: Overactivity reduced 67%.

Note: Overactivity was still substantially decreased eight days later when *no rewards* were used.

Scientific Application (p. 380)

Example 5

Pinpoint: Homework study time (11 and 13 year olds)

Record: Average 4.5 minutes homework per child per school day after four week's recording according to child's records. Parent's spot checks averaged 3.8 minutes.

Consequate: Television viewing time made contingent on homework time whether or not assigned. Each minute of homework or review time redeemable for six minutes of viewing time. Children kept own time logs. Given extra monetary reward when parent's record within two minutes of child's report.

Evaluate: Homework study time increased to thirty-two minutes per child per day, at which time parents changed the study/viewing ratio to 3–1 with no decrease in study time.

Professional Application

Example 6

Pinpoint: Littering (6th grade)

Record: Materials not put away—twenty-five daily (average one week)

Consequate: Large FRIDAY BOX instituted in classroom. Each student given responsibility for own materials—individually labeled. Materials not put away went in Friday Box. Friday Box opened one half-hour weekly—*only then could articles be recovered.*

Evaluate: After second week Friday Box, littering decreased to three incidents weekly.

Note: This procedure seems effective in all situations and at all age levels. An author had to wait four days to recover important research materials placed by his wife in the family Sunday Box. Also, the amount of material not taken from the box that is allowed to remain week after week provides a good indication of its worth to the litterer.

Professional Application

Example 7

Pinpoint: Fighting over toys (2- and 6-year-old boys)

Record: Children fought as to who owned particular toy (four times in A.M.); mother admonished children to share.

Consequate: Program instituted to teach children: (1) ownership and (2) sharing. Children told "ownership is when a toy belongs to you, and you can do anything you want with it," and "sharing is when you let somebody else use something that belongs to you." Children given separate toys (some for John, some for Marc, some for both), again admonished to share, and praised when they did.

Evaluate: Children initially hoarded their own toys (two weeks), then began to trade (three occurrences, two days), then to share (sixteen instances over four days). Fighting over toys diminished to an average of less than one per day.

Professional Application

Example 8

Pinpoint: Simple arithmetic reasoning (One male, 3.5; one female, 3)

Record: Completed arithmetic assignments zero

Consequate: Students learned numbers through pushing buttons that turned lights on and off. No verbal communication used. Tasks ordered and reduced to very small steps. Correct responses immediately followed by a tone. Food rewards given on preset schedule for correct responses. Incorrect responses resulted in short blackout on panel.

Evaluate: "Students" learned to match each of seven three-digit binary numbers with any of twenty-one possible combinations with good accuracy (less than five errors per hundred trials). However, it took hundreds of thousands of trials to learn.

Note: "Students" in this experiment were chimpanzees. These animals did not learn abstract concepts but responded to specific stimuli. This study gives additional hope for teaching the mentally retarded to achieve full potential.

Scientific Application (p. 381)

Example 9

Pinpoint: Talking, standing, blurting out, noisy inattention, turning around (Ten children—five different classrooms. Ages 6 years, 8 months to 10 years, 6 months. Teachers recommended most severe problem children in class.)

Record: Trained observers recorded inappropriate social behavior for six weeks. Average inappropriate behavior was 72%.

Consequate: Teachers: (1) made classroom rules explicit; (2) ignored behaviors that interfered with learning or teaching unless dangerous; (3) used withdrawal of approval as punishment; (4) gave praise and attention to behaviors that facilitated learning; and (5) attempted to reinforce prosocial behaviors *incompatible* with inappropriate social behaviors.

Evaluate: Average inappropriate behavior decreased from 72% to 19.5% over an eight-week period.

Note: Participating teachers were given a workshop in behavior modification during the experiment. Opportunities for each teacher to see daily observation graphs probably helped to increase effectiveness of the procedures.

Scientific Application (p. 374)

Example 10

Pinpoint: Vandalism (7th grade)

Record: Seven students wrote on or destroyed: (1) desks, (2) walls, and (3) school equipment.

Consequate: (1) Desks—students sanded and revarnished damaged desks, plus two others. (2) Walls—students washed *entire* wall. (3) School equipment—students contributed double financial value. All work strictly supervised and completed to satisfaction of teacher. Thereafter, students responsible for property upkeep, regardless of who caused damage. Parents *not allowed* to contribute to restitution in any manner.

Evaluate: Vandalism eliminated. Students' supervision of school property established.

Note: This is perhaps one of the oldest and most effective discipline procedures.

Professional Application

Example 11

Pinpoint: "Love note" passing—boy-girl talking (11th grade, biology class)

Record: Five intercepted notes in one week (three innocuous, two vulgar). Twenty incidents of talking during one class period.

Consequate: Friday field trip privilege contingent on "no more talking or letter writing."

Evaluate: Friday field trip denied two consecutive weeks, given third week after talking and letter writing stopped.

Note: Field trips were continued throughout year. However, trips were subsequently denied four times for talking—sometimes students forget.

Professional Application

Example 12

Pinpoint: Increases in speaking about oneself (3rd grade boys, thirty; 3rd grade girls, twenty-eight; 6th grade boys, twenty-one; 6th grade girls, twenty; 10th grade boys, twenty; 10th grade girls, thirty)

Record: Each child verbalized sixty sentences during individual session.

Consequate: Students instructed to begin sixty sentences with pronoun of choice. Researcher commented "good" *only* after sentences starting with the pronoun "I." No comment after any others.

Evaluate: Number of sentences beginning with "I" increased significantly.

Note: This study demonstrated effectiveness of simple approval. However, the study also indicated that the sex of a teacher may also be a factor in effectiveness of approval. *Adolescent* girls responded to praise from the male researcher (first-year medical student) to a greater extent than did adolescent males. With *younger* students, the *boys* began more sentences with "I," indicating a same-sex preference for younger children.

Scientific Application (p. 383)

Example 13

Pinpoint: Disruptive classroom behavior (9-year-old boy)

Record: Disruptions recorded by teacher.

Consequate: Disruptive behaviors ignored; appropriate behavior rewarded. Boy kept after school for extreme deviations
and sent home on later bus. This put child with students he did
not know and withdrew peer attention. Correct behaviors reinforced by teacher praise and peer approval (continuously in
beginning, more infrequently later on). Also, job of blackboard
monitor followed appropriate behavior.

Evaluate: Disruptive behaviors initially *increased* as pay-off
withdrawn. After initial rise, maladaptive behaviors progressively *decreased* and were eliminated by end of third week.

Scientific Application (p. 386)

Example 14

Pinpoint: Chewing-gum problems (8th grade, Special Education class)

Record: Five (average) gum wads under each desk. Gum wrappers observed on floor (six to ten daily).

Consequate: Gum privilege extended with admonition to "be responsible."

Evaluate: Six (average) gum wads under each desk. Gum wrappers on floor (eight to eleven daily).
If at first you don't succeed?

Consequate II: Group gum chewing Monday, Wednesday, Friday contingent on rules: Rule 1. "If an individual is caught chewing Tuesday and Thursday, individual will lose privileges of chewing gum for one week. He must also clean five wads from under desk." Rule 2. "If more than two wrappers are found on floor Monday, Wednesday, or Friday, entire class loses gum chewing privileges for one day."

Evaluate II: After three weeks, all gum wads removed from under all desks. Two wrappers Monday, Wednesday, and Friday observed on floor.

Note: If contingency had stipulated *no* gum wrappers, probably all wrappers would have been put away.

Professional Application

Example 15

Pinpoint: Disruptive noise (Large class)

Record: Absolute cacophony. *No* recording able to take place.

Consequate: Many children removed from class until class size became manageable. Teacher planned specific assignments and scheduled consequences. After small number of children brought under control, one child at a time added to class. Procedure started with limited number of children during special period while others normally out of room—later extended to entire day.

Evaluate: Teachers indicated procedure very effective.

Note: Teachers also stated that initial control of the *entire* group was absolutely impossible.

Professional Application

Example 16

Pinpoint: Boredom (10th grade, Spanish)

Record: Lack of enthusiasm for subject-matter acquisition— only two of twenty-three assignments completed in two-week period

Consequate: Friday football game instituted: teams chosen, rules established, points, yards, substitutions, etc., developed for correct *academic* responses. Game played on chalkboard with losing team providing "treat" for winners.

Evaluate: "Enthusiasm replaced boredom"—all assignments completed by second Friday.

Note: Any game can be used for any subject matter. It is best to choose a game specifically appropriate to the general outside interests of the student age group.

Professional Application

Example 17

Pinpoint: Show-off (8-year, 8-month-old boy)

Record: Three specific behaviors approved by peers. Out of seat twenty times per day, talking without permission eighteen times per day, five incomplete assignments (one week).

Consequate: Program initiated retaining approval from peers. Instead of receiving laughter for getting out of seat and talking, child allowed to tell jokes; instead of receiving attention for misbehaving, child received praises for proper behavior. Boy stayed after school as reward rather than punishment.

Evaluate: First week, talking decreased to two occurrences, left seat only once. Second through fourth week, *no* rules broken. Only one inappropriate behavior in fifth week.

Note: A great deal of "show-off" behavior is maintained by peer attention. If teachers remove one child from the group this often solves the problem.

Scientific Application (p. 380)

Example 18

Pinpoint: Off-task individual study (7th grade, Special Education class)

Record: Completion of work taking longer each day and extending into next period. (Average time increase—twenty minutes by end of third week.)

Consequate: All water-drinking privileges made contingent on finishing work on time. Water-drinking frequency increased considerably but functioned as a positive reward.

Evaluate: Increase in finished work in allotted time by end of fourth day.

Note: The contingent delivery of other materials previously not associated with proper study (crayons, pencils, colors) was later introduced to reward other academic behaviors.

Professional Application

Example 19

Pinpoint: Reading "bad" literature (10-year-old child)

Record: No instance of child reading "classic child stories" or factual book in two months.

Consequate: Parent cooperated with school by paying child 1¢ per page to read any book in family library. Child could take the $1.00 after 100 pages or buy any books of choice for 25¢ each (parents paid remainder).

Evaluate: Child read sixty-two pages of child's encyclopedia first week; thereafter, averaged approximately fifty pages per week from "good" books. Four month follow-up indicated reading rate also increased. Child "hooked" on scientific book series.

Note: The child in this study kept the records personally. Completion of each 100 pages was countersigned by mother and presented to father for payment on a check-type book that became very important to the child and was taken to school many times to show the teacher.

Professional Application

Example 20

Pinpoint: School failure (16-year-old boy)

Record: Failed all academic subjects first half of year. Parents and teachers unable to "motivate studying."

Consequate: School counselor developed system with parents' cooperation. Every teacher signed individual *daily progress report* (one small sheet) after each class. Decision of signing for appropriate social and academic behaviors based on teacher's criteria. Allowance, social engagements, car privileges contingent on number of signatures earned each day.

Evaluate: Better grades. C+ average attained for last six-week period of same year.

Note: Many parents offer rewards for good grades but cannot find a way to cut down the time interval so that rewards are meaningful in motivating the student. A complete academic term is very long for a student who cannot exhibit correct study patterns throughout one day.

Professional Application

Example 21

Pinpoint: Nail biting (Individual students—ages 6, 8, 9, 17)

Record: Excessive nail bitting (one instance of physical damage)

Consequate: *Negative practice*. Students practice *inappropriate behavior* at specific times (e.g., 8 A.M. for five minutes) in front of mirror. Parent or teacher delivered disapproval responses during nail biting sessions—"Doesn't that look terrible? Do you want people to see you bite your nails like that?" Children instructed to move hand up and down, biting repeatedly. During first session two children cried and wanted to stop.

Evaluate: Nail biting ceased after six to ten sessions.

Note: Behaviors such as nail biting are behaviors whose frequency has made them habitual. Concentrated negative practice probably serves as a stimulus by which the child begins to discriminate. The child learns to "think" as his hand starts to go up, and therefore inhibits himself. Negative practice has been used successfully in eliminating nose-picking, thumb-sucking, pubic scratching, tics, and other social improprieties.

Professional Application

Example 22

Pinpoint: Guffaw laughing (10th grade, six boys)

Record: Teacher's instructions elicited loud laughing from boys.

Consequate: Boys collectively taken out of room—brought back individually in front of class as girls applauded. Seating arrangements also changed to place each boy among group of girls.

Evaluate: Guffaw laughing ended.

Note: The same procedure of boy-girl seating was employed for the entire student body during general assemblies, resulting in considerable decrease in cat-calls and noise. It also helped boy-girl socialization.

Professional Application

Example 23

Pinpoint: Fear in young children (Separate studies concerning six hundred children, infants and school age)

Record: Overt signs of fear exhibited whenever children confronted fearful situations. Procedures reported from parent interviews and classified according to effectiveness.

Consequate: Following procedures reported effective by parents: (1) *Incompatible response.* Feared object or situation gradually introduced into child's presence while child engaged in fun activity; (2) *Gradual approach.* Child led by degrees (over a number of days) to come closer and closer to feared object or participate in feared activity; (3) *Modeling.* Feared activity or object made readily accessible to child while other children participated enjoyably.

Evaluate: *Incompatible responses, gradual approach,* and *modeling* eliminated about 85% of children's fears, according to parents.

Note: The following procedures were *not* successful: disapproval, social ridicule, scolding, verbal appeals, punishment, forcing child to participate, or changing the child's activity whenever he was afraid. When any fearful situation is forced on a child, fear may be *increased.*

Scientific Application (p. 386)

Example 24

Pinpoint: Fear of going to school (Fifty children—ages 4 to 16)

Record: All children frightened of going to school were referred to University Human Development Clinic over eight-year period. They had at least *seven* of the following ten behaviors: (1) first episode of school fear, (2) begun on Monday following an illness previous Thursday or Friday, (3) had begun with no warning, (4) more prevalent in lower grades (forty of fifty children were age twelve or under), (5) mother ill or presumed so by child, (6) child expressed concern about death, (7) parents communicate well, (8) mother and father happy and adjusted in most areas, (9) father shows interest in household management and problems, (10) parents easy to work with (school, church, clinic, etc.).

Consequate: Parents ignored bodily complaints (did not reinforce child's talk about feeling sick), merely made appointment with pediatrician for a time *not* during school hours or, if necessary, a quick examination on way to school. Child was taken to school usually by father, with school personnel instructed to keep child in room when parents left. Parents were told that child's difficulty transient, informed Monday would be difficult, Tuesday better, and by Wednesday, problem generally absent. Parents told not to discuss school attendance over weekend (most referrals late in week). Sunday night parent stated, "Tomorrow you go back to school," and discussion attempts were ignored. Monday morning child was dressed and given a light breakfast (nausea generally existed). No questions were asked about fear (parents therefore did not reinforce fear). Monday evening parents gave approval for going to school *and* staying at school (no matter how many times child cried, vomited, or tried to leave). Child also often seen briefly and explained advantages of going on in face of fear (getting right back on a horse after a fall, etc.).

Evaluate: All fifty cases responded with complete elimination of school fear. All cases followed for at least two years with no recurrences of fear.

Note: Any inappropriate behavior of recent duration with an acute onset is probably best handled immediately. Talking about the problem merely serves to intensify and prolong the behavior by giving a great deal of approval as well as reinforcing procrastination. The time to talk is after something has been done to change. *Talk should not take the place of action.* Of course, where any medical problems may be indicated careful examination is mandatory but should be handled by parents matter-of-factly. Most parents are perfectly capable of handling this type of school fear themselves. Should problems develop that you think extremely severe, then seek professional help immediately.

Scientific Application (p. 387)

Example 25

Pinpoint: Repeated crying (4-year-old boy, preschool)

Record: Eight crying periods each morning following mild frustrations. Whenever boy cried, teachers comforted him (picked up, talked softly, held on lap, etc.).

Consequate: Boy ignored unless "real grounds" for crying; given approval for self-help attempts.

Evaluate: One crying spell in five days after initial decrease.

Consequate II: Teachers again paid attention to crying (ten days).

Evaluate II: Crying almost reached original level during record phase.

Consequate III: Boy ignored when crying; given approval for self-help (ten days).

Evaluate III: Crying decreased to zero and low level maintained.

Note: The cause-and-effect relationship between adult approval and child behaviors is clearly demonstrated in this case. The reader may be wondering why one would deliberately produce inappropriate behavior in a student. In a research study, the experimenter must determine that a particular reinforcer is really causing a specific effect. In this case the reinforcer was attention—the effect, not crying. When a teacher is "sure" what produces a desired change in the classroom, this may be enough. However, the scientist must be certain. The reversal technique will be noted repeatedly in scientific investigations.

Scientific Application (p. 384)

Example 26

Pinpoint: Writing vulgar words (8- and 9-year-old neighborhood boy and girl)

Record: Two letters found by parents within one week; eight vulgar words written by boy, six by girl.

Consequate: Parents of girl talked to parents of boy. Boy's parents said, "You know kids nowadays, what can you do." Parents talked to daughter, explained proper time and place for verbal sexual discussion. Girl received special toys for bringing home notes.

Evaluate: Girl brought home four notes passed to her by same boy during next week. Wrote no more answers.

Note: Parents do not control all possible sources of reinforcement. Following the first week parents discussed notes brought home, indicated girl should ignore any note-passing behavior, and after initial time also spent time role-playing how to ignore note-passing behavior.

Professional Application

Example 27

Pinpoint: Asking about sex (Eighteen children, 4 to 7 years old)

Record: Children exhibited no factual information—a few "inappropriate" responses when questioned.

Consequate: Program instituted to teach:
1. Physiological functions with appropriate pictures from encyclopedia and other appropriate sources
2. Appropriate scientific terminology from same
3. "Improper terminology," i.e., language used in different settings and by various subgroups to describe similar processes
4. Value indoctrination, i.e., placing all the above within the value orientation of parents

Evaluate: Factual information concerning sex verbalized; identification and discrimination concerning use of various words within proper context (at least four occurrences for each child over two-week periods).

Professional Application

CHAP 6   CHANGING WRONG ASSOCIATIONS

Example 28

Pinpoint: Low-level skill achievement (9th grade, industrial arts class)

Record: No evidence of completed individual project or increased skills after fourth week of term

Consequate: Teacher continually threatened students with failing final grades for lack of industry.

Evaluate: Only *one* student of eight finished final project.

Note: Anxiety increases were observed during the last few days of class, as students frantically tried to finish projects. One boy was cut with a bandsaw two days before term ended. Students complained that they tried, but "didn't really know what the teacher wanted." This represents a situation in which the teacher "did not start where the student is." Thus, threats of disapproval did not produce constructive behavior; rather, threats produced anxiety and subsequent physical harm.

Professional Application

Example 29

Pinpoint: Noisy transition changing classes (8th grade)

Record: Length of time after bell rang that students took to be in seats steadily increased to eight minutes.

Consequate: "Record party" contingent on all students being in seats before final bell. One "pop" record (brought by students) played during Friday's class for each day all students in seats before final bell.

Evaluate: Extended record parties by end of third week.

Note: A decrease in other maladaptive responses was observed when one record was *deducted* from "Friday's list" for antisocial behavior from any student.

Professional Application

Example 30

Pinpoint: Rowdiness (6th grade)

Record: Average of eight disruptive behaviors during each ten-second observation.

Consequate: Students allowed play break with admonition: "I will let you play now if you promise to work afterwards." Students promised they would.

Evaluate: *In*effective study behavior (nine to twelve average for ten-second intervals).

Note: Rewards must come *after the fact*. After correct "work precedes play" contingency has been established, sequencing may then become effective (i.e., work, play, work, play, work, etc.).

Professional Application

Example 31

Pinpoint: Low frequency talking (4-year-old girl)

Record: Verbalization occurred only during 11% of all ten-second intervals observed (trained observers).

Consequate: Teacher attention to child contingent on talking; when child did not talk, she was ignored by teacher. Child also required to answer questions when requesting materials before receiving them (materials contingent on question answering).

Evaluate: Talking increased to average 75%.

Consequate II: Teacher attention to child contingent on non-verbalization; when child talked, child ignored by teacher. (Reversal of contingencies.)

Evaluate II: Talking decreased to 6%.

Consequate III: Again teacher gave attention for verbalizations, but stopped requiring talking before providing requested materials.

Evaluate III: Child's talking increased to 61%, dropped to 28% when questioning and further talking eliminated.

Note: Authors indicate that since talking dropped when teacher discontinued the questioning as requirement for receiving materials, it is clear that it was not the teacher's social approval alone that was responsible for the high rate of talking. They report that questioning the child and requiring several responses before allowing access to materials is crucial.

Scientific Application (p. 397)

Example 32

Pinpoint: Off-task during individual seatwork (Six elementary students, one first grader, two third grade classmates, three other classmates)

Record: Observers recorded 40% study time (percentage of on-task ten-second intervals) during thirty minutes of seat work. (Number of observations varied from seven to fifteen days.)

Consequate: Observer helped teachers by holding up small colored papers when children were studying. Teachers would go to the student and use verbal, facial, and contact approval.

Evaluate: Study behavior increased to average 75% for the six students.

Consequate II: Teachers stopped giving approval to study behavior.

Evaluate II: Average study behavior dropped to 34%.

Consequate III: Teachers again gave approval when observers signaled.

Evaluate III: Study behavior increased to 73%.

Note: Most teachers' attention to problem children was for nonstudy behavior during Record phase. It was also reported that classrooms were initially well controlled with a few students who did not stay on-task. Teacher approval was made contingent through observers' signals that later proved to be unnecessary and the cues were eliminated. The cues were initially used to make the teachers aware of contingencies.

Scientific Application (p. 384)

Example 33

Pinpoint: Crawling during school (Nursery school, girl 3.4 years)

Record: Girl spent 75% of time (observed two weeks) in off-feet position. Also avoided contacts with other children and adults.

Consequate: Nursery school teachers *ignored* girl when not standing; approached, praised, displayed interest when girl on feet. Disapproval techniques such as anger, shame, disgust, or disappointment not used.

Evaluate: Girl stood 75% of time during first week. During second week, up as much as other children.

Consequate II: Contingencies reversed. Teachers approved *off-feet* behavior.

Evaluate II: First day of reversal, girl off-feet 75% of time; second day 81.9%.

Consequate III: Return to praise for standing.

Evaluate III: First hour of first day, on-feet 75.9%; first hour of second day, 62.7%; by second hour, 100%. *No relapses observed.*

Scientific Application (p. 384)

Example 34

Pinpoint: Homework study (High school, 17-year-old girl)

Record: Grades monitored for one semester. Average grade D—with frequent failures.

Consequate: Flash cards developed by student to assist study in history, civics, Latin. Meals contingent (except breakfast) on success in responses to cards.

Evaluate: Within eight weeks grades rose from D to a B—average.

Note: Researchers noted the flash cards may have been reinforcing instead of the food. However, a follow-up at a later semester indicated grades had returned to a D average. Obviously, cards or grades alone were not sufficient rewards for this girl. Motivation must come from without before it gets "in." The question of how long it takes for motivation to "get in" for each individual is not known. However, it would appear that even constant rewarding is better than constant failure.

Scientific Application (p. 393)

Example 35

Pinpoint: Discriminating rules for visiting children (Thirteen children, 2 to 9 years old)

Record: "Total bedlam" (three visits from other children) reported by one parent who said, "If I have to put up with those neighbor's children again, I'll even stop letting their parents visit." Another parent, "I can't do anything with that child after she comes home from Grandmother's."

Consequate: *Difficult* program to teach parents to have enough courage to enforce their own rules with other children and also with visits to grandparents. *Simple* program to teach visiting children discriminations. "In this house you must follow (different) rules." Visiting children told when entered house about expectations and consequences: "If you play nicely, you may have a treat, and if you break our rules (carefully explained), you must leave."
Own children told "when we are home from grandparents' we have different rules."

Evaluate: Children learned to discriminate (rowdy, undisciplined, only in situations where allowed) and followed rules in orderly house after being sent home twice (average) first week. Own children took average of one day to "shape up" after visit to grandparents.

Note: Only adults' behavior presents problems in these situations. However, an initial strong positive approach with other parents, especially one's own, usually solves the problem. When adults do set strong limits with neighbor's children (especially if they pay off from time to time, children's good behavior), their house will usually be the one all the children "love to visit." When grandparents visit it is wise to give them a set of the child's rules when they arrive, making sure to correct grandparents' deviations immediately and gently. Children also learn different rules in different classrooms.

Professional Application

Example 36

Pinpoint: Physical aggression (Nursery school, twenty-seven 3 to 4-year-old boys)

Record: Physical aggression frequency during observation period totaled 41.2 incidents, verbal aggression 22.8, with total 64.0 incidents (one week observation).

Consequate: Teachers ignored aggression and rewarded cooperative and peaceful behaviors (interfered only when bodily harm was likely). Approval techniques replaced reprimands.

Evaluate: Total aggressive behaviors decreased—64 incidents to 43.4. (Physical aggression 41.2 to 26.0; verbal aggression 22.8 to 17.4.)

Consequate II: Following initial consequate, researchers told teachers experiment completed. However, observations again recorded three weeks later.

Evaluate II: After experimenters left, teachers not as consistent. Total number aggressive responses increased 43.4 to 51.6. Physical aggression increased 26.0 to 37.8. However, verbal aggression decreased 16.4 to 13.8. (Teachers found it harder to ignore fighting than to ignore verbal threats.)

Consequate III: Consequate I reinstated.

Evaluate III: Total aggression decreased 51.6 to 25.6. Physical aggression decreased 37.8 to 21.0; verbal aggression 13.8 to 4.6.

Note: This study substantiates the necessity of *absolute consistency*.

Scientific Application (p. 377)

Example 37

Pinpoint: Aggressive hitting (Preschool boys, private kindergarten)

Record: Teacher complained that boys went "out of control" during outside play periods (five children hurt in one week).

Consequate: Large punching bag dummy with red nose installed on playground.

Evaluate: No noticeable decrease in human hitting—six children hurt during week. Dummy punched frequently, especially in nose. (Actually, boys fought each other to take turns at dummy.)

Consequate II: Punching dummy removed. Individual boys isolated for duration of play period when observed hitting another child.

Evaluate II: After five days (seventeen isolations), hitting completely eliminated.

Note: Hitting, like other behavior, is *learned*. It is not a mystical entity deep inside everyone's system waiting to be released. The more children are reinforced for hitting, the more they will hit. Some people even develop a curious "self-fulfilling prophesy" in this regard. They sincerely believe that if they could just hit something they would feel much better. Thus, when frustrated, they hit something and, sure enough, they feel better.

Professional Application

Example 38

Pinpoint: Increasing math responses (6th grade, eighty-eight students)

Record: One hour spent on individualized math kit. 33.2 average correct responses.

Consequate: Correct responses during 20-minute work session earned 10 minutes of: (1) nothing, (2) math games, (3) earphone music listening, (4) group dance (four groups).

Evaluate: Gain scores for correct responses after one week: (1) no reward—minus 2.9, (2) math games—.4, (3) earphone music listening—26.1, (4) group dance—16.0.

Note: The contingent application of reward (music) served to cut the math period in half and still increase correct responses. It is interesting that individual earphone listening, which can be easily dispensed, was actually superior to the group dance in increasing correct math responses. Also, the teacher had been using math games "to help motivate," but on analysis math games did not function to increase responses.

Scientific Application (p. 391)

Example 39

Pinpoint: Striking other children with objects (9-year-old boy)

Record: Boy hit other children five times during four free-play periods.

Consequate: Adult assigned in vicinity. Boy praised and given donut when playing properly; when boy hit someone, supervisor instructed to hit him back with same object. During second supervised play period, boy hit another child in head with plastic baseball bat. Immediately, supervisor picked up bat and hit boy. Explanation to child: "When people are hit, it hurts."

Evaluate: Boy never observed hitting another child.

Note: This boy had been characterized as "having no conscience." Perhaps it would be more accurate to say that he did not realize the consequences of his own actions regarding pain. (See pp. 188, 194.)

Professional Application

Example 40

Pinpoint: Discriminating "courage" behavior (8-year-old boy)

Record: Boy home later from school after beating by "bully." Boy told his mother he didn't want to tell his father because he was a coward (one occurrence).

Consequate: Boy instructed in discriminating among fear, cowardice, courage. Boy told that: (1) fear is perfectly okay in some situations; given some examples, (2) cowardice is when one does not do what one thinks is right; again given examples, (3) courage is the ability to deal with big things (such as some of the problems the boy was trying to overcome at school).

Evaluate: Boy did not fight, yet maintained strong "self-concept," i.e., self-report to father, "I'm very afraid of that big fifth grader, but I know it's his problem not mine."

Note: Many modern parents are ambivalent concerning fighting. Some believe the child should fight, others believe that the child should never fight, and most believe the child should not start a fight yet should retaliate if put upon. Regardless of parental views, it seems much more important as far as the child is concerned that whatever the child does concerning fighting, he should still have a good "self-concept" regarding his behavior. Teachers can accomplish this by "labeling" for the child and then reinforcing whatever behavior they feel appropriate. However, consistency *must* be maintained.

Professional Application

Example 41

Pinpoint: Arithmetic achievement (6th grade, thirteen boys)

Record: Assignments completed during arithmetic period preceding recess averaged 4.2 (approximately nine incomplete assignments). Recess activity closely observed. All boys played 100% of the time during two-week period.

Consequate: Boys told if assignments not completed, they could not go out to recess.

Evaluate: Only four incidents of recess participation were earned during the next week (three for one child). Arithmetic assignment completion did *not* increase following application of contingency.

Consequate II: All boys instructed to work through recess and *denied* recess privilege. However, each boy allowed five minutes' play in gym after finishing two arithmetic problems correctly.

Evaluate II: Completed arithmetic assignments increased to nine by end of first week. By Tuesday of second week, all thirteen boys turned in assignments every day. After three weeks, accuracy reached an average of 80%.

Note: This application represents a discrimination many teachers fail to make. If the period of work is too long, the child cannot see the immediate rewards for his academic work; thus, behavior does not improve. It was apparent to the teacher that these thirteen boys (all retarded in arithmetic) really enjoyed recess. The teacher used recess contingently, but it did not work. The time span of work without reward for these particular boys was too long. When the rewarding activity was given following a short period of work, they all produced—even though regular recess was denied. To keep the boys coming back from the gym rapidly, the teacher occasionally rewarded them immediately with another period in the gym for prompt return. By the end of the second week, all boys were running back from the gym to work again. When using activities as rewards, it is important to pay very close attention to "structuring activities in time."

Professional Application

Example 42

Pinpoint: Excessive dawdling (5th grade)

Record: Three to five minutes to get "on-task" in individual study. (Average over eight days.)

Consequate: Teacher instituted multiple divergent token systems. Some children received paper money that bought "surprise gifts" at end of day. Other children received candies on various time interval schedules. Some children accumulated points written in notebooks. Reinforcers changed constantly. Varying token reinforcers "stimulated interest and created mode of excitement in classroom."

Evaluate: Individual dawdling decreased to approximately thirty seconds (average three days).

Note: Expectation level increased general classroom excitement toward goal achievement (receiving tokens), which was later modified by stretching the time interval using only exchange tokens. If students have previously been on a single token system, sometimes it is wise to alter the routine.

Professional Application

Example 43

Pinpoint: Isolate behavior (Girl, age 4.3 years)

Record: Varied repertory of well-developed skills pleased adults but did not gain child-child interactions. Observations during entire mornings by trained observers (one week) indicated: 10% child interaction, 40% adult interaction, 50% isolate.

Consequate: Maximum adult attention for child interaction. *No* attention for isolate behavior or adult interaction.

Evaluate: Over six days, child interaction increased to 60%, adult interaction decreased to 20%, time spent alone 20%.

Consequate II: Contingencies withdrawn.

Evaluate II: Child interaction *decreased* to 20%, adult *increased* to 40%, isolate 40%.

Consequate III: Contingencies re-established. Attention for interaction with children. Child interaction increased to 60%, adult decreased to 25%, 15% isolate.

Note: Follow-up observation showed girl to be maintaining the increased ratio of child interaction.

Scientific Application (p. 372)

Example 44

Pinpoint: High noise level—lunchroom (Grade school)

Record: Generalized noise (talking) at high level observed by principal. Other maladaptive behaviors developing, i.e., hitting, screaming, not staying at table until finished.

Consequate: Sound-activated switch (inexpensive circuit breaker device) connected to lights in lunchroom. When noise reached preset level (first day, 80 decibels; second day, 70 decibels, etc.), lights went off. When noise dropped, lights came on.

Evaluate: Selected noise levels maintained without *any* instruction. Children learned quickly to stay just beneath sound level setting.

Note: A similar device is available that can be set at any intensity level. This device sounds a shrill pitch until noise stops. Mechanical disciplinarians are absolute and effective. More important, they free a teacher's time for more productive interactions.

ofessional Application

Example 45

Pinpoint: Inappropriate behaviors (3rd grade, Adjustment class, seventeen 9-year-olds)

Record: Normal kinds of reinforcers (praise, grades) ineffective. Compliments from teacher resulted in children making faces at each other. Eight most disruptive children observed for one hour and forty minutes three days per week. Daily average of inappropriate behavior during three-week observation was 76% range 61%–91%).

Consequate: Reward program instituted for afternoon hours; activities included stories, records, arithmetic instruction, and group reading. Reward procedures explained to children every day for one week prior to consequate. Small notebooks taped to child's desk. Every twenty minutes teacher gave each child a score from 1 to 10. Points exchanged for playthings at end of one hour and forty minutes during first three days; days four through nine, points exchanged after two days. During next fifteen days, delay stretched to three-day period; for last twenty-four days, four-day delay. In addition to individual rewards, *group* points earned and exchanged for popsicle party end of each week.

Evaluate: Average inappropriate behavior decreased from 76% to 10% (range 3%–32%). Decline evident for every child.

Note: The total cost for entire program was $80.67. Teacher's reports and observer's records demonstrated profound difference in this classroom. The teacher also indicated that she had more time in which to teach. By pairing verbal praise with dispensing of points, the praise began to have a generalized effect even during the morning hours, when the token system was not in operation.

Scientific Application (p. 394)

Example 46

Pinpoint: Stuttering (Three adult males)

Record: Stuttering tabulated by analyses of two-minute intervals.

Consequate: Stuttering resulted in mild shock delivered to wrist.

Evaluate: Almost total reduction of stuttering. However, when shock removed, stuttering returned to original frequency.

Note: The use of shock as disapproval must be carefully controlled under appropriate supervision. This single scientific application (chosen from many) merely illustrates that the teacher has done only half the job when the inappropriate behavior is not replaced with appropriate behavior.

Scientific Application (p. 392)

Example 47

Pinpoint: Constant talking and disturbing others during study time (15-year-old boy, math class)

Record: On-task study behavior ranged from 3 to 45% with an average of approximately 25%.

Consequate: Boy took daily report card for teacher to check. Teacher marked "yes" or "no" to such items as acceptable use of class time, assignments completed on time, homework assignments, overall behavior good. When student earned all "yesses," he received snacks, television privilege, and permission to go outdoors. Even one "no" resulted in loss of privileges. (Child lived in a foster home for predelinquent boys.)

Evaluate: Study behavior rose to 95%; it remained high for six days of observation.

Consequate II: Student no longer received teacher's checks; he was told he would be granted privileges anyway.

Evaluate II: Study time dropped to 25% the first day, 10% the second day, and boy also got into one fight.

Consequate III: Privileges again made contingent on card signatures.

Evaluate III: Study time increased to 80% first day, dropped for three days until teacher assigned one "no" whereupon on-task study time increased to 100% and remained high for remainder of term.

Note: This well-controlled scientific study (one of three within same article using trained observers) indicates that home-based rewards can maintain on-task school behavior. Rewards were on a daily basis as it was necessary for the teacher as well as foster-parents to "prove" that they would, or could, be consistent. When no card was required behavior was disruptive; however, the teacher also had to assign a "no" before the lesson had been learned.

A subsequent experiment indicated that when cards were given only two days per week (reducing daily rewards) this also maintained a high level of appropriate behavior in class.

Scientific Application (p. 373)

Example 48

Pinpoint: Teaching lying behavior (11-year-old boy)

Record: Known misconduct; boy observed stealing $1.00 from sister's bedroom.

Consequate: Father took boy aside and with displeasure said, "Now, I want you to be honest with me, did you do it?"

Evaluate: Lie 1   Child, "No."
"Now, be honest!"

Lie 2   "No, I didn't do it."
"Don't lie to me."

Lie 3   "I'm not, really I didn't do it."
"I'm not going to tolerate any lying now."

Lie 4   "I'm not lying."
"Why were you in there?"

Lie 5   "Where?"
"The bedroom."

Lie 6   "Which bedroom?"
"You know which bedroom."

Lie 7   "No, I don't."
"Of course, you do."

Lie 8   "Dad, I really don't; I didn't do anything."
"You took it."

Lie 9   "What?"
"You know."

Lie 10   "I don't even have any money."
"Ah! Who said anything about money?"

Lie 11   "You did."
"No, I didn't."

Lie 12   "You said that I took Clara's money from her bedroom."
"No, I didn't."

Lie 13   "Dad, I didn't take it."
"How did you know it was money I was talking about?"

Lie 14   "I didn't.
    "You said, 'I didn't take Clara's money.' "
Lie 15   "No, I didn't say that."
    "What did you say?"
Lie 16   "I said, 'I didn't even know about Clara's
    money.' "
    "I'm not going to have you lie to me."
Lie 17   "I'm not lying, honest."
    "Now, once and for all, did you take it?"
Lie 18   "What?"
    "Clara's money."
Lie 19   "What money?"
    "I said I was not going to have any more
    lying."
Lie 20   "I'm not lying."
    etc., etc., etc., until
Truth 1   "Okay, okay, I did it."

Consequate II: Next morning. "Son, your behavior makes me very ashamed of you. You took your sister's money without her permission. Very few things are as serious as stealing, especially from a loved one. I choose not to give you the privilege of interacting with me or the family until you make retribution to Clara and this family. I know that you will think about this for a long, long time; I also know that you will pay back Clara and apologize to her and to the rest of us. I hope you can also think of a positive project that will demonstrate to us all the kind of person I know you are; right now you make us very, very sad."

Evaluate II: Boy exhibited "guilt" and engaged in project to earn back respect, i.e., positive familial interaction.

Note: Obviously consequate II should have been consequate I. Nothing is generally gained by playing detective or cross-examiner, except to increase lying. Even though most people can be caught in lies because they do not have good memories and/or are afraid and/or are young, this questioning process does not usually represent a worthwhile pursuit. If one knows for certain that a child has committed an inappropriate act, then the teacher should act on that basis. It does little good to get the child to admit it. If the teacher is not sure, the teacher should think through the possible consequences of the questioning process, i.e., to unwittingly teach lying.

Professional Application

Example 49

Pinpoint: Standing up, walking around (1st grade, forty-eight students, team-taught)

Record: Average of 2.9 children out of seats during each ten-second interval (291 children were counted [average] during twenty-minute period—twelve days.) Teachers told specific children to "sit down" an average of six times per twenty minutes. Whenever teacher told a child to sit down, the child did.

Consequate: Teachers instructed to tell children who stood up without good reason to sit down (average once every minute).

Evaluate: Amount of standing up *increased*. Each student sat down when told to sit down, but, overall, *more pupils stood up*. (Pupils standing per ten-second interval averaged 4.14.)

Consequate II: Procedure reversed, i.e., children told to sit down only six times per twenty minutes.

Evaluate II: Standing decreased to approximately original level (3.14 pupils standing per ten-second interval).

Consequate III: To demonstrate that teachers' comments "caused" the children to stand up, teachers again told children who were up without good reason to "sit down" (average once every minute).

Evaluate III: Standing up again increased to about same level as the first time teachers "paid attention" (3.94 per ten-second interval).

Consequate IV: *Vicarious approval* introduced. Teachers praised good *sitting*. Whenever one child stood up or walked around, teacher "caught" a sitting student working diligently and praised the "good" child.

Evaluate IV: Standing *decreased* (1.89 average).

Note: Praise delivered to individuals who were *not* standing was very effective in controlling the entire class. (What teacher hasn't noticed that thiry backs straighten when one child is complimented for sitting up straight and paying attention?) In this study the "good child" was used as a model for the group. ("Watch how quietly Susie gets her math counter!" "See how nicely Jim writes," etc.) Vicarious praise, however, was effective only for approximately thirty seconds. Even when first-graders "know the rules," it is necessary to deliver praise comments very regularly. It should be remembered that attention is extremely important to most children. Sometimes by paying attention to *inappropriate* behavior, you probably increase the very behavior you wish to eliminate.

Scientific Application (p. 391)

Example 50

Pinpoint: Disruptive social talking (Junior high school, six girls)

Record: Talking recorded on sheet of paper taped to teacher's desk (77% of time, three days).

Consequate: Teacher explained to class that talking during study time interfered with completion of work assignments (this had been done before). Class discussed importance of rules for study, agreed something must be done, and suggested very extreme alternatives. Teacher then stated: "Anyone caught talking in class during study time must leave the room." Five girls sent out during next two days.

Evaluate: Eightfold *decrease* in talking followed four weeks of contingency.

Note: One caution in using this type of procedure should be mentioned. The technique of removing students from a classroom (isolation) is effective only when the classroom provides many positive consequences (i.e., the student would rather spend his time in the classroom than be isolated). The girls in this classroom were *very concerned* with receiving approval from one another as well as from the teacher; thus isolation was effective.

Professional Application

Example 51

Pinpoint: Rest time disruptions (1st grade, nineteen children)

Record: Average inappropriate behavior 54% (trained observers, ten days). Teacher gave praise or reprimands twelve times during ten to fifteen minute rest period.

Consequate: Teacher contingently praised appropriate behavior, ignored disruptive behavior (twelve praise comments per day—only two reprimands in eight-day observation).

Evaluate: Disruptive behavior averaged 32%.

Consequate II: Teacher reprimanded so no one except disruptive child could hear (eleven per day—no praise seven days).

Evaluate II: Disruptive behavior averaged 39%.

Consequate III: Disapproval comments contingent on inappropriate behavior loud enough for entire class to hear (fourteen per day; no approval for five days).

Evaluate III: Disruptive behavior increased to an average of 53%.

Consequate IV: Teacher praised appropriate behavior, ignored inappropriate behavior (five days—twelve approval comments).

Evaluate IV: Disruptive behavior averaged 35%.

Note: In this scientific study, the teacher controlled disruptive behavior by praising and reprimanding quietly. Loud reprimands (yelling) increased rather than decreased the inappropriate behavior. A combination of approval for appropriate behavior and firm statements to the individual offender often serves to control young children very well. Quiet reprimands eliminate the possibility of the other children paying undue attention to the misbehaving child.

Scientific Application (p. 394)

Example 52

Pinpoint: Fear of failure, worrying (17-year-old girl)

Record: Girl reported "worrying constantly." Mother recorded average of twelve times per day daughter talked about upcoming "problems."

Consequate: (1) Time set for fifteen minutes of daily worry. Must worry "hard" during this time, imagining all the bad things that might happen. (2) Rank ordered all possible outcomes of failure in upcoming events. (3) Instructed to say "stop," subvocally, every time worrying started during other times of day and change to organized study routine immediately after recording one instance of worrying on worry card carried by girl.

Evaluate: Worrying increased to "constantly" (daughter's own statement, no actual record). Worrying during prescribed time seemed "silly."

Consequate II: Girl told worrying had probably actually decreased from "constantly," had actual record been made, to point that she could discriminate between when she was or was not worrying; therefore, worry could be counted.

Evaluate II: Worrying decreased to twice daily; fifteen-minute worrying period decreased to five minutes (worry time became negative).

Note: Eventually the worrying time became extremely silly as girl learned to plan constructive activities, and worry time was discontinued.

Professional Application

Example 53

Pinpoint: Teaching contractual agreements (9th grade, civics)

Record: Nothing

Consequate: Beginning of term each student wrote contract including amount of work to be completed for special class project as well as evaluation criteria for determining student's grade. Individual contracts exchanged among students. Entire class then chose a project and wrote one contractual agreement determining individual and collective responsibilities, including penalties for "illegal" behaviors. Teacher assumed role of interested bystander as students pursued class project. Disputes during course of project adjudicated in "class court" (some students did not do their share of work).

Evaluate: Effective learning judged by teacher on basis of *ex post facto* essays written by students.

Note: It is interesting that the predominant theme of most essays concerned "fairness." Written contractual agreements are very effective for this age group and can concern any cause-and-effect relationship between the parties (teacher/student, parent/student). Contracts specify contingencies ("If I do my work you promise to pay me," etc.) and may be used for individuals and/or groups. Exactly the same benefits accrue from such written contracts as from similar, more sophisticated adult agreements.

Professional Application

Example 54

Pinpoint: Hyperactivity (9-year-old boy, academic retardation)

Record: Home and classroom observations determined frequency and categories of hyperactive behavior—talking, pushing, hitting, pinching, moving, tapping, squirming, handling objects, i.e., did not sit still.

Consequate: A box, 6" × 8" × 5", equipped with counter and light, installed in classroom. Following ten seconds of appropriate behavior, light flashed, counter advanced, and boy received M & M or penny. Accumulated awards divided among classmates. Thus, other children received rewards for ignoring. Training session varied from five to thirty minutes; average rewards dispensed sixty to one-hundred.

Evaluate: Significant decrease in activity level (average decrease of 8.4 responses).

Note: The peer group in this study was used to reward the deviant boy. Thus, the group began to have a positive effect on him. Teachers can have an entire class help one or more children. Rewards can be given for both ignoring and paying attention. It is also suggested with *extremely* active children to: (1) use a stopwatch and start with as little as five seconds while counting to the child (verbal cues help the child perform in time); then reward immediately. Make sure the child does not get rewarded if he moves as much as an eyebrow. Gradually build the time sequence so child can remain still for thirty seconds or more; and (2) have the child practice the hyperactivity on purpose for five minutes a day to help the child discriminate between sitting still and moving.

Scientific Application (p. 395)

Example 55

Pinpoint: Positive verbalizations about oneself and positive social interactions (16-year-old boy)

Record: Boy avoided peer interaction; stated he did not like himself because his parents couldn't stand him; stated he was not good and no one could possibly like him (self-records indicated over twenty times per day debased self and no positive peer or adult contact—two weeks' records).

Consequate: To teach good "self-concept" (appropriate self-labeling), boy was instructed to: (1) record positive verbalizations, (2) list hierarchy of interests and good points (himself and parents), (3) carry list in pocket and read list whenever he caught himself in self-abasement (incompatible response), (4) initiate peer contact (one per day) based on similar peer interests, (5) interact verbally with parents ten minutes per day in positive way.

Evaluate: One close friendship within six weeks (average three to four positive contacts daily); joined boy's science club. After three weeks, he talked positively regarding parents.

Note: "Self-concept" usually relates to cognitive behavior and to a phenomenon called *labeling*, i.e., "I am a good person" as opposed to "I am no good" or "My student is a good person" versus "He is just a bad boy." Research regarding "labeling" seems quite conclusive in its implications regarding cause-and-effect relationships between labels and behavior. If a student gets the idea that he (she) is a "bad person," this will probably influence his (her) behavior. That is, the student will behave in accordance with this "self-concept."

One of the major theses of this book concerns the effect of positive as opposed to negative verbal expectations. For example, "I know you will do a good job" versus "Don't you dare try to cheat on your work." This is precisely what is meant by "catch the child being good and reward the student immediately." *Behavior that is reinforced increases.* If we catch students being good and reward them, we will probably have good students. If we only interact negatively with students, we create a negative cycle that is not only difficult to break but also probably actually produces more bad behavior.

Professional Application

Example 56

Pinpoint: Teaching beginning reading (Ten research studies employing four hundred children: retarded, slow readers, and unselected kindergarten and 1st grades.)

Record: Reading scores assessed prior to reading instruction.

Consequate: Programmed reading for periods of up to one semester.

Evaluate: No tutored children failed to read, with exception of one "normal" first grader and some (but not all) children with I.Q.'s below 50. One experiment showed relatively rapid acquisition of reading vocabulary by simple pairing of words with pictures. In another study, retarded children taught reading vocabulary to other retarded children with simple tutoring program. In other research, sight-reading vocabulary taught in sentence contexts to slow readers, retarded, and normal children. Two extension studies showed frequent alternation of programmed tutoring and classroom teachings more effective than less frequent alternation. One study indicated reinforcement proportion of approximately 20% more effective than higher levels.

Note: It appears that periodic withholding of approval develops a "hope" that is more effective than when the teacher reinforces all the time. The interested teacher can find literally hundreds of experiments in scientific journals concerning the effects of various reinforcement schedules.

The central issues related to programmed instructions seem little different from any other teaching-learning sequence. *One should begin where the student is.* Learning steps should be small, and adequate reinforcement and feedback techniques should be employed. Every teacher can individualize instructions and follow these systematic procedures.

Scientific Application (p. 380)

Example 57

Pinpoint: Sex-role behavior (175 boys, 85 girls; ages 5 years, 10 months to 6 years, 8 months)

Record: Series of ingeniously devised experimental studies recorded amount of play with same sex-typed toys as contrasted with opposite sex-typed toys or neutral toys. (Girls' toys included doll, pearl beads, high-heeled shoes, a mirror, and play make-up materials, cups and dishes, and a baby carriage with a doll; boys' toys consisted of boxing gloves, a tank, a racing car, a sword, a gun, a catcher's mitt and a baseball; neutral toys included a pegboard, three old blocks, and three pieces of tinker toys. The neutral toys were deliberately less inviting for purposes of the experiments.)

Consequate: Children observed peer and adult models playing with either "sex-inappropriate" or "sex-appropriate" toys. Some models gave approving or disapproving comments; i.e. "I don't want to play with those; they are girls' toys." Some models said nothing while playing with toys and others gave verbal cues as well as playing. (Five separate experimental studies were completed with excellent control groups.)

Evaluate: Even with little total time exposure to models (less than ten minutes), when children saw peer and adults playing with toys, they increased the time spent with toys. Children who saw models receive approval after playing with certain toys played more with these toys themselves (even when no approval was given to children). Children who observed others receive disapproval for playing with certain toys tended to avoid the same toys themselves. Children who observed someone giving themselves reasons for not playing with certain toys and who did not engage in play themselves were better able to gain similar control over their own behavior.

Note: These studies are extremely important for those who desire to increase or decrease the sex-role identity of children.

Society has changed very dramatically in the last few years, and it becomes more and more difficult to draw distinctions between masculine and feminine roles. However, adults who are concerned should label verbally and reinforce whatever they consider to be appropriate behavior from a very young age to discriminate or not discriminate differentiations that fit within the parents' value system. These studies clearly demonstrate the cause-and-effect relationship between: (1) supplying a child with the label, (2) modeling appropriate behaviors, and (3) producing same.

Scientific Application (p. 387)

Example 58

Pinpoint: Noncooperation (11th grade, English, five boys)

Record: No English assignments completed during two-week period. Students also refused to recite orally. Boys caught "shooting craps" in back of room.

Consequate: All boys sent to principal's office and given a "good talking to" concerning classroom responsibilities and advantages of learning English.

Evaluate: No change occurred in behavior. Boys became more noncooperative and began to mimic female teacher. Caught shooting craps twice during following week.

Consequate II: Teacher began to praise every class member who cooperated in giving oral recitations from selected literature.

Evaluate II: No change noted. Not one boy volunteered to participate in oral recitations. Teacher saw dice once but didn't catch boys in any games.

Consequate III: Everyone who participated in oral recitations allowed to bring any book or magazine to class for thirty minutes of private reading.

Evaluate III: One noncooperative boy brought a *Playboy* magazine to teacher after class and asked sarcastically: "If I read aloud from your book, can I read mine?" Teacher agreed. Next class session he did. Within four weeks all boys recited.

Note: The teacher also was able to shift these boys' interest from *Playboy* to *Hot Rod*, and after four months to sophisticated sports magazines found in the school library. This case demonstrates effective use of peer contingencies and approximations toward better literature through lack of censorship.

Professional Application

Example 59

Pinpoint: Use of illegal drugs (19-year-old boy)

Record: "Pot," two to three times weekly; LSD, two occurrences

Consequate: Boy began research on effects of drugs and was paid $5.00 for each two-page paper written.

Evaluate: LSD discontinued.

Note: This boy stated he found what he considered good evidence for discontinuing LSD but found conflicting evidence on the dangers of marijuana, so he decided not to stop. Many other young people with same contingencies have decided to give up all drugs because of legal, occupational, religious, and/or societal consequences. Many adults may desire to emphasize preventative measures, stressing what they feel to be more important issues than the medical effects of drugs. In these preventative programs, rewards are given for research concerning laws, community employment, church, and legal views.

Professional Application

Example 60

Pinpoint: "Bad attitude" (1st-grade boy)

Record: Child continued maladaptive responses just a little past point of instruction. Thus, when teacher said, "Stop talking," he did but continued *almost* to point of being disobedient. When teacher said, "Do not pick the flowers," he picked leaves. When she said, "Come here," he walked very slowly. When she said, "Quiet down," he did—still slightly louder than the group but not so loud as to receive punishment. This child (like so many others) delicately balanced upon the "edge of propriety." Punishment seemed not quite warranted, and reward seemed ridiculous.

Consequate: Teacher set up short lesson using *vicarious modeling*. Three names not duplicated in classroom were written on the board. The class was presented a new word, *attitude*. Teacher paired names with the new word:—"George has a *bad attitude*; Sam has an *all right attitude*; Tommy has a *good attitude*. When their teacher tells these three boys, 'Let's all pick up the mess,' George tries to get out of work or hides his mess in the desk, Sam cleans up his own mess—only his own—, but Tommy cleans up his own mess and then helps other children." The teacher talked through two such specific examples, then let children say what they thought George, Sam, and Tommy would do. (Children are usually very correct in these assessments, especially as they describe their own problems.) Teachers made several praising comments, stating: "I liked Tommy the very, very best." She then asked problem boy whom he would want for a friend. (The teacher now had a word, *attitude*, that she could use to describe this boy's behaviors in specific and general contexts—"That's a good attitude, Cort.") She now began rewarding *good attitudes* instead of being frustrated at not being able to find responses to deal with this child.

Evaluate: Child in question changed "attitude" when rewarded for proper verbal and motoric behavior.

Professional Application

Example 61

Pinpoint: Temper outbursts. (4-year-old boy—I.Q. recorded 72 and 80— possible brain damage)

Record: Frequency of objectionable behaviors varied from eighteen to 112 during sixteen one-hour periods (sticking out tongue, kicking, yelling, threatening to remove clothing, calling people names, throwing objects, biting, and hitting self).

Consequate: Consequences applied by mother in home two to three times per week for six one-hour sessions. Researchers helped mother by giving signals indicating: (1) she should tell her son to stop what he was doing, (2) place him in isolation for five minutes, or (3) given attention, praise, and affection.

Evaluate: Rate of objectionable behavior decreased (range one to eight per session). Isolation used four times; special attention given ten times.

Consequate II: No signals given; mother told to *"act as before."*

Evaluate II: Objectionable behaviors increased, but ranged well below original recordings (two to twenty-four per session). It appeared mother "learned." She reported more self-assurance, increased attention, delivered firm commands, and did not give in after denying a request.

Consequate III: Consequate I reinstated, except special attention for desirable play excluded.

Evaluate III: Objectionable behavior again *decreased* (almost identical to Consequate I, ranging from two to eight per session).

Note: No contact was maintained with the mother for twenty-four days after the experiment. She was given no instructions as to how to act and was given complete freedom to use any technique she desired. Later, three-session post contact check was made. Even after this long delay, the behaviors considered objectionable were still very low. The mother reported that her child was well behaved and less demanding. Isolation was used on the average of once per week. The mother's attitude toward her son was also considered to be more approving.

Scientific Application (p. 385)

Example 62

Pinpoint: Academic failure (General—twelve students, different classrooms, age range 11–14)

Record: Each student failed at least two academic subjects.

Consequate: Individual work-play routines developed with consent of parents. Students given special after-school assignments (approximately thirty minutes). Work immediately checked by parents and points assigned. Points were totaled each day to "buy" privileges and things (television watching, outside peer playtime; two children received money; one child—supper; one student—Saturday hiking plus one television program nightly; one student—time using "ham radio"). Time ratio for work-play approximately 1:4 in most cases. Thus, thirty minutes on-task work carried points worth two hours' activity or other reward.

Evaluate: Eleven of twelve students improved (average increase 1.5 letter grades in four months); one 14-year-old ran away from home—this student entirely on money contingency—parents later admitted they began to pay him before, rather than after, study sessions, i.e., he was manipulating them, rather than vice versa.

Note: This program is effective, but demands absolute cooperation from parents. Many parents will respond to such a program when they: (1) admit their child has a problem, (2) have some confidence in the programmer (teacher/counselor), and (3) will be *honest* in dispensing rewards.

Professional Application

Example 63

Pinpoint: Thumb-sucking (7-year-old girl)

Record: Thumb-sucking occurred 45% of time that the girl watched television or read (mother's records). Dentist indicated "bite" was getting worse.

Consequate: Mother, after hearing PTA lecture on "A positive approach with record-keeping," "caught" girl every time she had thumb in mouth. If thumb removed, girl received praise and special checks on prominently displayed chart in living room. (Checks were to be traded for bicycle—picture of bicycle at end of chart). Mother continued for fourteen days.

Evaluate: Thumb-sucking *increased* to 75%. Mother sought professional help from behaviorally oriented counselor stating, "I tried, but bribery just doesn't work."

Note: A cause-and-effect approach rests on record-keeping (data). In this case, the consequence did in fact work (changed behavior). Thumb-sucking *increased* 30%. The behavior change, however, was not in the direction desired by the mother (nor the dentist). Regarding the "bribery" issue, some people confuse the use of approval with a notion of "bribery." The girl in this case learned exactly what she was taught— (1) put thumb in mouth, (2) take thumb out of mouth, and (3) get rewarded. The girl was rewarded for what she was not supposed to do. Teachers must be careful not to reinforce the child by making a "deal" *after* the misbehavior has occurred or *after* the time for something to be done has passed. "If you stop dawdling and do your work, I'll give you free time," teaches dawdling. "Stop fighting, and you'll get a reward," teaches fighting. In each instance children are given approval to *stop* inappropriate behavior but actually learn to *begin* the inappropriate behavior so they can make a "deal" to stop so they can get a reward (generally on a partial schedule as we don't give in every time, and, thus, the child also learns persistence in misbehavior). Teachers should either use ignoring or disapproval to stop or extinguish the misbehavior. Teaching for incompatible responses using a positive approach involves setting up the reward beforehand.

Professional Application

Example 64

Pinpoint: Classroom "out of control" (6th grade, thirty students, beginning teacher)

Record: Average classroom study rate during first hour 25% (four days)

Consequate: Teacher had two conferences with principal, wrote assignments on board, changed class seating arrangement, watched a helping teacher demonstration (study rate 90% during demonstration).

Evaluate: Average classroom study rate increased to 48% (thirteen days). Teacher averaged only 1.4 contingent approval comments per day to entire class during the period.

Consequate II: Teacher instructed in principles of contingent approval; contingent approval comments increased to average of thirteen per session.

Evaluate II: Average study rate rose to 67% (fourteen days).

Consequate III: Teacher discontinued contingent approval comments.

Evaluate III: Study behavior decreased steadily to 45% by sixth day.

Consequate IV: Teacher reinstated contingent approval, averaging seventeen per session; decreased disapproval comments following nonstudy behavior.

Consequate IV: Study behavior increased average 77% (fourteen days).

Note: Three postexperimental observations indicated the study rates were being maintained at approximately the same level.

Scientific Application (p. 384)

Example 65

Pinpoint: Volunteering answers (6th grade, social studies class, four girls)

Record: Number of times girls volunteered during two-week period: zero. Only six questions answered when specifically directed toward them. Sociograms indicated girls isolates.

Consequate: Activities developed with approval from teacher and classmates. Girls recited alone from assigned book, read passages for parents, who praised accomplishment, then read for teacher alone. Girls' voices recorded and positive verbal approval given by teacher for effective talking. Recording later played for entire class, who praised performance. Teacher also praised interaction with other children. Additionally, small groups of girls worked on projects. Each group started with one fearful girl and one girl who modeled appropriate behaviors —number of students gradually increased.

Evaluate: Volunteering in class increased from nothing to an average slightly below rest of class.

Note: These procedures are closely related to many learning situations in which initial fear is gradually reduced by participating in the fear-producing activity (or approaching the feared objects) in small steps, receiving approval for behavior that is *incompatible* with avoidance.

Professional Application

Example 66

Pinpoint: Rehearsal effectiveness (High school band)

Record: *All* stops by conductor constituted disapproval responses (traditional rehearsing procedure).

Consequate: Band director marked two notated musical scores (equal difficulty and unfamiliar to band) with periodic pencil checks that divided musical phrases. During first score, director stopped at each checkpoint, delivered *disapproval* responses regardless of performance quality. During second score, director stopped at checks and delivered specific compliments to performers.

Evaluate: Compliments produced "a better performance and rehearsal attitude." Rehearsal time judged for equal performance level: disapproval = thirty-three minutes; approval = nineteen minutes.

Professional Application

Example 67

Pinpoint: Fighting during recess (12-year-old boy)

Record: Teacher watched through window and recorded number of days boy hit other children (four out of six days observed).

Consequate: Every time boy hit another child, he was taken into principal's office and given one hard swat with paddle.

Evaluate: Playground fighting *increased* after consequences.

Consequate II: Procedures changed. Boy allowed talking privilege (five minutes) with principal every day he behaved well on playground.

Evaluate: Fighting behavior decreased to zero over four weeks.

Note: Sometimes severe punishment can be actually rewarding to a child. There are children who associate any attention given by authorities or adults as indications of approval. (This is not as absurd as it seems—remember, we discipline those we care about.) Some children receive only negative attention. The application of approval following *good* behavior changes this wrong association.

Professional Application

Example 68

Pinpoint: Rebelliousness, disagreements, and refusal to talk to parents (11.5-year-old boy, large for age)

Record: Summer camp and school behavior in sharp contrast to misbehavior at home. (Young man reported camp and school misbehavior punished immediately; related interesting activities contingent on good behavior; therefore, no problem.) Boy indicated obedience only when father angry, as father oblivious to misbehavior except when in a "sour mood."

Consequate: Counselor enlisted boy's aid in "experiments." Boy to be on lookout for situations when he could disagree or disobey, then to stop and imagine to himself that father was so angry he was ready to attack verbally and physically. It was explained that if he could control his behavior by imagining an angry father, he probably would not have to face an actual one. Role-playing practice in imagery produced reactions similar to when he actually faced an angry father. Further treatment focused on the boy accepting authority of his father, even when unreasonable.

Evaluate: Home situation improved. First nine days boy reported using the "little trick" anywhere from ten to twenty-five times. The first week father had even taken him to an auto show and spent an enjoyable day. (It was pointed out that present obedience and restriction in freedom would result in more freedom later—delay of gratification.) Following some weeks, boy took father more into account (turned down volume on record player so it wouldn't disturb father, etc.). During the fourth week, an argument developed that was so violent the boy didn't want to return home. Father stayed away from boy for a while with improvement in relations continuing. Boy received more freedom; it became unnecessary to use "imagining father angry" technique as father became more reasonable and son less inclined to disagree on every little thing.

Note: A professional behavioral therapist helped this boy over a five-month period. The most significant factor appears to be that the boy, by pretending the father was angry, was able to tell himself that disobedience would lead to disapproval. This method of having children "talk to themselves and imagine potentially good or bad results" is a method of assisting in the development of self-control, especially if the thoughts are immediately followed by approval. This technique can be enhanced as teachers teach children to "label" many aspects of their behavior and follow the reproduction with approval. The results may not be as dramatic as the present case, in which the use of a thought "trick" improved a terrible home situation; but with continued communication parents and teachers are able to assist children in self-control procedures.

Scientific Application (p. 380)

Example 69

Pinpoint: Using adoption to control adults (16-year-old girl)

Record: Girl used statements concerning her adoption to "get her way." Engaged parents in "proving their love" and providing "payoff" (seven instances in one month).

Consequate: Parents instructed to ignore all talk concerning adoption, to leave girl's presence when subject brought up unless girl verbalized approval statements, and to prepare for extreme test.

Evaluate: Girl ran away; she returned the following weekend.

Consequate II: Girl instructed by parents that parental approval would continue to be contingent on good behavior, not on genetic involvement.

Evaluate II: The use of "adoption" to control parents ceased.

Note: Many children at all ages use adult concern, worry, or guilt to change the adults behavior. The child learns one of several perverted associations. "When I get punished and act hurt long enough, someone will give in," i.e., good things happen after I suffer. "They love me, so if I act nasty long enough they'll give up," i.e., to stop the negative behavior adults provide payoff. This reinforces the adults as obnoxious behavior stops, but children are reinforced for persisting in negative behavior for longer and longer periods. "When I get their goat anything is likely to happen," i.e., child's payoff *is* the anger of the adults (parents or teachers).

Professional Application

Example 70

Pinpoint: Disruptive behaviors—talking, fighting, out of seat, throwing objects, noisy (7th grade, thirty students, beginning teacher)

Record: Class met daily for forty minutes; had five-minute break followed by a forty-five minute session. Observation during first thirty minutes of session showed study behavior to average 47% (twenty-five days). Teacher gave contingent approval average of six times, disapproval for disruptive behaviors over twenty times per session.

Consequate: Teacher increased attention to study behavior, decreased attention to off-task behavior. Contingent approval increased to nine times per session, disapproval to nine per session.

Evaluate: Study behavior increased to average of 65% (six days). Noise level, disruptive behavior remained high.

Consequate II: Teacher placed chalk mark on board when students disturbed class. Each mark reduced class break ten seconds (twenty-four marks canceled break).

Evaluate II: Study behavior increased to 76% (twenty-four days). Noise dropped.

Consequate III: Teacher eliminated disapproval contingencies (chalk marks). Attention to disruptive behavior was increased.

Evaluate III: Study average dropped immediately; noise level increased.

Consequate IV: All procedures reinstated.

Evaluate IV: Study rate increased to 81% (maintained for remainder of study).

Note: The overall noise level remained high even when there was a large gain in on-task study behavior. It was necessary in this well-controlled scientific study to add a disapproval contingency (deprivation of break time for inappropriate behavior) before the classroom was brought under control. It should be emphasized that approval for good behavior can provide a positive atmosphere for learning even when disapproval procedures are employed.

Scientific Application (p. 384)

Example 71

Pinpoint: Unfinished assignments, bothering neighbors, playing (2nd grade, two boys referred by teacher)

Record: Trained observers recorded average of 47°₀ inappropriate behavior.

Consequate: Teacher and class formulated rules. Rules repeated six times per day for two weeks.

Evaluate: Little decrease in inappropriate behavior (average 40%).

Note: Apparently just knowing (being able to repeat rules) is not effective.

Consequate II: Teacher attempted to ignore inappropriate behaviors (teacher not entirely successful). Continued to repeat class rules every day.

Evaluate II: Behavior worsened. Average inappropriate behavior for four observations 69%.

Consequate III: Teacher praised prosocial behavior, repeated classroom rules, ignored inappropriate behavior.

Evaluate III: Inappropriate behavior *decreased* (average of 20°₀). Combination of procedures effective in reducing inappropriate behavior.

Consequate IV: Teacher instructed to act as she had in September. (Observers monitored entire year.)

Evaluate IV: Inappropriate behavior increased same day teacher changed (averaged 38%).

Consequate V: Rules, ignoring, and praise reinstated for remainder of school year.

Evaluate V: Inappropriate behavior again decreased (averaged only 15% for last eight-week period).

Note: Many teachers who believe they use more approval than disapproval do not (monitored by trained observers in classroom). It is necessary to practice delivering responses and to give yourself time cues or cues written on material you are teaching. A mark on every page can remind you to "catch someone being good." It is interesting to note that one boy reported in this study was seen during the entire year by a professional counselor. This boy responded in the same way to consequences as did the other boy who was not seen. It would seem that the teacher is capable of handling many behavioral problems generally referred to counselors, if responses are well developed and applied contingently.

Scientific Application (p. 391)

Example 72

Pinpoint: Following instructions (Kindergarten, 5 students)

Record: Students followed teachers' instructions 60% of the time during five days recording. Instructions included: pick up the toys; sit down; come and get a paper and pencil; write your name on the paper; fold your paper; bring your paper to my desk; put your chair on the table; get your mat out; lie down; be quiet.

Consequate I: Teacher attended students who followed rules (within 15 seconds) by giving verbal approval. Teacher tried to catch children being good during act of following instructions (6 days).

Evaluate I: Instructions followed increased to average of 78%.

Consequate II: Teacher no longer caught students being good, acted as during Record phase (five days).

Evaluate II: Average instructions followed equalled 68.7%.

Consequate III: Attention given specific children for following rules again as in Consequate I.

Evaluate III: Average percent of instructions followed 83.7%.

Note: Instructions were followed when the teacher caught the children being good and gave verbal approval for following rules. Whether or not children continued to follow rules is specifically dependent on the extent to which consequences follow desired behavior.

Scientific Application (p. 398)

Example 73

Pinpoint: Walking in street (1.5- to 4-year-old boys and girls)

Record: Various occurrences (parent's self-report)

Consequate: Children spanked, yelled at for going into street, given approval for verbalizing comments concerning "not going into street"; taken to edge of pavement and taught discrimination if pre-verbal, i.e., child put on grass, given approval; taken barely onto pavement spanked, yelled at. Children taught that when they hold parents' hands, then and only then may they walk in or across streets, parking lots, etc.

Evaluate: ?

Note: The strength of reinforcement required for teaching should be in direct proportion to the danger involved. (It seems unwise to put both dirty hands and potential death into the same "no-no" basket.) Sometimes complete supervision or instilling fear is the early alternative to potential danger; sometimes teaching for discrimination is advisable (i.e., concerning knives, hot stoves, scissors, electricity, poisons, water, etc.). *The adult must decide what is important.*

Professional Application

Example 74

Pinpoint: Talking out, standing (5th grade, 28 students)

Record: Students averaged 43.3°, talk-outs, 5.5% out-of-seat behaviors during English period, and 39.2% talk-outs, 10.0°₀ out-of-seat during math period (14 days observation).

Consequate I: Individual contingencies applied only during English period. Reinforcement included free time with choice to participate in desired activities (tutoring, reading, assisting teachers, record listening, viewing filmstrips).

Evaluate I: Average talk-outs decreased to 2.8%, out-of-seat decreased to .3% during English period. Observations during math indicated talk-outs 24.8°₀, out-of-seat 4.1°₀. Individual contingencies during English only, slightly modified the same behaviors during math.

Consequate II: Contingencies removed (five days).

Evaluate II: During English, talk-outs increased to 24.8%, average out-of-seat to 6.6°₀. During math period, talk-outs averaged 30.2%, out-of-seat 8.8°₀.

Consequate III: Group contingency applied to English period only. Five or more rule violations for entire class resulted in entire class losing free-time privileges (five days).

Evaluate III: During English period, average talk-outs decreased to 1.8°₀, out-of-seat to .1°₀. During math period, talk-outs averaged 15.0°₀, out-of-seat 1.7°₀.

Consequate IV: Contingencies removed from English class.

Evaluate IV: Talk-outs 3.4%, out-of-seat .4% during English. During math period, talk-outs averaged 20.1%, out-of-seat .3%.

Consequate V: Group contingency reapplied to both English period and math period. Five violations for entire class resulted in entire class losing free-time privilege (five days).

Evaluate V: Inappropriate behavior decreased to lowest level during both English and math periods. During English, talk-outs averaged .4%, out-of-seat, 0%. During math period, talk-outs averaged 1.0%, out-of-seat 0%.

Note: Both the individual and group contingencies had an impressive effect in reducing two bothersome behaviors. When the actual number of talk-outs is counted (rather than percentage of observed intervals), the results are even more impressive. During an average 40-minute English or math period, there was a difference of at least 180 fewer talk-outs during the least effective contingency. Results also indicate some carry-over to math period when contingencies were applied to English. Group contingencies are easier to apply than are individual contingencies (record keeping), and both were equally effective.

Scientific Application (p. 383)

Example 75

Pinpoint: Embarrassment (10th-grade music, three girls)

Record: Self-evaluation indicated students possessed "no musical talent." Students refrained from individual singing, stating "My voice sounds funny," or "I cannot carry a tune."

Consequate: Twofold program to: (1) teach all students discrimination between (a) possessing ability and (b) performing before class, and (2) teach entire class role-playing to deliver approval feedback to "insecure students."

Evaluate: Students learned to participate in activities, even though they did not possess even moderate "talent." Class also taught to smile, nod heads, keep eye contact, and approvingly reinforce a terrible performance. Teacher played role of extremely poor singer while class learned to "put a performer at ease" by *not* responding to performer's fear and avoidance with fear and avoidance, but with approving reinforcement. Shy performers began participating regularly. One girl stated: "I have always known I've had a lousy voice, but now I love to sing."

Note: Students in upper grades who have a problem with embarrassment in relation to any activity have *learned* this embarrassment from someone. It is usually learned traumatically. For example, the young child sings and enjoys himself until one day he shockingly learns his voice sounds terrible, whereupon he stops singing.

Unfortunately, some teachers do not understand the importance of teaching discriminations, and therefore continuously prepare many youngsters for disillusionment—some for catastrophe. Dedicated to well-intended censorship, many teachers pretend that no one is different from anyone. "Celia has only one arm, but in my classroom she has two, just like everyone else." "Fred has a lisp, but in my classroom we ignored his impediment." "Spencer is a Negro, but in my classroom everyone's skin is the same." It is unfortunate that these children must get out on the playground where other children do not censor: "Hey, Celia, what happened to your arm?" "Gosh, Fred, you talk funny." "Why are your hands white, Spencer?" Some children even make fun of these differences. Yet where can children learn to accept differences proudly and not make fun? —certainly not in a classroom in which differences *do not exist*. Children can easily be taught discrimination of differences. Much more important, they can be taught *acceptance* and *respect* for differences. This learning, however, will not come from censorship.

Professional Application

Example 76

Pinpoint: Arithmetic problem-solving (7th-grade boy, 13 years old)

Record: Number of completed correct problems per minute = .47, attention to assigned work averaged 51% (five days recording). Each day's assignment corrected and returned the following day.

Consequate I: Student given immediate praise, correct answers marked for each two problems completed (two days), four problems completed (next two days), eight problems (next two days). Final two days of treatment student completed 16 problems before receiving approval.

Evaluate I: Correct answers per minute increased to 1.36. Average percentage attending behavior increased to 97%.

Consequate II: Teacher returned to original procedure: gave student daily worksheet, corrected assignment, and handed back the following day without immediate approval (five days).

Evaluate II: Rate of correct answers *decreased* to .98. Percentage of attending behavior *decreased* to 82%.

Consequate III: Teacher again instituted immediate feedback. Five problems prior to approval (first day), ten (second day), fifteen (third day). Student completed all twenty problems before receiving approval (last two days).

Evaluate III: Correct arithmetic answers per minute increased to 1.44. Percentage of average attending behavior increased to 97%.

Note: This study demonstrates that when the teacher starts *where the student is* and gradually trains the student to delay feedback, the student's on-task behaviors may increase at the same time. The teacher in this case used a "fixed-ratio" schedule that was adjusted either every day or every other day.

Scientific Application (p. 387)

Example 77

Pinpoint: Lawbreaking (Forty delinquent boys, average age 17.8, lower socioeconomic)

Record: Average age at first arrest 13.5; average number arrests 8.2; total time incarceration 15.1 months. All boys arrested approximately same age, same nationality, equal number of months in jail, similar residence and religious preferences.

Consequate: One group participated in consequences, one "control" group did not. Boys were not in school (most of them should have been) and met on street corners or other places of frequent occupancy. Each boy was offered job and told that the researcher wanted to know "how teenagers felt about things." Boys who participated were rewarded with food, cokes, money, or tokens, depending on each individual case. No punishment was employed. Occasionally, bonus rewards given for prompt arrival, proper verbalizations, and spontaneous interest.

Evaluate: Groups were compared three years later. Consequate group averaged 2.4 arrests, other group 4.7; average number of months in jail 3.5 for consequate group, 6.9 for other group. Illegal acts committed by consequate group less frequent and much less severe.

Note: In this particular study, consequences were *not* directed toward criminal behavior itself but represented an attempt to teach prosocial behavioral patterns. When a boy did not appear, the researcher would meet him out on the street and bring him to the lab. It is sometimes important for the teacher to go after a child and bring him where he should be. Any peer group such as the above juvenile group can exercise tremendous pressure toward group conformity. Often peer rewards must be broken down or changed if the teacher is to succeed.

Scientific Application (p. 398)

Example 78

Pinpoint: Low level English achievement (High school dropouts, 17)

Record: No academic performance; all students out of school during summer.

Consequate: Students contacted on city streets during summer were induced to "try coming to school a few days for rewards." Local merchants donated: (1) food—hamburgers, cokes, malts, sandwiches, etc., (2) music—records and passes, (3) free time, (4) teacher attention, and (5) grades. Students were assigned a different consequence each day.

Evaluate: 14 boys completed English requirements during the regular year and decided to return to high school in the fall.

Note: Of special interest in this study was the disparity between stated preferences and actual behavior. At the beginning of summer, all boys were presented paired items from a reinforcement menu and asked which they would work for (e.g. would you work harder for a McDonald's hamburger or 10 minutes of free time?). All classes of items were paired with all other classes. The order of preference at the beginning of the summer was: (1) food, (2) music records and passes, (3) free time, (4) grades, and (5) teacher attention. At the end of the summer, the same questionnaire was given all boys. The order of preference as stated by the boys was the same at the beginning of the summer as at the end; however, accurate records kept on the actual work output of each boy indicated that during the first week of summer school they indeed worked harder for material rewards and food, but during the last week of summer school the most work was actually produced when followed by *teacher attention*.

Professional Application

Example 79

Pinpoint: Tardiness following recess (5th grade, 25 students)

Record: Teacher and one student recorded the number of students late for noon, morning, and afternoon recesses. Average number of students late for noon recess was 7.2 (13 days). Average number late for morning recess was 3.7 (21 days). Average number late for afternoon recess was 3.9 (27 days).

Consequate I: Students were studying patriots and were excited about being Today's Patriot. Teachers introduced Today's Patriot Chart. Chart (posted on the board at the end of each day) listed those who got back to classroom on time after noon recess. Chart only for noon recess, did not include morning and afternoon recesses.

Evaluate I: Students late decreased dramatically. Only three students were late after noon recess during the 19 days the chart was in effect. However, average number late after morning recess was 3.3; after afternoon recess, 3.7.

Consequate II: Patriots Chart expanded to include morning recess. Names appeared on chart only if students on time for both morning and noon recesses.

Evaluate II: No student was late during the 10 days the chart was in effect for either morning or noon recesses. Average 3.2 students continued to be late for afternoon recess.

Consequate III: Teacher again raised criterion for inclusion on Patriots Chart to on time for all three recess periods.

Evaluate III: No one was late after any recess period during five days criterion.

Consequate IV: Teacher informed class that students had done so well chart no longer needed. Teacher could "count on them" to remain patriots.

Evaluate IV: Noon tardiness averaged 5.0 for five days, tardiness after morning recess, 2.6, and after afternoon recess, 2.6.

Consequate V: Teacher reinstated chart for all three recess periods.

Evaluate V: Not one person was late after any recess during the five days the chart was in effect.

Consequate VI: Class voted to post an Un-Patriots Chart (those students who were *late*) instead of Patriots Chart. Teacher posted chart every second day for six days, every third day for six days, and every fifth day for last week of project.

Evaluate VI: One student was late after one recess during the final 18 days of the project.

Note: This study indicated that many teachers can carry out specific projects without the help of outside observers. Also, if the consequence has some meaning to the student and is consistently applied, the results are predictable. Many teachers have used "good" charts of some kind but they are seldom as precise and consistently applied. The specific name given to the charts is meaningful to the students if they have been studying an area and are allowed to decide the name of the chart as well as on criteria for inclusion on the chart in conjunction with the teacher.

Scientific Application (p. 383)

Example 80

Pinpoint: Children manipulating parents (Three children and mothers trained in Child Development Clinic. A 6-year-old boy attempted to force parents to comply with his wishes. A 4-year-old boy considered excessively dependent at home, aggressive in nursery school. Another 4-year-old extremely stubborn in presence of mother but not with other adults.)

Record: Each mother observed while interacting with son.

Consequate: Mothers instructed: (1) in delivery of approval techniques, (2) to ignore inappropriate behavior, and (3) to respond with praise and affection for appropriate behavior. Mother A responded positively to child *only* when he did not attempt to force compliance. Mother B ignored child's dependency, responded approvingly to independent behavior. Mother C ignored oppositional behavior, responded to cooperate behavior. Later, Mother C was instructed to isolate son in empty room for at least five minutes immediately following oppositional responses.

Evaluate: First two boys' behavior improved markedly through mothers' attention to appropriate behavior and ignoring inappropriate responses. The third boy improved only after isolation.

Note: This is a good example of differential treatment. The teacher should always remember that it is necessary to structure for each student. It should be noted that the use of disapproval (isolation) was necessary for one child before improvement took place.

Scientific Application (p. 402)

Example 81

Pinpoint: Academic underachievement (25 underachievers, 8 to 12-year-olds, average age, 10.1)

Record: 30 children were originally selected for summer program; five moved. The average educational level of mother was 7.0, the fathers' was 7.2. Average income was $3,800. 40°₀ of children came from broken homes (separation, divorce, or death). California Achievement Test averaged 1.5 years below norms. Overall grade point average for preceding year was 1.47 (D grades). Total work time (percent of assigned classroom time engaged in academic activities) averaged 39°₀ (dropped last day to 18%). Rate of work output (number of exercises and problems done divided by number of minutes) averaged 1.40 problems attempted per minute. Accuracy of output (number of problems and exercises done correctly divided by total attempted) averaged 50°₀ (fifteen days recording of all 25 students). Teachers and aides averaged 13 approvals per hour, 27 disapprovals per hour. Instructional responses (requests, commands, and rules) averaged 55 per hour.

Consequate I: Students were given personalized booklets with 50 squares per page (three colors of pages). Points were awarded by teacher checking the appropriate number of squares in booklet. Academic work was reinforced by assigning points for *accuracy* (⅔ of total) and *speed* of working (⅓ of points). Social behavior reinforced by getting to work quickly (20 pts.), working for 10–20 minutes continuously (20 pts.), working while fight or noise going on nearby (10 pts.), raising hand (5 pts.), obtaining permission to leave desk (5 pts.). Inappropriate behaviors were given warning first and then 10–50 pts., fine taken, two fines resulting in "time-out" with contingency to finish one assignment without points to work way back into system. Points were redeemable as follows: First 25 points (green) paid for lunch (no child missed lunch entire summer); yellow points earned school store (candy, gum, toys, supplies, goldfish, clothes, jewelry, makeup kits, baseballs, games of many kinds, etc.); red points earned field trips occurring on Friday afternoon (fishing, boating, swimming parties, farm trip, bank, hospital, and pet shop). Teachers passed out store items while giving approval and urging continued success. Teachers and aides paired approvals for academic and social behaviors while giving points in books Program lasted for 29 days of summer term.

Evaluate I: Total work time increased from 39% to 57% average. Rate of work increased from 1.4 assigned problems attempted per minute to an average of 3.35. (SRA reading workbook .97 to 2.9, SRA spelling .90 to 2.34, SRA Reading Lab .28 to 1.43, Merrill Workbook 1.37 to 2.7, spelling workbook .80 to 1.72, math workbook 2.01 to 6.19, math worksheets 2.65 to 4.84); accuracy increased from 50% correct to 70% correct (SRA reading workbook 32.4% to 62.2%, SRA reading lab 30.9% to 64.9%, Merrill Workbook 53.3% to 68.2%, spelling workbook 52.0% to 68%, math workbook 51.6% to 72.9%, math worksheets 58.7% to 75.1%, spelling tests 46.7% to 71.9%). Teachers and aides during Consequate I averaged 47 approvals per hour, 7 disapprovals per hour, and 17 requests, commands, and rules per hour.

Consequate II: Teachers eliminated the point system but continued approval for appropriate academic and social behavior (children received candy, toys, lunch without contingencies during nine days of program as during Record phase).

Evaluate II: Time at work average dropped to 42%. Problems attempted per minute *increased* to 5.5. Accuracy increased to 73%. Teachers and aides decreased approvals to 27 per hour, disapprovals increased to 9 per hour, and requests, commands, and rules to 16 per hour. CAT scores averaged .42 years higher at end of summer than at beginning.

Note: The normal classroom routines during the Record phase were producing less and less work prior to the introduction of the point system. There followed a substantial increase in achievement with the dual introduction of the points and change in teacher verbal approval from an approval ratio of approximately 33% to one of 87%. Six weeks of contingent points and high verbal approval did not maintain a high work rate after the points were withdrawn. These teachers unfortunately did not maintain the same high approval rate during Consequate II. Perhaps if the teachers had maintained the same rate and ratio of approvals, then the work time might have remained as high after the points were withdrawn. The rate of work output increased steadily during the six weeks of contingent points and stayed even after the points were withdrawn.

It appears that six weeks' contingent reinforcement was able to maintain a high rate of work output even after withdrawing the reinforcers (things and activities), providing that teachers remained predominately positive and used verbal approval. The same is indicated for accurate work. Students reached a high level of accuracy during the point system and maintained the same level with social and academic verbal contingencies. The authors also report that during the Record phase teachers were spending more time in trying to eliminate disruptive inappropriate behaviors, but that during the Consequate phase they shifted to teaching behaviors. The students were also able to learn to interact in positive ways with both teachers and academic materials. Even though the work time dropped after the point system was withdrawn, students maintained a high work rate and high accuracy rate, perhaps indicating that the interaction with academic materials became more reinforcing to the students. It is interesting to note that the sudents were able to maintain accuracy and rate of problems completed, using less time in on-task work. Perhaps, as with the teachers, the students were able to spend less time and achieve better results following a precise and well-implemented program of contingent reinforcement.

Scientific Application (p. 378)

Example 82

Pinpoint: Academic "apathy" (11th grade, history, poverty level backgrounds)

Record: *No* evidence of *any* study behavior. Five days constant harassment.

Consequate: Teacher left *all* books and teaching materials home, sat at the desk, looked at students, and said nothing. Teacher continued procedure day after day throughout *one entire week*. Did not attempt to teach, control class, or respond in any way.

Evaluate: During the second week, two students timidly brought books to class and asked what to do. Teacher brought the two students to front of room and began teaching. As days passed, other students joined the small learning group. By end of six weeks, every student was involved. Last seven students came into learning group on same day.

Note: Much is said in education about students establishing their own goals. This study is an excellent example of this concept at its most basic level—for there is an infinite distance between zero and one. Most students do not know what their goals are. If they can engage a teacher in battle, this often becomes their goal. In the above case, students were left with nothing. In time, they began to want something, anything, even school work. Ignoring takes a temporal patience many teachers could well develop. Concerning these students, it should be noted that children who live in extreme deprivation meet boredom and apathy as an old friend. Perhaps more sophisticated students would have developed goals during this long period that excluded the teacher entirely.

When a teacher decides to accept the contingencies (goals) of the student peer group, he should do so in full knowledge of possible results. When speaking of "children establishing their own goals," it would seem wise for teachers to think this concept through. Most often this cliché indicates that the teacher *decides* to let children *decide* certain innocuous things. "You may choose any color you wish—you may not color on the wall." If, from the beginning, goals were left *entirely* to children, formal education would cease to exist. Knowledge and/ or decisions cannot exist in a vacuum—"Tell me something you *do not know.*"

Professional Application

Example 83

Pinpoint: Physical abuse of mother (15-year-old boy)

Record: Boy placed in county juvenile detention center for physical abuse of widowed mother, throwing her out of house, threatening others with a gun. Boy stated that he only wanted to play his guitar and be left entirely alone.

Consequate: (1) Guitar lessons contingent on assigned work tasks. Guitar removed if tasks not completed. (2) Communication sessions developed between mother and son, using boy's music as subject matter. Also, music paired with talk sessions to decrease high emotional responses. (3) Role-playing sessions between counselor and mother to establish correct verbalizations.

Evaluate: Case terminated after four weeks (guitar was removed once); no beatings, arrests, or verbal abuses.

Note: The mother in this case was being unwittingly controlled by her son. In her words, "Every time I try to talk with Fred and explain how I feel, he somehow turns my words against me and then goes into his room to listen to music; I am deeply concerned that he just doesn't understand me." Many adults, as the widow in this case, try to reason and explain their feelings, yet become "used" by young people. Reinforcing this insensitive behavior is certainly unproductive for adults and does little but produce a kind of "sadism." It seems extremely unproductive when adults allow young people to use divorce, adoption, lack of love, peer or sibling comparisons, etc., to get their way. In this case, the mother had fallen into the trap of "trying even harder to make her son understand her." It should be noted that after the boy's verbal and physical abuse stopped and he was rewarded for *appropriate* behavior (i.e., household duties, clearing the yard, not arguing, etc.), he did start to "understand" his mother.

Scientific Application (p. 391)

Example 84

Pinpoint: On-task attention, academic accuracy (14 third-grade children, age 10.1 average, I.Q. average 75, 2.58 arithmetic achievement level)

Record: Each day students worked 100 arithmetic problems drawn randomly from pool of 5,000 items containing equal numbers of addition, subtraction, multiplication, and division. Students worked 20 minutes per session. Average on-task behavior 80%, average disruptions 8%, median percent problems correct (number correct divided by number attempted) = 55%, median number of correct problems = 50% (six sessions).

Consequate I: Teacher circulated through three rows of children once per minute, gave tokens for attending to work task. Each child earned 12 to 16 tokens per 20 minute session; tokens could be exchanged for choice of candy, ice cream, inexpensive toys, high interest activities, field trips (14 sessions).

Evaluate I: On-task attending behavior increased during seven days to over 90% last day; disruptions averaged less than one per day; median percent of problems correct remained approximately constant (54%), as did median number of correct problems (50%).

Consequate II: Teacher continued to circulate among three rows once each minute giving tokens *not* for attending but for accuracy and rate of work. Students could now earn one token for seven correct problems, also bonus tokens (21% to 30% of problems worked correctly one token, 31% to 40% two tokens up to eight for 91% to 100% correct and two additional tokens for perfect paper). Students earned 10 to 18 per day (12 sessions).

Evaluate II: Attending behavior dropped to between 50% and 70%, disruptions rose to high of 20%. However, median percent of problems correct rose to 76%, median number correct remained approximately constant (50%).

Consequate III: Teachers again gave tokens for attending, *not* for accuracy of work.

Evaluate III: Attending behavior rose slightly from previous phase (average approximately $= 73°_0$, disruptions approximately 3%, median percent problems correct $= 72°_0$, median number correct problems $= 50\%$).

Consequate IV: Teachers gave tokens both for attending (on-task) and correct work.

Evaluate IV: Attending behavior increased to between $80°_0$ to $85°_0$, disruptions decreased to 1%, median percent problems correct $= 80\%$. Median number of correct problems increased to approximately $65°_0$.

Consequate V: Teachers again returned to giving tokens for correct work only, not for attending behavior.

Evaluate V: Attending behavior dropped to approximately 63%, disruptions rose to approximately $10°_0$, median percent of problems correct rose to $83°_0$, median number of correct problems approximately 56% (five sessions).

Consequate VI: Teachers again gave tokens both for attending and correct work.

Evaluate VI: Attending behavior increased steadily to a high of 86%, median percent problems correct 82%, median number of correct problems rose to high of $68°_0$ during last two sessions (seven sessions).

Note: The authors in this scientific study, and an additional study with the same age children, demonstrated that reinforcement contingencies applied to on-task behavior consistently increased attending behavior and decreased disruptions but had little effect on accuracy of math computations. Alternately, contingencies placed on correct work produced an increase in accuracy but the number of correct problems remained the same, and attending behavior decreased while disruptions increased. Contingencies placed on both attending behavior and accuracy of work increased attending behavior and number of problems correctly completed as well as the percentage of problems worked correctly.

These two excellent studies indicate the importance of the teacher specifying the precise behaviors to be reinforced. The teacher should not expect automatic improvement in academic achievement if the teacher decreases or increases inappropriate social behavior. Conversely, the students will not magically behave in socially appropriate ways just because they are making accurate academic responses. The teacher must determine what is going to be reinforced in what combinations and structure for both academic and social improvement.

Scientific Application (p. 381)

Example 85

Pinpoint: Off-task, low achieving students (7th grade, 12 students)

Record: Students off-task 56.4%, teacher academic approval = 49.9%, teacher social approval ratio = 3.0% (ten days observation).

Consequate I: Eight students were taken from the room and received daily group counseling (four were given behavioral counseling through role-playing, modeling appropriate classroom behaviors, and received reinforcement for verbalizing appropriate classroom behavior; four students were given "client-centered" counseling, and were helped to verbalize and interpret classroom behavior.) Four students remained in room as a control group to check effects of group counseling.

Evaluate I: Four students in behavioral counseling increased on-task behavior 6.8%. Four students in client-centered counseling increased on-task behavior 2.2%. Control group decreased on-task behavior 11.3% (Average off-task for all 12 = 57%). Teachers' academic approval ratio = 11.7% and social approval ratio — 1.5%.

Consequate II: Counseling continued for both groups (4 weeks) teacher instructed in contingent use of approval techniques.

Evaluate II: Behavioral counseling group increased on-task behavior an additional 38.1%, client-centered counseling group increased on-task behavior an additional 27.7%, no-contact control group increased on-task behavior 40.7% (average off-task for all 12 = 21.3%). Teacher academic approval ratio = 62.2%, social approval ratio = 62.4%.

Consequate III: Counseling continued; teacher continued attention for both academic and social behavior and also instituted a token reinforcement system (tokens were given for appropriate social behavior, redeemable on Friday afternoons for doughnuts, soda pop (2 weeks).

Evaluate III: Behavioral counseling group increased on-task behavior another 7.8% (2.1% = total off-task), client-centered increased on-task behavior another 10.8% (total off-task = 18.5%), control group increased on-task another 5.7% (total off-task = 19.6%). Average off-task for all twelve = 13.4%. Teacher academic approval ratio = 76.3%, social approval ratio = 86.7%.

Consequate IV: Counseling discontinued, teacher instructed to behave as before the study began (1 week).

Evaluate IV: All 12 students increased inappropriate behavior (41.2% off-task). No significant difference between three counseling groups.

Consequate V: Teacher reinstituted approving academic and social behavior, also reinstated token system.

Evaluate V: Average on-task behavior for all 12 students averaged 93.2% Teacher's academic approval ratio averaged 42.8%, social approval ratio averaged 91.1%.

Note: This study indicates that the teacher is the major instigator of both appropriate and inappropriate behavior even on the seventh grade level. It also indicates that counseling outside the classroom for classroom behavioral problems is probably not effective unless the teacher reinforces appropriate classroom behavior. Even though behavioral counseling was more effective than client-centered, behavioral counseling had little effect until the teacher used contingent approval. The study also indicated that the teacher is better able to change behavior where the problem occurs (in the classroom).

Scientific Application (p. 391)

Example 86

Pinpoint: Developing a study routine (Thirty-six teenage students, girls and boys)

Record: Average grade level considered by both teachers and parents to be at least one letter grade below potential (average grades = C—).

Consequate: Students were asked to indicate amount of time each felt appropriate to achieve goal (raising grades). Total time indicated was cut by 40%, after which a contract signed by pupil, teacher, and parent. Specific routines developed to aid in concentration:

1. *Underlining*
First it was explained that learning to underline or to outline were *not* the same as learning assigned material (many students have developed negative reactions particularly to these two activities). If students want to learn to draw lines it should be done with many colored pencils, a ruler, and blank paper. If students want to outline, the daily paper will do just as well as school material.

2. *Concentration*
The important aspects of study are *on-task* concentration and repetition of materials not fully learned (asking oneself questions and answering as the material is studied—talking to oneself). On-task study time determined by each student before beginning to study material. Students also noted the number of their distracting thoughts (no student was able to complete *six* minutes of study time with fewer than eight distraction marks). On-task study time was increased in following manner: Each student purchased a timer (kitchen timer, $4.00 to $7.00) with his own money and set aside only weekday study times that fit individual schedule (weekends free from nagging parents appealed to all students).

3. *Study place*

Students chose a "study-place" where only study would take place. If necessary, other members of family used the same spot, but the student with the problem could study only there and nowhere else in the house. A straight-backed chair was chosen, with attempts made to place chair facing a corner or blank wall. Prominent signs were constructed warning family members (including parents) to stay away during study time. Distractions such as music (radios, "hi fi") were eliminated (these do *not* increase studying effectiveness). Only one book or one set of materials was taken to study place for each study session.

4. *Distraction cards*

Students used 5 × 8 inch cards labeled as to date, time started, time finished, session number, as well as open space for distractions (distracting thoughts or interruptions). Students chose a pleasant activity to engage in during break times (reading, eating, listening to radio, talking with friends, telephone calls, etc.), got materials ready, removed watches and other indicators of time, filled in the card, set kitchen timer for six minutes, and began to study. Whenever the student was distracted in any way (defined by student to help teach discrimination between on-task and off-task behavior), the student marked in space provided for distractions and also wrote in longhand at the bottom of card, "Get back to work." After having first noticed a distraction (competing sound, daydreaming, thinking of opposite sex, etc.), initial inclination is to go back to work; writing little note "Get back to work" prevents this for a moment and serves to make concentration more desirable, discriminations more complete.

5. *Timer* (positioned so students couldn't see face)

When the timer rang, the students stood up immediately, took the timer, and moved away from study area. Reset timer for two minutes, then engaged in "fun" activity until timer again sounded; whereupon students went through same routine filling in new card. This procedure was repeated until the total time period allotted for study passed. Students changed from six-minute study session to nine-minute study session when num-

171

ber of distraction marks (and corresponding self-written work instructions) numbered two or fewer.

6. *Study schedules*

Students were permitted three-minute break for nine-minute study period. Each time distractors had been reduced to two or below, students moved up scale (study six, break two; study nine, break three; study twelve, break four; study fifteen, break five; study eighteen, break six; study twenty-one, break seven; study twenty-four, break eight; study twenty-seven, break nine; study thirty, break ten; study thirty-three, break eleven; study thirty-six, break twelve; study thirty-nine, break thirteen; study forty-two, break fourteen; study forty-five, break fifteen) until reaching maximum. Students were strongly encouraged to never study longer than forty-five minutes while using a fifteen-minute break for pleasant activities. This routine builds strong study skills as well as gives approval rewards following each small study session.

7. *External rewards*

Some parents/students used extra incentives (movies, car privileges, staying out time, money, family outings) for moving up study scale *while maintaining absolute honesty*. Of course, many students were delighted with a routine that didn't start with amount of homework to be finished but with amount of time to be studied (when no homework was available or required, student reviewed materials for test).

Evaluate: Average grades (thirty-one students) increased to B within three school terms. Follow-up indicated twenty-four students maintained this level or above during entire following school year. Five students who did *not* improve admitted to never getting with the program. Seven students who did not *maintain* grade level did not consistently adhere to program primarily as results of *parents* who did not change their normally punitive, nagging reaction; who expressed doubts as to mental capabilities of their children or effectiveness of program; and who did not encourage positively through words and extra incentives. Five students with parents falling into above category succeeded in spite of parental negativism and lack of support. (All later confided to school personnel they were going to prove to their parents that they were not "stupid" and continued the program in spite of lack of support. Three of these finally set up study places in friend's or relative's homes away from "distracting" influence of negative parents.)

Note: This routine has been used successfully with junior high students, upper-level grade school students, college students, and professionals who need to learn discrimination between on-task study as opposed to clutter. Most students do not enjoy their rest or fun times because they begin to feel "guilty" about not doing work. Alternately, when they attempt to study, they begin to feel sorry for themselves because they are not out having a good time!

Professional Application

Example 87

Pinpoint: Dishonesty (Any classroom, anywhere)

Record: Three students caught cheating on first exam of term.

Consequate: F grades assigned without explanation.

Evaluate: Same three students caught stealing "ditto master" of second exam from typist's wastebasket.

Consequate II: Each student asked to write short theme stating reasons for cheating.

Evaluate II: Same three students caught cheating in falsifying laboratory manual.

Consequate III: Students asked to prepare confessional speech to be delivered before entire class. Parents of two students strongly objected, stating such treatment "would not only be a terrible experience, but damage children's reputations." Principal received call from school board member, after which students, parents, and teachers instructed to meet in principal's office. At meeting, all students denied any cheating whatsoever. Teacher presented first themes of confession. Parents of one student immediately placed her in private school. Parents of second student persuaded principal to allow daughter to withdraw from course. Parents of third student did not come to meeting Teacher required this girl to make confessional statement before class. She did, but broke down crying before finishing. She later told teacher it was the worst thing she ever did in her life. Much later, she told the teacher that it was *second* worst thing she ever did in her life.

Evaluate III, IV, V, VI, etc.: *The science of behavior is predictable.* You know all three of these students, regardless of age, sex, or position.

Fictional Application

PART III

A POSITIVE APPROACH

CHAPTER 7

DEVELOPING RESPONSES

The teacher has many reinforcers that can be used contingently across time to teach desired behaviors. However, merely reading, talking, and thinking about consequential responses does not produce optimum results. The development of effective responses takes *practice*. Consider for a moment the tremendous practice it takes for a poet to choose the precise word, for a musician to turn a beautiful phrase, for an actor to deliver a line effectively. Practice in developing responses cannot be overemphasized. Just talking to yourself while looking into a mirror is very effective. A tape recorder can also be valuable in developing response skills. At first you will notice some tension—you will feel awkward and perhaps a little childish. Nevertheless, practice. A good place to start is with the words "thank you." Practice saying "thank you" with as many inflections as possible—from extreme sarcasm to sincere appreciation.

If one desires to express a sincere feeling, one must make sure the real intent will be expressed. Those people whom we consider warm and sensitive are people who have developed great skill in expression. Most often, expressions are not overtly practiced; yet all teachers (having been often misunderstood) should be sure to communicate their thoughts and feelings most effectively. Considering all the time we spend in front of the mirror on physical appearances, is it not incongruous we do not use some of this time to develop effective personal responses? After patient practice in role-playing, the teacher will begin to notice exciting new skill in the development of responses. Sometimes a teacher may choose to practice with another person who desires to be helpful in giving the teacher appropriate feedback.

Other than subject matter itself, responses available to the teacher can be classified in five categories: (1) words (spoken-written), (2) physical expressions (facial-bodily), (3) closeness (nearness-touching), (4) activities (social-individual), and (5) things (materials, food, playthings, awards). The following lists have been developed as possible *approval* models for the teacher. The teacher should select and develop those reinforcers deemed usable as specific behavioral contingencies for the age and grade level of students involved. Start with one or two responses, develop thoroughly, and evaluate in the classroom before developing others.

APPROVAL RESPONSES

Words Spoken: Approval

Words

Yes	Correct
Good	Excellent
Neat	That's right
Nice	Perfect
O.K.	Satisfactory
Great	How true
Fascinating	Absolutely right
Charming	Keep going
Commendable	Good responses
Delightful	How beautiful!
Brilliant	Wonderful job!
Fine answer	Fantastic!
Uh-huh	Terrific!
Positively!	Swell
Go ahead	Beautiful work
Yeah!	Tasty
All right	Marvelous!
Nifty	Exciting!
Exactly	Pleasant
Of course	Delicious
Cool	Fabulous!
Likeable	Splendid
Wonderful	Well-mannered
Outstanding work	Thinking
Of course!	

Sentences

That's clever.
I'm pleased.
Thank you.
I'm glad you're here.
That's a *prize* of a job.
You make us happy.
That shows thought.
We think a lot of you.
You're tops on our list.
That's good work.
Remarkably well done.
You're very pleasant.
That shows a great deal of work.
Yes, I think you should continue.
A good way of putting it.
I like the way __(name)__ explained it.
That is a feather in your cap.
You are very friendly.
That's an excellent goal.
Nice speaking voice.
That's a nice expression.
It is a pleasure having you as a student.
That's interesting.
You make being a teacher very worthwhile.
That's sweet of you.
Well thought out.
Show us how.
You're doing better.
You are improving.
You're doing fine.
You perform very well, __(name)__ .
That's very good, __(name)__ .
I'm so proud of you.
I like that.
This is the best yet.
That's the correct way.
That's very choice.
You do so well.
You're polite.
Thinking!

Relationships

Nice things happen to nice children.
That is very imaginative.
You are worthy of my love.
That will be of great benefit to the class.
I admire it when you work like that.
That is original work.
I appreciate your attention.
You've been a fine credit to your class.
I commend your outstanding work.
We are proud to honor your achievement.
That was very kind of you.
You catch on very quickly.
Obedience makes me happy.
That deserves my respect.
You demonstrate fine ability.
That is clear thinking.
You should be very proud of this.
That was nice of you to loan her your _____ .
I wish you would show me and the class how you got such an
    interesting effect.
I like that—I didn't know it could be done that way.
Permission granted.
That's a good job—other children can look up to you.
Let's watch him do it.
He accepts responsibility.
That *was* a good choice.
Show this to your parents.
I know how you feel—should we continue?
I'm happy your desk is in order.
Why don't you show the class how you got the answer?
That's a good point to bring up,   (name)   .
I agree.
Let's put this somewhere special.
I'd like this in my own house.
My, you have a nice attitude.
Now you're really trying.
Keep working hard,   (name)   .
You've improved.
Your work appears so neat.
You're a good person.
If at first you don't succeed, try, try again.
Thinking!

Words and Symbols Written: Approval

Bravo!

Improvement

Fine

Good

Neato

Very good

O.K.

Passing

*

X

✔

Thoughtful

100°'

Good paper

Very colorful

☺

Well done

Great!

Wow!

A-1

Perceptive

Good work

☆

Correct

+

Satisfactory

Nicely done

Very concise

Complete

A, B, C, D

Enjoyable

Excellent

Outstanding

☞

[Colored pencil markings]

Superior

Congratulations

Yeh

Show this to your parents.

[Honor rolls]

For display

[Rubber stamps]

Rules

In formulating rules, remember to:

1. Involve the class in making up the rules.

2. Keep the rules short and to the point.

3. Phrase rules, where possible, in a positive way. ("Sit quietly while working" instead of "Don't talk to your neighbors.")

4. Remind the class of the rules at times *other* than when someone has misbehaved.

5. Make different sets of rules for varied activities.

6. Let children know when different rules apply (work-play).

7. Post rules in a conspicuous place and review regularly.

8. Keep a sheet on your desk and record the number of times you review rules with class.

Expressions: Approval

Facial

Looking
Smiling
Winking
Nodding
Grinning
Raising eyebrows
Forming kiss
Opening eyes
Slowly closing eyes
Laughing (happy)
Chuckling

Widening eyes
Wrinkling nose
Blinking rapidly
Giggling
Whistling
Cheering
Licking lips
Smacking lips
Pressing lips affirmatively
Rolling eyes enthusiastically

Bodily

Clapping hands
Raising arms
Shaking fist
Signaling O.K.
Cocking head
Skipping
Rubbing stomach
Thumbs up
Shaking head
Jumping up and down
Shrugging shoulders
Circling hand through air (encouragement to continue)

Hand/finger to face, eyebrows, eyes, nose, ears, mouth, cheek, lips, hair, forehead
Grabbing
Bouncing
Dancing
Stroking motions
Opening hands
Flipping head
Taking a fast breath
Expansive movements of hands
Hugging self

Closeness: Approval

Nearness

Nearness concerns physical proximity and ranges from geographical separation—through noticeable contact—to embracing.
Interacting with class at recess
Eating with children
Sitting on desk near students
Sitting within the student group
Standing alongside
Walking among students
Gently guiding
Pausing—while transferring objects

Touching

Hand on hand
Ruffling hair
Touching head
Patting head
Pinching chin
Touching nose
Patting back
Patting shoulder
Touching arm
Straightening clothes
Hugging
Touching hand
Shaking hands
Squeezing hand
Patting cheek
Nudging
Helping put on coats
Retying sashes

Walking alongside
Combing hair
Tying shoes
Quick squeeze
Dancing
Rubbing back of neck
Gently raising chin
Leaning over
Touching hurt
Kissing a hurt
Putting face next to child
Tweaking nose
Tickling
Cupping face in hands
Gentle pull at hair
Running finger down person's nose
Guiding with hand

Activities and Privileges: Approval

Individual

Leading student groups
Representing group in school activities
Displaying student's work (any subject matter)
Straightening up for teacher
Putting away materials
Running errands
Caring for class pets, flowers, etc.
Collecting materials (papers, workbooks, assignments, etc.)
Choosing activities
Show and tell (any level)
Constructing school materials
Dusting, erasing, cleaning, arranging chairs, etc.
Helping other children (drinking, lavatory, cleaning, etc.)
Reading a story
Exempting a test
Working problems on the board

Answering questions
Outside supervising (patrols, directing parking, ushering, etc.)
Classroom supervision
Omitting specific assignments
First in line
Assisting teacher teach
Leading discussions
Making gifts
Recognizing birthdays
Grading papers
Special seating arrangements
Responsibility for ongoing activities during school holidays (pets, plants, assignments)
Decorating room
Presenting hobby to class
"Citizen of the Week" or "Best Kid of the Day"

Social

Movies
Decorating classroom
Presenting skits
Playing records
Puppet shows
Preparing for holidays (Christmas, Thanksgiving, Valentine's Day)
Making a game of subject matter
Outdoor lessons
Visiting another class
Field trips (subject matter)
Planning daily schedules
Musical chairs
Competing with other classes
Performing for PTA
Dancing
Going to museums, fire stations, courthouses, picnics, etc.
"Senior Sluff Day"
Participating in group organizations (music, speech, athletics, social clubs)
Talking periods
Recess or play periods
Early dismissal
Parties
Talent shows (jokes, readings, music, etc.)

Things: *Approval*

Materials

Books—appropriate level
Pets
Bookcovers
Book markers
Coloring books
Crayons
Paints
Pencils with names
Chalk
Flowers
Buttons
Pins
Pictures
Colored paper
Iguana
Counting beads
Games
Stuffed animals
Cards
Stars
Chips
Kites
Balloons
Jacks
Striped straws
Windmills
Miniature animals
Farm set and farm animals
Plastic toys (Indians, animals, soldiers, etc.)
Jump ropes
Musical toys
Wind-up toys
Hand puppets
Marbles
Building blocks
Lego
See N' Say toys
Lincoln Logs

Beads
Gum ball machine
Balls
Sand toys (bucket, shovel, etc.)
Play money
Banks
Peg board and peg towns
Telephones
Silly Sand
Silly Putty
Play Dough
Pick-up sticks
Blocks
Jack 'n box
Bath toys (boats, rubber ducks, etc.)
Pounding blocks
Doctor kits
Nurse kits
Tops
Tool bench and tools
Tinker toys
Fire engine
Yo-yo
Boats
Trains and equipment
Bean bags
Cars and gas stations
Racing cars
Trucks
Tractors
Steam shovels
Dolls and equipment (bottles, clothes, etc.)
Doll houses
Doll furniture
Talking dolls
Buggies
Kaleidoscopes

Flashlight
Strollers
Kitchen equipment (play stove, sink, refrigerator)
Comic books
Food mixes
Utensil sets
Household items (pots, coffee can, paper rolls, cardboard boxes, etc.)
Dishes
Money (exchangeable, token)
Stamps
Cleaning sets (carpet sweepers, brooms, etc.)
Play furniture (table, chairs, etc.)
Purses
Umbrellas
Costumes
Jumping beans
Ice cream maker
Popcorn maker
Cotton candy maker
Cash register
Switch board
Electric football, baseball, basketball, hockey
Cowboy dolls and equipment
Knights, castles, and equipment
Model kits (cars, planes, ships, etc.)
Pinball machine
Bicycle
Tricycle
Music boxes
Rocking horse
Bird houses
Ant houses
Bug houses
Suit cases
Wall decorations
Knickknacks
Sewing machine
Sewing boxes

Typewriters
Playing cards
Record player
Walkie-talkie
Records
Stationery
Calendars
Musical instruments
Bulletin boards
Desk organizers (notes, books, pencils, etc.)
Cameras and equipment
Photo album
Label maker
Pencil sharpener
Stapler
Autograph book
Date book
Address books
Pencils
Pens
Radios
Tape recorders
Watches
Vanity sets
Jewelry
Masks and wax disguises
Perfume
Bath powder
Bath oil
Hats and clothes
Make up
Hair ribbons
Hair bands
Hair barrels
Hairdryers
Belts
Jewelry boxes
Puzzles (jigsaw, trauma tower, dice cube, wooden cube, solitaire, pyramid, mad maze, three dimensional, etc.)
Collections (coins, rocks, glass, leaves, stamps, etc.)

World globe
View master
Telescope
Microscope
Erector set
Trains
Science kits
  Frog dissecting kit
  Chemistry set
  Slide preparing kit
  Geologist's kit
  Biological kit
  Radio kit
  Computer kit
  Electric builder kit
  Rock identification kit
  Magnetic kits
  Body kits (man, woman, heart, head, skeleton, eye, ear, etc.)
Creative craft kits
  Origami (paperfolding)
  Wood burning
  Hand bag decorating
  Embroidery
  Découpage
  Wall decorations
  Marquetry
  Mosaics
  Pillow
  Clay
  Yarn
  Ceramics
  Beads
  Leather
  Colored pipe cleaners
  Cloth
  Rock polishing
  Papier mâché
  Wood
  Felt
  Tile
  Glass
  Paper

Art sets
  Oils
  Watercolors
  Pastels
  Chalk
  Colored pencils
Bowling equipment (ball, shoes, etc.)
Swimming equipment (fins, face mask, etc.)
Kickball
Golf equipment (clubs, balls, etc.)
Ping pong equipment
Pool table
Football equipment
Baseball equipment
Tennis equipment
Skiing equipment
Ice skates
Roller skates
Scuba diving equipment
Sleigh
Toboggan
Class pictures
Swing
Swing sets
Slide
Boxing gloves
Striking bag
Body building equipment
Horse shoe set
Croquet set
Badminton set
Tackraw
Darts
Tether ball
Camping equipment (sleeping bag, lantern, stove, etc.)
Fishing equipment (rod, reel, etc.)
Aquariums
Money
Juke box

Food

Jaw breakers
Chocolate creams
Cake
Lemonade
Popcorn
Peanuts
Ice cream
Cookies
Sugar-coated cereals
Apples
Crackers
Raisins
Candy kisses
Fruit
Life savers

Lemon drops
Sugar cane
Candied apples
Candy canes
Candy corn
Animal crackers
Soft drinks
Milk
Marshmallows
Gum
Juices
Lollipops
Popsicles
Candy bars
Potato chips

Awards

Citations
Athletic letters
Plaques
Pens
Subject-matter prizes (books, science hardware, subscriptions, etc.)

Medals
Cups
Report cards
"Good-Deed" charts

DISSAPPROVAL RESPONSES

The following lists gleaned from actual classroom observations contain *disapproval* responses. The teacher should study these lists carefully in order to achieve two important discriminations: (1) to recognize responses that one may be unwittingly using and wish to eliminate or replace with incompatible approval responses, and (2) to plan carefully, responsibly, and cautiously the application of disapproval. The authors believe most of the following should *never* be used. *The teacher must discriminate.* Even a pleasant "hello" can be a scathing indictment if the tone and intensity of the voice cause that effect.

Words Spoken: Disapproval

This list includes naggings, sarcasms, bitternesses, dishonesties, and other ineffectual teacher responses whose angry delivery generally demonstrates that the *teacher*, not the student, has the problem.

Impractical
Be prompt
Work faster
Try to understand
Do your homework
Do your best
Unclear explanation
Don't you want to do things right?
It can't be that difficult
You're too slow
Stop talking
Behave
Pay attention
Don't
Wrong
Stupid
Be still
Follow directions
Think for a change
Use some thought
No, that's not what I said
Would you like to get paddled?
You don't understand because you don't listen!
If I find you chewing gum once more, you'll wear it on your nose
Be quiet and sit down
You're gutless
That's ridiculous
Meaningless
Absurd
Bad
Nonsense
Too vague
Try harder
Unacceptable
That's not right
Incorrect
Needs improving
Unsatisfactory

Poor
Undesirable
You should be ashamed
Useless
That's not clear
I dislike that
Don't be silly
That's terrible
What is this?
Is this something?
Quit making messes
Let's throw this away
That's not mature
I can't read anything you write
Haven't you learned how to spell?
Grow up
You're not doing as well as you used to
Horrible
Absolutely not!
Shh!
Stop
Listen to me
Maddening
Be quiet
Raise your hand
Stop that laughing
I'll have no more talking
Apologize now
Sloppy
Shut up!
I'll show you who's boss
One more time and you'll get it from me
Finish it now
No talking
I'll slap you silly
Look for the answer
Leave her alone
You march straight to the office
Keep your eyes on your own paper
You lack interest
I'll give you something to cry about
You *couldn't* have done worse
I do not like this
It's not up to requirements

I will not repeat it
I'm not telling you again
You're dull
That's ugly
You idiot
You're a laughingstock
It's hopeless for you
Why are you a fraidycat?
You're cheap
Snob
You're worthless
You're rude
Don't be crabby
You're disgusting
You little monster
Don't laugh at me
Cut it out
You're dumb
You're filthy
You naughty boy
Mock me and you won't hear the end of it
You're narrow-minded
That's childish
Simple Simon
No! No!! No!!!
You haven't applied yourself
Your work isn't acceptable
Get your parent to sign this bad paper
What do you mean you're not finished?
Stand up straight
Just try that once more
Anyone else!
Learn that!
You'd better get on the stick
So you're tardy again!
Speak when you're spoken to
Smart alec
You *must* be confused
I don't see your point
You know what happened the last time you did that
You do this over
You know better than that
Play fair
Don't cause problems

You're never dependable
That wasn't the right thing to do
Well, we'll never do this again
If you had a brain in your head, you wouldn't say that
Do it!
You think you're the only one here?
You're bad
Poor stupid oaf
Wrong again
You're doomed to failure
You're wrong all the time
You don't know anything
You make me sick
You're just an inadequate person
Impertinent
You're not thinking
You haven't been paying attention
Wipe that silly grin off your face
I guess I shouldn't expect any more from *you*
You're just plain boring
You have a dirty mind
Terrible! Terrible!
This isn't what *I* had in mind
You know that's wrong
Stupid nonsense
You'd *better* try harder
People never change

Expressions: Disapproval

Frowning
Curling lip
Lifting eyebrows
Looking at ceiling
Furrowing brows
Smirking
Lowering eyebrows
Shaking finger or fist
Wrinkling mouth
Squinting eyes
Staring
Wrinkling forehead
Nose in air

Puckering lips
Wrinkling nose
Pounding fists on table
Laughing
Shaking head
Turning away
Gritting teeth
Biting lips
Squinting eyebrows
Looking sideways
Closing eyes
Clicking tongue
Pushing mouth to one side

Pointing finger
Putting hand behind ear
Grimacing
Sniffing
Tightening jaw
Sticking out tongue
Twisting side of mouth
Cackling
Snickering

Turning head away
Letting out breath
Raising lips
Hissing
Fingers in front of lips
Nodding head (no)
Showing teeth
Pulling in bottom lip

Closeness: Disapproval

Closeness disapproval concerns corporal punishment and ranges from threatening approaches—through spankings—to severe physical beatings.

Activities and Privileges: Disapproval

Disapproval concerning activities and privileges constitutes various degrees of *deprivation*. Deprivation ranges from withholding of privileges—through isolation—to social incarceration.

Isolation
Ostracism
Silence periods
Sitting in corner
Staying after class
Writing misbehaviors
Standing in front of class
Leaving room
Extra work
Staying in from play
Being last to leave
Sitting in hall
Being sent to principal
Eating alone in lunchroom
Away from friends
Pointing out bad examples
Apologizing to class
Writing letters of apology
Bringing parents to school

193

Things: Disapproval

Concerning things, disapproval refers to inanimate materials that are damaging to the body: (1) intense noises (ear damage), (2) heat (fires and stoves), (3) chemicals (poisons), and (4) objects in motion (knives, cars, bullets, radiation). Obviously *none* of these should ever be used by the teacher (even washing a child's mouth out with soap can sometimes cause tissue damage).

CONCLUSION

Teaching and learning should be exciting and satisfying for both teacher and student. The innovative teacher has too many positive and effective resources available to resort to shoddy and punitive measures. Many experienced teachers state that almost all of their earlier punitive consequences could have been handled in a more positive manner. A teacher who truly cares will practice developing *positive* responses.

LEARNING AND
OBSERVATIONAL
MANUAL

INTRODUCTION TO PART IV

This *Learning and Observational Manual* provides an extension to *Teaching/Discipline: A Positive Approach For Educational Development*, Second Edition. Each chapter serves a separate purpose and may or may not be applicable to various instructional objectives.

An increased emphasis on practicum learning for students and the availability of planning periods, preschool workshops, and in-service sessions for teachers have expanded the demand for activities designed to teach application of behavioral techniques.

It is unfortunate that some of these activities are considered unproductive and that specific techniques used in workshops and classes never produce changes beyond the verbal reports of, "There were some good ideas presented," or "That activity was really interesting."

In an attempt to develop more effective learning tasks which can be justified by specifying and producing measurable changes in teacher behavior, which in turn will produce changes in student behavior, data pertaining to these objectives has been compiled by the authors over the past eight years and is presented to the reader in the following chapters.

A selected coverage of behavioral changes in actual classroom behavior as a function of in-service teacher workshops is found in Chapter 8, "Teachers as Learners." This chapter is specifically included to provide workshop directors, school administrators, supervisors, and classroom instructors with a *general* overview concerning the effects of workshop participation.

Activities concerning observational techniques and recording procedures may be found in Chapter 9, "Learning Through Observation." This chapter is intended to provide students, teachers, and researchers interested in detailed recording procedures more objective recording instruments aimed toward greater validity and reliability. Masters of all forms are available from the authors.

Chapter 10, "Outline for Learning," contains a series of learning activities for college classes and in-service workshops. It is written specifically for students in educational methods and educational psychology courses as well as participants in pre-service, in-service, or other workshop experiences. Learning activities are provided to encompass from one to fifty-two hours and are designed to enhance classroom applications of behavioral principles. Individual topics and activities may be organized for various time periods and in different sequences depending upon instructional objectives.

CHAPTER 8

TEACHERS AS LEARNERS

The application of behavioral principles to practical problems confronting teachers has seen phenomenal growth and acceleration during the past decade (see Selected Bibliography). Scientific investigations dealing with students and teachers have demonstrated the many changes possible when classroom teachers systematically apply behavioral principles in teacher-student interaction patterns. Research indicates that the teacher is probably the most powerful and perhaps the most important controller of classroom behavior. Teachers have been able to induce "happier" classroom environments, increase classroom control, and enhance social and academic achievements. Many varied contingencies have been used by teachers to decrease inappropriate behaviors which compete with learning as well as to increase appropriate behavior. Behavioral principles have been applied to programming of academic subject matter and the more informal but necessary teaching of social behavioral skills.

All teachers are, in fact, modifiers of behavior. The behavioral scientist is able to systematically observe any classroom and demonstrate effects of the teacher's reinforcement patterns whether or not the teacher has a technical knowledge of behavioral principles. While it is true that teachers who are competent usually have developed, through modeling or trial and error, effective means of classroom control and subject matter presentation, it has also been demonstrated that even the most proficient teachers make "mistakes of reinforcement." Thus workshops have proliferated which have as their goal more efficient application of behavioral principles in classroom teaching. The premise of these workshops is that through learning behavioral techniques teachers will be better at their jobs—better able to insure academic and social improvement and better able to prevent potential problems which might interfere with learning.

The extent to which successes or failures occur in pupils' learning can probably be attributed to the degree of success the teacher achieves in arranging the total school environment. It is also assumed that successes or failures concerning workshop effects should be demonstrated in observable classroom results. Therefore, precise workshop methods should be assessed as to effectiveness and durability. Specific effects should be demonstrated concerning environmental change as well as documented procedures used in the interaction between those who learn to teach and those who are doing the teaching. These procedures must be demonstrated when teachers, or potential teachers, are participants in in-service or pre-service workshops and classes which focus on behavior modification.

The workshop learning experiences developed over the past few years attempt to apply the results of many quantitative, practical, and experimental studies to the general problem of teacher training. Development of precise observational data extended and revised from the initial beginnings in earlier studies (Becker, Madsen, Arnold, and Thomas, 1967; Madsen, Becker, and Thomas, 1968; Madsen, Becker, Thomas, Koser, and Plager, 1968; Thomas, Becker, and Armstrong, 1968) has made it possible to assess changes in teaching as a function of workshop experience. Observational techniques and skills have been used to systematically analyze the behaviors of teachers subsequent to workshops in the application of behavioral principles in classroom instruction. These projects have demonstrated that, when teachers change their pattern of interaction with students, change in teacher behavior results in change in pupil behavior.

SELF-REPORTS VERSUS ACTUAL BEHAVIOR

Most individuals working in education seem convinced that the learning environment should be a relatively positive place where students learn "to be nice people and take joy from learning." In fact, many teachers, administrators, counselors, and others have been asked to respond to the question of whether or not they believe the classroom atmosphere should be predominantly positive (approving) or negative (disapproving). Responses overwhelmingly indicate that school personnel believe that teachers should be predominantly positive. Over 99 percent of 5,686 respondents "strongly agree" or "agree" on questionnaires that teachers should have a positive classroom environment. Ninety-seven percent also agreed that a strong indicator of a positive environment would be where more approving than disapproving comments are heard directed by the teacher toward student behavior (tabulations from forty-four workshops). However, this human self-report data is in sharp contrast to results based upon actual classroom observations.

Interaction patterns based on definition of approval and disapproval between students and teachers observed by trained personnel show an entirely different distribution of results. Less than 8 percent of 6,849 teachers (kindergarten through high school) actually dispensed more approval for appropriate than disapproval for inappropriate social behavior. This difference between verbally stated values and actual behavior seems even more disparate when it is realized that trained observers used the teachers' own definitions of appropriate and inappropriate student behaviors.

It is amazing that actual interaction patterns of teachers with students are so different from the intended outcomes. Results indicate clearly that there are definite differences between the verbal reports of values and actual in-class overt behaviors. This disparity also indicates that whether or not a teacher reports via questionnaire that the teacher "likes" a workshop may have nothing to do with actual in-class teaching behavior. Preworkshop classroom observations indicate that 92 percent of the teachers dispense more disapproval and mistakes of reinforcement than they dispense approval for appropriate social behavior. Computations of the percentage of observation intervals in which reinforcement behaviors occur indicate that the approval ratio is less than 50 percent in 92 percent of the cases. It should be noted that many teachers are not as negative in dealing with academic behavior (34 percent do give more approval than disapproval to appropriate academic behavior). The computation for the approval ratio is based upon the amount of approval dispensed relative to all reinforcing behavior and does not depend upon the absolute frequency of reinforcing behavior. Thus the approval ratio is based upon the percentage of approval teacher behavior independent of the total frequency or amount of behavior. It has also been observed that, the higher the grade level, the more time the teacher spends questioning, stimulating, or explaining rather than reinforcing appropriate social behavior.

Perhaps it is not surprising that some pupils begin complaining about teachers and teaching practices before they begin to seriously evaluate any other aspect of their lives. Indeed, it appears that only occasionally are reports of excellence voiced. The thoughtful person may look past apparent idiosyncrasies and trivia to ask some basic questions: Why is this educational situation extant? Are most teachers committed to misery for themselves as well as their students? Do people enter the teaching profession to promote ineffectual learning? It appears true but unfortunate that several important changes occur with many teachers in that short period of time while passing from a naive idealist to "practitionaire." The desire to be a good teacher often gives way first to disillusionment, then to cynicism, and perhaps on to despair. The culmination is sometimes complete resignation and apathy. (Madsen, Madsen, and Driggs, 1971, p. 61.)

A systematic analysis of some of the variables within the learning situation which could bring teacher behavior in line with their own values appears needed.

EARLY DEVELOPMENT OF WORKSHOPS

Early workshops were conducted with volunteers and were less systematic than the outline in Chapter 10. Teacher involvement time in an early study was sixteen hours during one-hour early morning sessions twice weekly (Becker, Madsen, Arnold, and Thomas, 1967). Teachers were asked to complete a programmed text, the *Analysis of Behavior* (Holland and Skinner, 1958), plus selected behavioral readings and research articles. Teachers were then given quizzes and participated in general discussions. The final portion of the workshop included application of behavioral principles to the teachers' own classrooms with discussions of different ways to structure environmental contingencies. Subsequent workshops have generally included in some form aspects of the same four components:

1. Learning behavioral principles and theoretical constructs
2. Learning applications demonstrated by others (reading, videotape, or film)
3. Discussing and role-playing behavioral applications
4. Classroom practice (Madsen, Becker, and Thomas, 1968)

Establishing a training sequence

A series of workshop presentations including observational feedback with a variety of teachers led to the conclusion that merely hearing about, or even learning to repeat the principles of behavioral classroom management (90 percent accuracy on criterion tests over behavioral techniques and practical examples), was not an effective method of changing classroom behavior. A series of observational studies based upon comparison of pre-training with post-training in-class observations of teachers from kindergarten through high school in thirteen counties led to questioning the traditional learning sequence. The traditional learning sequence generally involves understanding principles as opposed to emphasizing actual participation. Using hindsight, it should be clear that behaviorists especially should not be deluded into thinking that there is some magic in the learning of "words," even if the words are behaviorial and substantiated by test papers indicating a 90 percent criterion level. However, this is a difficult lesson to learn—especially by those who have been reinforced for many years to memorize, analyze, and repeat theories and facts. The results cited led to additional studies designed to assess at least some of the questions raised during the thirteen workshops concerning amount of time necessary for change, particular sequences of training, and necessity for periodic feedback.

Effects of workshop duration

Thirteen teachers in grades one through twelve in four separate schools volunteered for participation in a classroom management program. Four hours of baseline observations were conducted in the teachers' classrooms by trained observers using previously validated observational categories (see Chapter 9). A behavioral workshop of eight hours duration (four sessions) was conducted for all thirteen teachers followed by an additional four hours of observations with feedback in the classroom environment. Follow-up observations (four hours) during two subsequent school years were completed on teachers who remained in the system (N = 10). An additional group of teachers approximating those in the experimental group were observed without benefit of a behavioral workshop.

Ratings of teacher reinforcement behaviors were completed by trained observers in the classroom environment. Teacher results were based upon the percentage of observed intervals (ten seconds) during which specified classes of behavior occurred (sixty minutes each observation period). Each teacher provided a list of rules that the teacher maintained within the class setting so that each teacher's response to inappropriate behavior was rated only with respect to the teacher's own classroom rules. Observers were trained to 80 percent reliability prior to baseline observations (see Chapter 9).

Total teacher contact time was eight hours in four sessions. The first session consisted of a discussion involving the principles of classroom management based on reinforcement principles. This general orientation included questions and answers specifically directed toward behavior modification principles. Attempts were made to eliminate difficult jargon and keep discussions on a nontechnical level.

The session also included a lecture on principles of behavior modification and examples of research in which the principles had led to changes which teachers had desired. Teachers were provided a handout entitled "Catch the Child Being Good" which stressed:

1. Rules for specific classroom learning situations
2. Approval for appropriate behavior
3. Ignoring inappropriate behavior
4. Disapproval strong enough to stop misbehavior that could not be ignored[1]

---

[1] Summarized in "Classroom RAID: Rules, approval, ignore, disapproval: A cooperative approach for professionals and volunteers," by Madsen, Madsen, Saudargas, Hammond, Smith, and Edgar, *Journal of School Psychology*, VIII, 1970, 180–85.

The remaining six hours were conducted by graduate students enrolled in school psychology and counselor education programs. These sessions consisted of (1) role-playing classroom situations, (2) discussions of specific answers to classroom problems, and (3) open discussion of any questions, reservations, value conflicts, or hostile behaviors.

In the second and third sessions, workshop participants were provided with graphs from their own classroom observations. Results were discussed individually with each teacher, and questions were answered with specific reference to individual classrooms. General problems were then brought before the entire group. The last session was devoted to role-playing, applying the behavioral principles which were presented and discussed in the workshop. General constructive criticism followed each role-playing session.

Results of the workshop experience indicate that approval to appropriate student behaviors increased from an average of 16.4 percent to 27.1 percent. The amount of disapproval decreased from an average of 11.1 percent to 6.1 percent, and the number of mistakes of reinforcement decreased from an average of 6.4 percent to 3.9 percent.

The approval ratio is another method used to compare teachers. There are limitations to any measure; however, the percentage of approval as a ratio of the total amount of reinforcement given by the teacher allows the researcher to use a direct measure which is independent of total amount of behavior. This is important, as the absolute frequency of approval and disapproval given by teachers is generally higher in the lower grades and decreases as students become older. Computation of approval ratios allows comparisons among teachers from kindergarten through high school.

The average approval ratio (across all thirteen teachers for fifty-two observations) prior to workshop experiences was 43.6 percent. This approval ratio increased to 70.7 percent following the workshop experience, although individual differences were apparent. Eleven of the thirteen teachers were able to increase their approval ratios as a function of the workshop experiences (average increase of 27.1 percent). The approval ratio dropped for one teacher from 74.6 percent to 50.1 percent and for another from 53.2 percent to 49.4 percent. Follow-up observations (four) taken during the next school year (six months later) indicated that the teachers were able to maintain their approval ratios, at least in the presence of observers. The approval ratio for the ten teachers who remained in the school system increased from 39.7 percent to 65.1 percent following the workshop experience and remained at 63.9 percent eighteen months later. During follow-up, the absolute frequency of behavior indicated that approval responses were slightly higher and disapprovals were slightly lower, but mistakes of reinforcement were higher than during the post-workshop observations.

This study indicated that results of the workshop seemed to carry through the summer session and into the next academic year. Results also indicated that many teachers across different levels (K-12) could effectively modify their own classroom behavior. Verbal self-reports following the workshop and during the next school year from teachers, principals, and students indicated that classrooms had become a more pleasant setting for school work for both teachers and students.

The effects of this workshop did not, in this short period of time, remove mistakes of reinforcement but did demonstrate the importance of involvement and actual participation as opposed to the ability to merely repeat principles.

Effects of training sequence

In another training workshop, it was determined that the sequence of training should be investigated. By now it had been decided that there were three main components for this particular method of teacher training. The components included:

1. Teachers receiving or reading about principles and concepts of behavioral analysis
2. Teachers using role-playing, with feedback, to practice developing approving and disapproving behaviors
3. Teachers functioning as teachers within classrooms monitored by those conducting the workshop

It should be remembered that the common teacher-training sequence within teacher-training institutions of higher learning is as follows: Theory is presented in lectures and texts, principles are applied and analyzed in mini-teaching or micro-teaching situations, and, lastly, the teacher goes out into the classroom as an intern under the watchful eye of an experienced teacher who is to give the new teacher feedback and extend practical effectiveness in the classroom. The question was posed as to what would happen if the sequence of presentation were varied.

The traditional sequence was contrasted with two varying sequences using a series of volunteers. Observations included three hours of baseline observation, then the workshop, followed by post-observation. The sequence of presentation that resulted in the greatest change varied from the traditional sequence. The largest observed gains were demonstrated by teachers who followed this sequence:

1. Four hours of self-critical videotape feedback based on observational categories
2. Four hours of discussion of the principles of applied behavior analysis in a practical way
3. Four hours of role-playing and actual practice in the principles involved

The second most beneficial sequence was:

1. Role-playing and practice
2. Videotape observation
3. Discussion of principles

The least effective sequence was:

1. Discussion of principles
2. Role-playing and practice
3. Self-evaluation

This study involved sixteen teachers who received training and six control teachers who received no training. All twenty-two teachers taught K–3 in three rural county schools. Pre-observation included three data points with a minimum reliability on every point of 85 percent. Six teachers participated in each of two workshop sequences while four teachers participated in a third sequence, with six teachers receiving no workshop experience. Half of the teachers had participated in a twenty-hour introductory workshop in behavior modification the preceding year which made it possible to check effectiveness concerning the carry-over from the previous workshop as well as observe any additional results.

Six weeks were used for presentations, in three two-week subsections. Each of the three training groups spent two weeks in each of the three methods used in training, for four meetings each with a minimal meeting time of six hours in each section. In sum, all of the sixteen teachers received a minimum of eighteen hours of instruction and training. Six teachers, serving as controls, received no training during this period. The three groups were as follows:

1. Discussion of Principles. A copy of *Teaching/Discipline: Behavioral Principles Toward A Positive Approach*, was provided each teacher. A programmed text, based on selected portions of the book, was also utilized. This method was basically the traditional academic, theoretical approach.

2. Practice and Role-playing of Principles. Each teacher was instructed in what was being observed in her classroom performance by use of her own pre-observation records. Behaviorally, her teaching actions were pinpointed and discussed. Learning principles were discussed. Particular situations of problems in the classroom were role-played by the instructor and teachers. Application of the principles involved was subsequently explained, discussed, or clarified.

3. Self-evaluation and Observation. Prior to each group session, a ten to fifteen minute videotape was made of each teachers actual classroom situation and her teaching, including the controls. These individual teacher tapes served as the basis for the four meetings for each group. Each was observed and evaluated in terms of the behavioral principles involved. Each was discussed, and alternate ways of applying the principles were presented.

Each of the micro-groups received essentially the same instruction and experience in each procedure, limited only by the differences of the teachers involved in each subsection and the instructor's ability of exact replication. Each method of training was received by each group, but in different sequences. A total of three instructors were used, each one presenting the same procedure three times, once for each group.

All twenty-two teachers were women. Roughly half had had less than three years teaching experience, half had had four or more years. They ranged in age from twenty-one to fifty-six. The county system had participated in an in-service workshop in methods of classroom management the previous summer. No observations were taken but all county teachers participated. One-half of the twenty-two teachers participating in the present study had previously attended the former workshop; the others had not. All twenty-two teachers had degrees from colleges or universities in the Southeastern United States. Eight of the teachers were currently taking courses toward a Master's degree; two had earned their Master's degree. Three were recent graduates and were unmarried, four were divorced or separated, and the remainder were married. Seventeen had children of their own. Number of children per teacher ranged from one to ten; ages of children from eighteen months to twenty-nine years. Thus, it was assumed that these teachers represented a cross section of most kindergarten through third grade elementary teachers in the United States.

Results on pre-observations indicated the infusion of behavior principles into the county system from the previous workshop sessions (see Table 8–1). The control group in this case might have functioned as an indicator of the benefits of an additional session six months after the initial session or the amount of communication for training teachers. The initial approval average for the eleven naïve teachers was a great deal higher than would have been expected on the basis of observations of many other teachers prior to experience in the use of behavioral principles and almost identical to the teachers who had twenty prior hours of workshop experiences. Average approval ratio for those without the workshop was 68.2 percent and for those with the workshop 64.6 percent. The average approval ratio for those given the additional experience increased from 64.6 percent to 89.1 percent ($N = 16$) while the average approval ratio for those not receiving the additional workshop increased from 68.1 percent to 77.9 percent. Fourteen of the sixteen teachers participating increased approval ratios, while five of the six controls also increased their approval ratios. It appears that, when the majority of teachers in an elementary school are in a workshop, the principles are communicated and modeled from the teachers receiving the workshop to those who are not. Further research needs to be completed to ascertain the critical mass necessary for behavioral principles to be used by the other teachers.

The absolute frequency of approval, disapproval, and mistakes of reinforcement indicate changes during the course of the work-

Table 8–1   *Percent of Observed Intervals During Which Behavior Occurred*

Workshop II	Approval		Disapproval		Mistakes		Approval Ratio	
	Pre	Post	Pre	Post	Pre	Post	Pre	Post
Experience (N = 16)	12.8%	20.6%	4.7%	2.0%	2.3%	0.5%	64.6%	89.1%
With Workshop I (N = 8)	13.0	22.7	2.9	1.8	2.3	0.8	71.4	89.8
Without (N = 8)	12.5	18.4	5.4	2.8	2.6	0.3	58.8	85.7
Control Teachers (N = 6)	15.2	20.8	4.2	4.4	2.9	1.5	68.1	77.9
With Workshop I (N = 3)	14.4	19.6	4.3	5.8	4.1	2.7	63.1	70.0
Without (N = 3)	16.0	22.0	4.0	3.0	1.8	0.3	73.5	86.8
Sequence 1 (N = 4) Workshop II	16.6	17.2	2.1	0.9	2.2	0.5	79.6	92.4
Sequence 2 (N = 6) Workshop II	11.7	28.2	2.9	2.4	2.1	0.4	70.2	90.9
Sequence 3 (N = 6) Workshop II	11.3	15.2	8.2	2.3	2.3	0.6	51.1	84.3

shop. The workshop participants increased the average absolute percentage of approvals from 12.8 percent to 20.6 percent, decreased the average disapproval observed from 4.7 percent to 2.0 percent, and decreased the average mistakes of reinforcement from 2.3 percent to 0.5 percent. The control teachers increased their average observed approvals from 15.2 percent to 20.8 percent and decreased mistakes of reinforcement from 2.9 percent to 1.5 percent; however, there was not an average decrease in the use of disapprovals and the control teachers increased from 4.2 percent to 4.4 percent.

Exactly one-half of the workshop group ($N = 6$) and one-half of the control group had received the prior summer's experience. When the results are broken down in this manner, it may be asked whether these teachers were contributing most of the change in either the experimental or control group. The results indicate very little difference between those who had received the prior workshop and those who had not. The major difference apparent in the differing sequences of training appears to be an increase in the overall dispensing of approvals. The approval ratios following training were not very disparate (92.4 percent, 90.9 percent, and 84.3 percent). The real differences appear to be in the increase in approvals for sequence 2 from 11.7 percent prior to the workshop to 28.2 percent following the workshop experience. These results indicate the importance of allowing the teacher to learn the observational categories early in instruction rather than later, if the purpose is to increase the overall reinforcement activity level. It will be noted that the teachers in sequence 1 decreased overall reinforcement from a pre-workshop level of 20.9 percent (approval plus disapproval plus mistakes) to a level following the workshop of 18.6 percent. Sequence 3 decreased the overall reinforcement level from 21.8 percent to 18.1 percent while sequence 2 (the group starting with self-observation and evaluation of videotapes) increased from 16.7 percent to 31.0 percent. While mistakes of reinforcement were less than 1 percent in all three groups, the overall use of disapproval was significantly less in group two. The exact effect of an increased frequency of reinforcement is not yet clear and needs further research. However, modification of further workshops to include instruction and training on specific observational categories was initiated as a result of this study.

An important sidelight of this study concerns the often repeated assumption that, if a teacher increases approvals, then disapprovals will decrease. This does not appear to be substantiated by present data. Instead, there is an increase in overall reinforcement level. The observation training and instruction appear to be much more critical than previously expected.

TEACHER ATTITUDES AND CLASSROOM BEHAVIORS

Results of the preceding project led to a workshop outline which included a variety of experiences stressing observation and participation rather than verbal understanding of principles. An interesting aspect concerning self-report of attitude change was designed prior to collection of data and built into that project. While the project was designed to change classroom behavior and did not deal at all with changes in the self-report of teachers' attitudes, "attitudes" of the teachers were changed significantly following training in behavioral techniques. The Minnesota Teacher Attitude Inventory (MTAI) was administered before, during, and following treatment for all participating teachers. *Buros' Fourth Mental Measurement Yearbook* indicates for those that rely on test scores that the MTAI is a testing instrument of exceptional quality.[2] The test consists of 150 items which have been designed and tested for the purpose of revealing a teacher's attitude toward teaching. The scores reflect the philosophy of the test authors, which could best be characterized as child-centered and permissively oriented. This test was used because in many educational circles, especially where the philosophy of education is considered "child-centered," behavior modification techniques are evaluated as being incongruous with good education, perhaps even inhuman, or too controlling (see Chapter 3). In addition there has been little reported evidence in the area of teacher-training workshops in behavior modification that instruction which facilitates a change in teacher performance also affects self-report measures of attitudes. The MTAI Manual states:[3]

[2] Oscar K. Buros, *Fourth Mental Measurement Yearbook*, Highland Park, N.J.: Gryphon Press, 1953, p. 801–2.
[3] W. W. Cook, C. H. Leeds, and R. Callis, *MTAI Manual*, New York: Psychological Corp., 1951, p. 4.

Information available to date indicates that attitudes of adults are rather resistant to change. This seems to hold true for the attitudes measured by this Inventory. It should be remembered that teacher-pupil attitudes are simply indicators of the teachers' classroom behavior, and that the mere inculcation of better attitudes by instruction may not produce any change in behavior.

The changes in reported "attitude" as scaled by the MTAI indicated that teachers who received the workshop experience increased from 37.8 correct to 48.7 correct. The control group, however, had a decrease from 54.8 correct to 40.4 correct (correct answers as indicated by the inventory). These results appear contrary to the test authors' contentions that "attitudes are not changeable as a result of instruction."[4] However, in this particular behavioral program teachers were helped to change their classroom behaviors and the self-reported attitudinal changes followed. Correlational analysis of each individual teacher's performance change, in both direction and degree with scale attitudinal change, substantiated this finding. Regarding specific teachers, it was found that fourteen of the sixteen teachers in the workshop changed. This can perhaps be explained by the fact that the self-reported attitudes improved as they were no longer incongruous with the actual classroom behaviors in terms of increases in approval behavior. Alternatively, the control teachers were aware of the training, were being observed and videotaped, and, while their classroom behavior did in fact improve toward a more positive teacher-student interaction pattern, they were verbally less satisfied as they interacted with the teachers who participated in the workshop. When given the opportunity at the conclusion of the workshop to express their own attitudes toward teaching, the control teachers expressed less satisfaction.

Results from the attitudinal inventory need to be further explored in additional research studies; however, present results seem to indicate that the old adage, "You can act your way into a new way of thinking faster than you can think your way into a new way of acting," was certainly true for fourteen of the sixteen teachers who participated in this workshop.

[4] Cook et al, *MTAI Manual*, p. 4.

WORKSHOP DEVELOPMENT AND OBSERVATIONAL RESULTS

A two-week in-service workshop conducted for thirty-two teachers comprising the entire staff of a rural elementary school supplied the opportunity to develop aspects of the workshop instructional model. This workshop was especially designed to ascertain the effects of continual observational feedback to teachers involved. The major focus of the workshop involved (1) learning behavioral principles, (2) learning observational categories pertaining to classroom reinforcement, and (3) role-playing and practicing techniques to be employed later in the classroom. The focus was on a practical approach that could help teachers handle problems expected in the opening of a newly integrated school with a great disparity in both the academic abilities and the socioeconomic status of blacks and whites.

The major innovation within this workshop was the long-term observational recording and the graphic feedback given to teachers. Teachers were observed on the average of three times per week during the entire school year and were provided observational graphs indicating their percentages of approval to appropriate behavior, disapproval to inappropriate behavior, and mistakes of approval and disapproval reinforcement. Concurrent recording of the behavior of eighty-four students was also completed throughout the year. The amount of inappropriate behavior (off-task) was recorded for those students selected by their teachers. The selection was determined by observing students whose behavior interfered with learning (their own or another's). Results of observations for both teachers and students were reported to the teacher approximately once a week in small group sessions.

Pre-observations prior to workshop experiences were not possible in this study, so a sample of comparison teachers was matched on age, race, socioeconomic status of classroom, grade level, years of teaching experience, years since degree awarded, and number of children in the class. This matching was continued during the next two school years and observations completed over an extended period of time. Since observers are constantly being trained and a series of teacher workshop experiences are continually in progress, an almost precise matching was possible except for the variable concerning socioeconomic level of students. Therefore, four additional teachers were matched with four of the original twenty-eight so that socioeconomic ability could be averaged across two classrooms with teachers similar in all other aspects.

During this same school year, it was also possible to work with another project that included only first-grade teachers working in predominately black classrooms. Very similar workshop experiences were conducted by the same personnel. Each project was supervised by an on-the-job psychologist who was responsible for observational scheduling and graphic and verbal feedback sessions for teachers, as well as periodic videotaping for self-evaluation.

The results and comparisons between teachers who had behavioral workshops in two separate counties and the matched teachers indicated the effectiveness of the combination workshop-follow-up procedures as shown in Table 8–2.

The approvals, disapprovals, and mistakes of reinforcement indicated by the comparison teachers match very closely the average approval ratio for most teachers observed prior to workshop experiences in behavioral techniques. It should be noted, however, that the project teachers who were being observed approximately three times per week and given videotape feedback and weekly graphic feedback for the first one-half of the school year were spending on the average 19.9 percent of their time in reinforcement behaviors with an approval ratio of 84.4 percent and less than 1 percent mistakes of reinforcement. The effect on the three students whom they considered to be potentially the most disruptive was quite dramatic. The average off-task behavior for the eighty-four students observed was 24.4 percent. This should be placed in perspective by indicating that, in most well-controlled classrooms where a great deal of academic learning is accomplished, the average off-task is approximately 20 percent for the entire classroom. Thus, in a school which had a complete socioeconomic range of students, 60 percent white and 40 percent black, in the first year of integration and a potentially disruptive student body, the behavior of students referred by teachers was very close to the average in other well-controlled classrooms. However, in the comparison classroom, the average off-task student behavior for the ninety-six referred students was approximately the same for most referred students. (It has been our experience that, when a student approaches 50 to 60 percent off-task, he is generally well known to teachers, counselors, principals, and other referring agencies in the community

Table 8-2   Reinforcement of Student Behavior With and Without Workshops and Feedback in Behavioral Techniques*

	Approval	Disapproval	Mistakes of Rein-forcement	Total Rein-forcement	Approval Ratio	Percent Off-Task Student Behavior
Project I Leon County, Florida N = 28, K–6 Observations = 1,408	16.8	2.5	0.6	19.9	84.4	24.4**
Comparison Teachers Southeastern United States N = 32, K–6 Observations = 1,042	7.0	17.9	5.2	30.1	23.2	59.5**
Project II Orange County, Florida N = 15; First grade Observations = 492	41.0	4.0	0.9	45.9	89.3	18.3‡

* The average reliability across all 3,352 observations was 88 percent, with a range from 73 percent to 100 percent, computed by comparing each symbol within each interval and dividing total agreements by total agreements plus disagreements.
** The average off-task behaviors are recorded for these students whom the teacher referred as to children with problems.
‡ The average off-task behaviors were recorded for the entire classroom.

and school system.) Students engaging in this much disruptive behavior will usually have a lengthy evaluation in their cumulative folder and also will have received some label from school professionals (brain damaged, hyperkinetic, learning disabled, retarded, emotionally disturbed). The average off-task behavior for the comparison teachers' classrooms was 59.9 percent. Of course, teachers generally seek out professionals because they do in fact have behavior problems in their classes and this result is not generalizable to all classrooms under all situations.

The second major point of this study concerned differences between the approval ratio of the comparison teachers (23.2 percent) and the mistakes of reinforcement (5.2 percent). The comparison teachers were using reinforcement (disciplining) 30.1 percent of the time, which was 10.2 percent more often than the teachers who participated in the workshop. However, the off-task percentage for their referred children was over half as low (24.4 percent compared to 59.9 percent) when compared to the workshop-trained teachers. This effect appears to be based upon the lower ratio of approval responses and the higher rate of reinforcement mistakes. The differential effects of increasing approvals and/or decreasing mistakes need to be experimentally isolated; however, it is clear that a combination of high approval with low mistakes of reinforcement has a greater effect on pupil behavior with less interaction by the teacher.

Results of this project are also instructive in that these first grade teachers were instructed to maintain higher levels of approvals to see if there would be an attendant decrease in off-task behavior. This proved to be the case, as the classroom averages were 18.3 percent, which was slightly lower than the K–6 comparison teachers. The precise effects of almost continuous approval need to be ascertained. The attendant decrease from approximately 24 percent to 18 percent may not be worth the additional 26 percent increase in intervals during which reinforcement is administered.

The foregoing study was primarily concerned with reinforcement following social behavior and did not deal with academic reinforcements for correct or incorrect materials. Naturally, there were individual differences among teachers. However, all twenty-eight of the workshop teachers maintained an approval ratio which averaged approximately 80 percent, ranging from 53 percent to 100 percent.

Academic and social reinforcement

Most of these workshop observations were devoted to recording teacher reinforcement functions regarding appropriate or inappropriate social behavior. A workshop conducted for twenty-eight special education teachers included pre- and post-observations which recorded academic as well as social reinforcement.

The special education workshop included three pre-observations for all special education teachers at both the primary and secondary levels. The workshop lasted five days and included many of the learning activities described in Chapter 10. All teachers were given a formal academic content pre-test and post-test. Results indicated that the post-test increase was 15.1 questions from an absolute mean correct on the pre-test of 20.1 to 35.2 on the post-test, an increase of 74.6 percent over the initial mean level.

Results from these teachers are instructive as well as similar to many subsequent observations (see Table 8–3). Many teachers are less negative when responding to academic behaviors than in responding to social behaviors. Notice that the approval ratio for academic feedback prior to workshop experience is approximately twice as high as that for social behavior. Both academic and social reinforcement were able to be increased as a function of the workshop. It is instructive to note that the total amount of social reinforcement increased from 12.3 percent to 15.3 percent of intervals observed, while the amount of academic reinforcement actually decreased. The percent of students' inappropriate social behaviors dropped from 34.6 percent to 27.3 percent. Observations were taken immediately before and immediately after the workshop experience.

The importance of isolating the social and academic behaviors appears critical. This isolation provides a teacher with the technique of reinforcing hard work and staying on-task without pressuring students concerning the correctness or incorrectness of their academic responses. Alternatively, a teacher may reinforce good academic achievement without paying off a student for wasting a great deal of time even though all problems and exercises are correctly done. This assumes, of course, that the teacher is attempting to teach good work habits as well as academic achievement.

Table 8-3 Student-Teacher Interactional Changes As A Function of A Teacher Workshop in Behavioral Principles (N = 28)

	Approval		Disapproval		Mistakes		Approval Ratio		Amount of Reinforcement		Percent Off-Task Average Across Class	
	Pre	Post	Pre	Post	Pre	Post	Pre	Post	Pre	Post	Pre	Post
Social Behavior	3.9%	8.3%	6.8%	5.8%	1.6%	1.2%	31.7%	54.2%	12.3%	15.3%	34.6%	27.3%
Academic Behavior	7.4	8.4	4.1	1.5	0.3	0.0	62.7	84.8	11.8	9.0		

Expansion for a county system

A rural, small town, county system provided the opportunity to assess the effects of a four-day in-service workshop followed by three observation and feedback sessions during the academic year (three observations with feedback to each individual teacher).

A complete school district comprised of 175 teachers and administrators was divided into groups and proceeded through the workshop sequence. The sequence included a one-week workshop followed by three observational feedback days during the school year. Data from the schools were analyzed by school (three elementary schools with twelve, sixteen, and forty teachers; one junior high with forty-one teachers; and one high school with thirty-nine teachers).

The total amount of reinforcement dispensed was approximately 20 percent for both social behavior reinforcement and academic behavior reinforcement, with a tendency for teachers at all levels to be much more positive in the reinforcement of academic behaviors when contrasted with social behaviors (see Table 8–4). There was also a tendency to make more mistakes of reinforcement (approval mistakes) when interacting with the pupils following social behavior. Generally teachers do not make mistakes when referring to the correctness or incorrectness of academic material. In addition, the percentage of student off-task behavior was not very high.

One clear conclusion from the foregoing data and other studies in this area is that the precise effects of academic versus social approval and/or the effects of mistakes of reinforcement in maintaining appropriate academic and social behaviors in students has not yet been completely determined. Many studies need to be designed which separate the effects of one variable by holding constant other variables within the classroom environment. However, some tentative conclusions may be drawn. Approval for social behavior, even with a workshop and follow-up observational sessions, is not very high. When compared to other workshop-trained teachers with additional follow-up, it appears that the precise amount of behavioral training is still not fully explored. Other studies in this series indicate that, when volunteers are involved with these kind of experiences, the results are more noticeable as well as longer lasting.

Table 8–4   Teacher Observations Following Workshop and Three Feedback Sessions

Social Behavior	Approval	Dis-approval	Approval Mistakes	Dis-approval Mistakes	Total Reinforce-ment	Approval Ratio	Average Percent Off-Task
Elementary (N = 53)	8.1%	10.1%	1.6%	0.3%	20.1%	40.2%	13.8%
Junior High (N = 33)	10.1	10.9	3.3	0.6	24.9	40.1	14.7
Senior High (N = 33)	5.7	5.9	2.2	0.6	14.4	39.6	14.2
Academic Behavior							
Elementary (N = 53)	20.3%	6.0%	0.0%	0.1%	26.4%	76.9%	....
Junior High (N = 33)	13.6	3.0	0.2	0.0	16.8	80.1	....
Senior High (N = 33)	14.5	3.5	0.1	0.0	18.1	80.1	....

Some teachers do not change

A training problem was made manifest during a study aimed at determining if some optimum level of reinforcement could be achieved by changing the approval-disapproval ratio (Vanderbeck and Madsen, 1968). Seven teachers had volunteered for participation and a series of projects were developed incorporating the specific problems presented by the teachers.

The study was intended to show that a classroom with a high percentage of inappropriate behavior could be brought under control by changing teacher contingencies. The authors also hoped to determine the most appropriate ratio of teacher approval and disapproval for maintaining pupil behavior. The teacher was a twenty-five year old man with two years teaching experience. He was a volunteer who stated he was very interested in the program and convinced the entire experimental staff of his "good" intentions. The study took place in a third-grade class with an average of thirty-one children attending daily. The project also included an attempt to hold teacher total approval and disapproval behavior constant while the ratio of approval to disapproval was varied.

Observers within the classroom tabulated both teacher and student behavior (classroom average) with high reliability. Three months were used to acclimate the teacher and class to the observers. (This long period was probably not necessary but at that time it was decided to take no chances.) Following baseline, the teacher learning phase was initiated. This phase included twelve hours of interaction on an individual basis which covered theories and principles supporting the study, relevant previous research, and daily feedback pertaining to the children's graphs and the teacher's own behavior. The experimenter sat in the classroom for five half-days with immediate discussion of the teacher's use of approval, disapproval, and mistakes of reinforcement. A series of reversals were planned to follow the initial high-approval high-disapproval phase which was to be controlled for absolute frequency. *The teacher didn't change.* During the first, high-disapproval phase, daily graphic feedback as well as sample lists of child behaviors which warranted disapproval were discussed. Three morning training sessions were added. Experimental observations were taken throughout the afternoon during the math period, where direct verbal and written feedback together with encouragement for use of reinforcement was given.

Additional teacher helps were initiated when it became apparent during the next, high-approval, phase that the teacher, despite his hand counters, daily feedback, and discussions, was not able to reduce disapproval to less than 20 percent. At this point a cueing system was begun during the morning session. A two-foot pointer was extended whenever the teacher had neglected to deliver an approval comment for a sixty-second period. Seven cueing sessions totalling over three and one-half hours were completed during this phase. Discussions and examples of written approval comments continued to supplement the verbal and graphic feedback. These techniques were also failures. The next alternative, a token system, was devised contingent on the teacher's behavior. Money was given to him for appropriate delivery of either approval or disapproval, depending upon the experimental phase, with punishment for an excess of errors of approval during the disapproval phase and disapproval during the approval phase. The available amount of money was in excess of $100.00, but he was able to earn only $23.35. The final attempt to bring the teacher's behavior under control involved the use of role-playing with the intern, the teacher, and the experimenter in four two-hour sessions. This procedure gave the teacher practice in emitting various types of approval and disapproval and focused on the specific child behavior problems which had been observed in the classroom. Results of the experiment indicated that the teacher's behavior was still not enough under control to answer the initial question concerning the most appropriate approval ratio. It was true that the contingencies and procedures applied did make some changes in teacher behavior but not to the extent demonstrated by other teachers with similar procedures. This study indicated that additional parameters concerning the most effective procedures in changing teacher behavior need to be investigated.

Based upon data from the workshops reported thus far and an analysis of many other workshops of a more informal nature (i.e., with less data), it became apparent that there were perhaps a number of important components to a workshop experience in behavioral principles—specifically, those components designed to reduce the disparity between ideas and behaviors in the classroom. It became evident, as indicated above, that there are a number of teachers in every workshop who never do improve in the classroom even though they want very much to alter their behavior. Thus, during the last two years, additional experiences have been developed that appear to be important if a teacher is subsequently going to change behavior. This conclusion is based on data obtained from teachers in more than thirty workshops.

TEACHERS AS BEHAVIORAL CONSULTANTS

An important aspect concerning the use of behavioral principles to promote the arrangement of an environment where effective learning can take place requires the local system to continue follow-up after the initial training. The best situation appears to be an hierarchical model of training which allows the consultant "to work himself out of a job" and let the local school district personnel conduct all future training sessions.

An excellent prototype was begun in a large public school system. Pupil personnel within the staff development section of this county system chose approximately thirty-five counselors, teachers, and administrators to participate. Two workshop directors assisted by thirteen persons conducted an in-service workshop for these people, directed toward preparing them to conduct similar workshops with teachers within the county system. Teachers had been assigned to work in schools which had been recently integrated. The particular program focused on *A Behavior Modification Workshop in Human Relations* and was designed to involve teachers in practical techniques directed toward classroom management and human relations problems. Experience in the practical application of behavioral techniques within actual classes, including videotaped analysis, theoretical discussions, and role-playing, prepared participants to conduct similar workshops with other county personnel. Following the initial prototype two-week workshop, observational data on all participants was gathered by the thirteen behavioral specialists. Data included white-black interactions, small group interactions, scores on tests, and classroom observations. Data were analyzed and the thirty-five persons were assigned on the basis of the data to teams of two or three. Each team conducted two workshops for twenty to thirty local teachers. The directors and assistants correlated the training and assisted the county personnel. This expansion model resulted in the training of over 750 teachers during the six-week time period. Subsequently, these local county personnel have also conducted over twenty additional workshops without additional training or contact from the consultants, except for consultants providing a videotape library and some additional materials.

Since the initial expansion workshops, local personnel have conducted regular thirty-hour workshops with approximately twenty-five teachers per group, thus reaching directly over 500 additional teachers. These local persons function as consultants to Title I, Title III, and Title IV programs in the local district as well as serving as behavioral engineers in solving problems created in desegregation of the schools.

Long-term results

Preceding workshops were tailored to the needs of individual schools or districts but generally included the following three-phase program:

1. Pre-observations of participating teachers (baselines). Three to five observations are considered minimal; however, more extensive observation is sometimes limited by available funds. This problem has been solved in some school systems by training local personnel in observation techniques.
2. Workshop experience (see Chapter 10). Research indicates that a four-day program can have long-lasting effect, especially if followed by periodic feedback and help in the classroom. Lasting results are difficult to maintain with a one- or two-day introduction or four or five days spread out throughout the year.
3. Post-workshop observations with graphic and/or videotape feedback to the individual teacher followed by random intermittent checks with teachers. The best post-workshop experience involves allowing the teacher to observe classroom interaction behavior via videotape with immediate observational analysis.

Three workshops which were conducted over the past few years have at least one-year follow-ups on results of teacher workshop experience. The first involved teachers who volunteered for participation in a classroom management program. Four hours of baseline observations were followed by a workshop of eight hours duration (four sessions) and an additional four hours of classroom observations. Four-hour follow-up observations during the subsequent school year were completed on all ten teachers who remained in the system. Pre-observations, averaged across teachers, indicated an approval ratio of 40 percent. The workshop experience increased the ratio to 64 percent. Six months later, in the next school year, with each teacher interacting with completely different classes, these teachers had maintained the same level of approval. The follow-up approval ratio was still 64 percent. This improvement was maintained without any intervening conduct. It should be remembered that these teachers were volunteers and desired to improve classroom atmosphere. The workshop was conducted by graduate students and was also one of the shortest conducted. Difference in results when compared to longer initial workshops is indicated by the inability of teachers to eliminate their mistakes of reinforcement. Most long-term workshops serve to eliminate almost all mistakes of reinforcement to less than 1 percent.

The second workshop demonstrating long-term results involved the entire teacher population of a small county. This workshop experience involved twenty hours of workshop training, classroom observations of all teachers, an additional training sequence of sixteen hours during the school year, and a follow-up check on maintenance of behavior during the subsequent school year. Data for the teachers remaining in the system after a three-year interval indicated that the approval ratio for appropriate behavior on observation one following initial training was 54 percent and following the subsequent training the ratio had increased to 81 percent. The two year follow-up indicated that the teachers maintained approximately the same ratio of 81 percent. The teachers had actually increased the amount of approval to appropriate behavior while also decreasing the disapproval to inappropriate. Thus a positive approach to classroom management appeared to remain consistent after two years. Observations in this study were based upon four one-hour observations in the classroom at random time intervals.

The third workshop for which long-term data exist involved one entire elementary school. Teachers were observed two years after the termination of an initial workshop, with the results shown in Table 8–5. Twelve teachers were included in the workshop.

Table 8-5   Teacher-Student Interactions

	SOCIAL REINFORCEMENT					ACADEMIC REINFORCEMENT				
Teacher	Approval to Social	Dis-approval to Social	Social Mistakes	Ratio of Approval	Average On-Task Student Behavior	Approval to Academic	Dis-approval to Academic	Academic Mistakes	Ratio of Academic	Combined Ratio (Academic and Social)
1	29.1%	3.0%	0.0%	90.7%	88.5%	3.9%	0.0%	0.0%	100.0%	90.6
2	12.7	5.7	0.0	70.0	86.0	22.0	3.0	0.0	88.0	80.0
3	11.1	4.3	2.2	62.9	68.6	25.4	5.3	2.2	77.1	72.3
4	12.7	0.6	0.3	93.7	77.9	28.0	1.9	0.3	92.9	93.1
5	9.3	0.3	0.6	91.6	83.1	12.3	2.4	0.5	80.4	84.8
6	8.4	5.0	0.0	62.8	78.8	17.9	2.0	0.0	89.9	79.0
7	8.6	1.4	0.3	83.3	77.3	17.4	0.9	0.2	93.9	90.1
8	12.4	3.0	0.0	80.6	80.3	20.1	1.1	0.0	94.6	88.7
9	26.6	5.3	0.0	83.4	82.0	22.0	1.4	0.0	93.9	87.9
10	14.9	5.4	0.3	72.2	79.9	25.1	3.1	0.4	88.0	81.4
11	35.7	3.4	0.0	91.2	90.8	30.7	1.6	0.0	95.1	92.9
12	24.9	5.3	0.0	82.5	89.0	19.6	0.3	0.0	98.6	88.9
TOTAL AVERAGE	17.2%	3.6%	0.3%	82.3%	81.8%	20.4%	1.9%	0.3%	93.9%	87.8%

227

Ten had participated in a two-week summer workshop two years earlier. The remaining teachers, and the original ten, participated in a two-day follow-up workshop and received continual observational feedback during the interim year (average sixty-four observations). The initial workshop and follow-up training, including video and observational feedback, were based upon the training principles and learning activities reported in Chapter 10. During the second year, all twelve teachers participated in a half-day workshop. All twelve teachers also received individual contact with a behavioral consultant approximately once a month and received graphs of observational results approximately every two weeks. In addition, training procedures were designed to help teachers maintain a positive learning atmosphere in their classrooms. This was accomplished through discussions, role-playing, videotape analysis, and specific suggestions for the implementation of positive techniques.

The behavioral consultant emphasized (1) making classroom rules repeatedly explicit, (2) ignoring minor behaviors which interfere with learning, (3) using disapproval and—when necessary—isolation (time-out) and withdrawal of approval, (4) giving approval to behavior which facilitates learning, and (5) reinforcing prosocial behavior incompatible with inappropriate social behavior. The observational schedule for these teachers included feedback twice weekly from October through December and observation with no feedback for January, February, and two weeks in March, followed by twice weekly feedback for the remainder of the school year. The year following the workshop (one year later), remaining teachers received a two-day workshop at the beginning of the school year and were given observational feedback approximately once a week during the entire year. Overall, ten of twelve teachers (180 total observations) maintained an 80 percent approval ratio for both the academic reinforcement of appropriate skill development (correct learning responses) and social reinforcement of appropriate behavior that did not violate the classroom rules or interfere with the learning of other students. In addition, eleven of the twelve teachers had less than a 1 percent rate of mistakes of reinforcement.

It should be noted that four of the twelve teachers did not have an 80 percent reinforcement interaction ratio. The social reinforcement interaction represented one-half of the total reinforcement interactions observed during this school year. The academic re-inforcement ratios are generally higher for teachers trained in behavioral techniques. Perhaps these teachers tend to dispense less social reinforcement as control is more easily achieved. Eight of the twelve teachers used more academic reinforcement. Compara-tively, the lowest ratio of social reinforcement for these teachers is higher than 92 percent of all other teachers observed. The average social reinforcement ratio for all other teachers observed was 24.9 percent compared with the average of these twelve teachers of 82.3 percent.

Academic reinforcement ratio averaged 93.9 percent compared with 82.3 percent for social reinforcement. When the reinforcement interactions for both academic and social behavior are combined, two of the twelve teachers fall below the arbitrarily determined 80 percent criterion level. However, even the lowest teacher among these twelve, with a ratio of 72.3 percent, is 50 percent higher than the average of most teachers (observations of over 6,500 teachers).

The frequency of the behavior observed is the percent of ten-second intervals during which the behavior occurs while the ratio of reinforcement is the percent of reinforcement which was positive (approval) whether or not the total frequency of behavior was either high or low (see analysis of teacher observation in Chapter 9).

Concerning the effect of these teacher behaviors on students, it should be observed that the average percent of students on-task was 81.8. Every teacher was able to maintain an average on-task per-cent much higher than most untrained teachers. Average on-task student behavior of about 80 percent is generally considered to represent a well-controlled classroom. Comparisons between trained and untrained teachers matched on teaching experience and grade level indicates the effectiveness of the training procedures. This effectiveness is apparent in both the increase of appropriate student classroom behaviors as well as increasing the positive, or approval, behavior of the project teachers. There is a direct relationship between the positive teacher ratio and the amount of inappropriate student behavior. Generally, the higher the positive teacher ratio, the greater is the student's responsiveness to the learning situation. Behavioral improvement seems to be directly related to the amount of attention teachers give to appropriate academic and social behavior.

TEACHER AIDES

Observational data on teacher aides provide the opportunity to test the effect of behavioral training on supportive personnel. Twelve teacher aides working with the follow-up teachers indicated that the training for the aides (ten to twelve hours of training) increased their positive interaction patterns with students but did not enable them to reach a level comparable to the teachers with whom they worked. The aides did get better as the year progressed and became more and more similar to the regular teachers. However, more time should be spent with aides in techniques of behavioral control early in the school year if a high ratio of social reinforcement is to be achieved by paraprofessionals.

Results indicate that aides are fully capable of interaction with students on a level comparable to teachers and that they are able to reinforce positively both social and academic behavior. The overall reinforcement ratio for the aides (average of twelve) was as follows:

Social Ratio 74.2%	Approval to Appropriate Social Behavior 17.3%	Disapproval to Inappropriate Social Behavior 4.4%	Mistakes 1.6%
Academic Ratio 80.4%	Approval to Appropriate Academic Behavior 13.3%	Disapproval to Inappropriate Academic Behavior 1.7%	Mistakes 1.7%

The above results demonstrate that aides are significantly higher in approval ratio than the average for over 6,500 *regular* teachers, that is, aides in this school were able to develop and maintain a classroom atmosphere which was more positive in orientation than 92 percent of all teachers observed.

MAINTENANCE OF APPROVAL INTERACTIONS

The precise amount of follow-up interactions with teachers who have demonstrated competencies in behavioral methods of classroom reinforcement is as yet unknown. Teachers in many studies did receive periodic observational feedback. However, it is important to realize that principals and supervisors in every school district could provide the same feedback to their own teachers. How long it takes for the teachers' behaviors to become self-reinforcing enough to maintain the behavior across long periods of time with no external feedback is unknown. It is probably unrealistic to expect teachers to maintain positive interactions with students if the persons interacting with the teachers are negative and disapproving. It would be expected that the teachers' behaviors would extinguish with no approval from peers and supervisors. Present data show that teachers are able to maintain a high level of approval and reduce mistakes of reinforcement when some feedback is given. Other research has indicated that the greatest changes are produced when specific criteria for academic approval and social approval are set and results are reported to teachers (Saudargas, 1972; Grandy, 1973). Principals, supervisors, counselors, psychologists, and others may serve the function of observing and reporting observational results following the setting of specific criteria in conjunction with the individual teachers.

Since there are many differences in both individual teachers and studies, partial data give only an indication of the variables concerning interaction patterns of teachers. Continuing research in delineating these variables is clearly necessary and desirable.

CHAPTER 9

LEARNING THROUGH OBSERVATION

It has been stressed repeatedly by those interested in behavioral analyses that data must be collected regarding overt demonstrable behaviors. Often teachers in the field are able to devise their own recording instruments in regard to specific problems to be corrected within their own classroom. In most cases this is preferable, but to sensitize the teacher or potential teacher to individual effects of reinforcement, more elaborate procedures should be used. In addition, researchers must maintain even greater rigor as well as some uniformity in observation data in order that their findings may be transmitted in a systematic manner to others in the area. Regardless of intent or dissemination, observational data must be both accurate and reliable.

CATEGORY DEVELOPMENT

Prerequisites to accurate behavioral observations include mutually exclusive category definitions which are precise enough to allow observers to note and record the behavior reliably. The general rules which are followed in developing observational categories for inappropriate student behaviors are that categories should:

1. Reflect behaviors which interfere with classroom learning by limiting the time (individual or group) students are on-task in the classroom.

2. Involve behaviors which violate rules, written or implied, established by the teacher.
3. Reflect particular behaviors a teacher desires to change (increase or decrease).
4. Refer to overt behaviors which can actually be observed in order to limit the potential for inferences made by the person doing the observing.
5. Be similar in some important way—either topographically (appearing similar) or logically (conceptual class).
6. Be mutually exclusive so that observational recording of one category of behavior will not be confused with another category.
7. Be limited so that the observer can rapidly decide and record the classes of behaviors observed.

Observation which is accurate and reliable requires observers who are extremely proficient in recording procedures. Indeed, recording of behavior should become almost automatic. Therefore careful study of behavioral categories as well as continued practice either in the classroom or with videotape is required.

OBSERVER MATERIALS AND RULES

Each observer should be equipped with (1) a pencil (always better than a pen as corrections are sometimes required), (2) something to write upon (a clipboard is generally best), (3) a means for accurately assessing the passage of small increments of time,[1] (4) observation sheets with space for the date, time, activity, person or persons being observed, and a section for inferences or other comments, and (5) a pair of sunglasses. Observers should always record all information—never leave any item blank.

Observers need a special signal which identifies them readily to school personnel and also serves as a signal for teachers and students to refrain from interacting with them. Sunglasses are excellent for this purpose. Sunglasses also partially hide the observer's

---

[1] A stopwatch or watch with a sweep hand is useful. More sophisticated equipment might include electronic recording devices or prerecorded cassette tape signals for observation. Also, two or more observers listening to the same cassette eliminate unreliability due to time differences as the signals can state, "Line one, observe. . . . Record. . . . Line two, observe. . . . Record. . . , and so on. Small timed lights have also been used successfully.

eyes from the teacher and class so that the person being observed is generally unaware of the scrutiny. Teachers should be instructed to refrain from introducing or otherwise referring to the observers when they come into the classroom. Teachers should also be instructed to say nothing and ask no questions of any observer when the sunglasses are over the eyes. When the observer is part of the school staff, for example, a counselor, psychologist, or administrator, the observer will remove the sunglasses before speaking to any of the students or teachers. Thus the sunglasses serve a dual purpose in identifying the observer and signaling to inhibit verbal interaction. Research within many classrooms indicates that observers are effectively ignored by the students in primary classes after about three or four hours of observation, while intermediate and high school classes take about four to eight hours of observation and teachers somewhat longer.

It is axiomatic that observations are not as accurate (valid) prior to the time the class and teacher became accustomed to observers taking data. But, even though interaction patterns are somewhat less frequent during the first phases of observation, the general ratio of approval/disapproval reinforcement is generally similar even during initial observations.

The goal for observers is to become as unobtrusive as a piece of furniture. Teachers should try to be as natural as possible with the class and, except for brief answers to observer's questions prior or subsequent to observation, refrain from interacting with or even mentioning the observers, especially when the class is watching. It is preferred that teachers who are to be observed not have a specific time schedule for the observations. This would only increase initial anxiety and limit observational accuracy. It is recommended that teachers understand the purpose of the observation and be given feedback as soon as possible concerning the results of the observations, preferably immediately following observations.

Observer instruction summary

Observers should be provided with the following instructions:

1. Wear sunglasses when observing. This signals teachers, students, and others that you will not interact with them. During the time of the observation there should be *no* talking or inter-

action with the teacher and questions or recording problems should be settled before entering the classroom whenever possible. If teacher interactions become necessary, make certain that the sunglasses are removed and that observations cease for a short time. Should a teacher initiate interaction during an observation, generally ignore it until the observation is concluded.

2. Sit silently and as immobile as possible when observing. Change location quietly and only when absolutely necessary. If you are observing a particular student or students who change locations then you may have to change if you are unable to hear the verbal interactions.

3. Your goal as an observer is to become a piece of furniture. Take great care that you do not become a reinforcement variable with reference to the behavior of students or teachers in the classroom.

4. Make no differential responses to students, i.e., laughing at wisecracks, answering questions directed toward you, smiling at student's responses, or changing position of head or eyes when addressed. Make the minimal movement necessary to see the student, teacher, or other person you are recording. Social behaviors by students either on entering or leaving the classroom or the school should be ignored as well as behaviors directed toward you while you are in the halls. *Remember*, if ever you decide to talk to another observer, the teacher, or your supervisor, then please remove your glasses.

5. Discussion of any student, by name or otherwise, except with proper school personnel or your immediate supervisor, is a breach of professional conduct.

6. Please conform to the general faculty dress standards of the school in order that your dress does not become a variable and/or interfere with the task of observation.

7. Look only at observation forms during recording intervals and ignore any noises from the person or persons observed.

8. Remain as unsubjective and unbiased as possible at all times. The main objective is for two people watching the same behavior to agree that the same behaviors occurred (reliability). Record what the person does without trying to think what he should have done. Your time will come.

Teacher observation forms

Teacher forms are self-contained and provide for a complete analysis which can later be graphed, summarized, or presented verbally to the teacher who has been observed. Observations of teacher reinforcements following student behavior are more easily understood when the appropriate symbols are related to the two-by-two teacher contingency table (page 242). The teacher observation symbols are placed in the appropriate boxes to facilitate learning. The order of the symbols is identical to the placement on all teacher observation forms; therefore, symbols are directly transferred from the following contingency table to the observation forms whenever an observer is recording teacher reinforcement.

RECORDING PROCEDURES

Before observation begins, all identifying data should be completed. This generally includes recording the name of the teacher(s) and/or student(s) being observed, the date, the time, and name of the observer.

The general activity is recorded at the top of the sheet and the nature of the on-going classroom (for individual) activity is recorded under the column marked activity. Each time there is a change in activity, such as from reading to math, from group discussion to seatwork, this change should be recorded in the activity column. Activities can be recorded using a number and letter code.

BEHAVIORAL CONTINGENCY INTERACTIONS: TABLE 1

| | | SOCIETAL AGENTS BEHAVIOR | |
		Approval	Disapproval
	APPROPRIATE (On-Task – Social & Academic)	**YES** (No When No Disapproval) (1)	**NO** (Mistake) (2)
	INAPPROPRIATE (Off-Task – Social & Academic)	**NO** (Mistake) (3)	**YES** (No if Payoff Or When No (4) Approval)

STUDENT BEHAVIOR

FORM A: TEACHER OBSERVATION

Observer_____   Teacher _____
Reliability Observer _____   Grade or Subject _____
No. in Class or Group_____   Date _____
General Activity_____   Time: Start ____End _____
Length of Observational Intervals in Seconds _____
Record Intervals in Seconds _____   Page _____of _____

TIME	ACTIVITY CODE	(1)	2-RECORD	(3)	4-RECORD	(5)	6-RECORD	COMMENTS
1		OBSERVE NOW	As Aa Ds Da / As Aa Ds Da	OBSERVE NOW	As Aa Ds Da / As Aa Ds Da	OBSERVE NOW	As Aa Ds Da / As Aa Ds Da	
2			As Aa Ds Da / As Aa Ds Da		As Aa Ds Da / As Aa Ds Da		As Aa Ds Da / As Aa Ds Da	
3			As Aa Ds Da / As Aa Ds Da		As Aa Ds Da / As Aa Ds Da		As Aa Ds Da / As Aa Ds Da	
4			As Aa Ds Da / As Aa Ds Da		As Aa Ds Da / As Aa Ds Da		As Aa Ds Da / As Aa Ds Da	
5			As Aa Ds Da / As Aa Ds Da		As Aa Ds Da / As Aa Ds Da		As Aa Ds Da / As Aa Ds Da	
6			As Aa Ds Da / As Aa Ds Da		As Aa Ds Da / As Aa Ds Da		As Aa Ds Da / As Aa Ds Da	
7			As Aa Ds Da / As Aa Ds Da		As Aa Ds Da / As Aa Ds Da		As Aa Ds Da / As Aa Ds Da	
8		OBSERVE NOW	As Aa Ds Da / As Aa Ds Da	OBSERVE NOW	As Aa Ds Da / As Aa Ds Da	OBSERVE NOW	As Aa Ds Da / As Aa Ds Da	
9			As Aa Ds Da / As Aa Ds Da		As Aa Ds Da / As Aa Ds Da		As Aa Ds Da / As Aa Ds Da	
10			As Aa Ds Da / As Aa Ds Da		As Aa Ds Da / As Aa Ds Da		As Aa Ds Da / As Aa Ds Da	
11			As Aa Ds Da / As Aa Ds Da		As Aa Ds Da / As Aa Ds Da		As Aa Ds Da / As Aa Ds Da	
12			As Aa Ds Da / As Aa Ds Da		As Aa Ds Da / As Aa Ds Da		As Aa Ds Da / As Aa Ds Da	
13			As Aa Ds Da / As Aa Ds Da		As Aa Ds Da / As Aa Ds Da		As Aa Ds Da / As Aa Ds Da	
14		OBSERVE NOW	As Aa Ds Da / As Aa Ds Da	OBSERVE NOW	As Aa Ds Da / As Aa Ds Da	OBSERVE NOW	As Aa Ds Da / As Aa Ds Da	
15			As Aa Ds Da / As Aa Ds Da		As Aa Ds Da / As Aa Ds Da		As Aa Ds Da / As Aa Ds Da	
16			As Aa Ds Da / As Aa Ds Da		As Aa Ds Da / As Aa Ds Da		As Aa Ds Da / As Aa Ds Da	
17			As Aa Ds Da / As Aa Ds Da		As Aa Ds Da / As Aa Ds Da	TOTALS:	As____ Aa____ Ds____ Da____ / As____ Aa____ Ds____ Da____	

FORM B: TEACHER OBSERVATION

Observer _____   Teacher _____
Reliability Observer _____   Grade or Subject _____
Number in Class or Group _____   Date _____
General Activity _____   Time Start _____ Time End _____
Length of Observation Intervals in Seconds _____
Record Intervals in Seconds _____ Page _____ of _____

TIME	ACTIVITY CODE	INTERVALS					Comment
		1 - Record	2 - Record	3 - Record	4 - Record	5 - Record	
1		As Aa Ds Da As Aa Ds Da	As Aa Ds Da As Aa Ds Da	As Aa Ds Da As Aa Ds Da	As Aa Ds Da As Aa Ds Da	As Aa Ds Da As Aa Ds Da	
2		As Aa Ds Da As Aa Ds Da	As Aa Ds Da As Aa Ds Da	As Aa Ds Da As Aa Ds Da	As Aa Ds Da As Aa Ds Da	As Aa Ds Da As Aa Ds Da	
3		As Aa Ds Da As Aa Ds Da	As Aa Ds Da As Aa Ds Da	As Aa Ds Da As Aa Ds Da	As Aa Ds Da As Aa Ds Da	As Aa Ds Da As Aa Ds Da	
4		As Aa Ds Da As Aa Ds Da	As Aa Ds Da As Aa Ds Da	As Aa Ds Da As Aa Ds Da	As Aa Ds Da As Aa Ds Da	As Aa Ds Da As Aa Ds Da	
5		As Aa Ds Da As Aa Ds Da	As Aa Ds Da As Aa Ds Da	As Aa Ds Da As Aa Ds Da	As Aa Ds Da As Aa Ds Da	As Aa Ds Da As Aa Ds Da	
6		As Aa Ds Da As Aa Ds Da	As Aa Ds Da As Aa Ds Da	As Aa Ds Da As Aa Ds Da	As Aa Ds Da As Aa Ds Da	As Aa Ds Da As Aa Ds Da	
7		As Aa Ds Da As Aa Ds Da	As Aa Ds Da As Aa Ds Da	As Aa Ds Da As Aa Ds Da	As Aa Ds Da As Aa Ds Da	As Aa Ds Da As Aa Ds Da	
8		As Aa Ds Da As Aa Ds Da	As Aa Ds Da As Aa Ds Da	As Aa Ds Da As Aa Ds Da	As Aa Ds Da As Aa Ds Da	As Aa Ds Da As Aa Ds Da	
9		As Aa Ds Da As Aa Ds Da	As Aa Ds Da As Aa Ds Da	As Aa Ds Da As Aa Ds Da	As Aa Ds Da As Aa Ds Da	As Aa Ds Da As Aa Ds Da	
10		As Aa Ds Da As Aa Ds Da	As Aa Ds Da As Aa Ds Da	As Aa Ds Da As Aa Ds Da	As Aa Ds Da As Aa Ds Da	As Aa Ds Da As Aa Ds Da	
11		As Aa Ds Da As Aa Ds Da	As Aa Ds Da As Aa Ds Da	As Aa Ds Da As Aa Ds Da	As Aa Ds Da As Aa Ds Da	As Aa Ds Da As Aa Ds Da	
12		As Aa Ds Da As Aa Ds Da	As Aa Ds Da As Aa Ds Da	As Aa Ds Da As Aa Ds Da	As Aa Ds Da As Aa Ds Da	As Aa Ds Da As Aa Ds Da	
13		As Aa Ds Da As Aa Ds Da	As Aa Ds Da As Aa Ds Da	As Aa Ds Da As Aa Ds Da	As Aa Ds Da As Aa Ds Da	As Aa Ds Da As Aa Ds Da	
14		As Aa Ds Da As Aa Ds Da	As Aa Ds Da As Aa Ds Da	As Aa Ds Da As Aa Ds Da	As Aa Ds Da As Aa Ds Da	As Aa Ds Da As Aa Ds Da	
15		As Aa Ds Da As Aa Ds Da	As Aa Ds Da As Aa Ds Da	As Aa Ds Da As Aa Ds Da	As Aa Ds Da As Aa Ds Da	As Aa Ds Da As Aa Ds Da	

SOCIAL REINFORCEMENT

Symbols	Total No. Observed	÷	Total Intervals Observed	=	% Intervals Behavior Observed
As =		÷		=	_____ %
Ds =		÷		=	_____ %
(As) =		÷		=	_____ %
(Ds) =		÷		=	_____ %

Social Approval Ratio: $\dfrac{As}{As + Ds + (As) + (Ds)}$ (OR) ÷___+___+___+___= %

Academic Reinforcement

Symbols	Total No. Observed	÷	Total Intervals Observed	=	%Intervals Behavior Observed
Aa =		÷		=	_____ %
Da =		÷		=	_____ %
(Aa) =		÷		=	_____ %
(Da) =		÷		=	_____ %

Academic Approval Ratio: $\dfrac{Aa}{Aa + Da + (Aa) + (Da)}$ (OR)___÷___+___+___= %

$$\text{RELIABILITY} = \frac{\text{Total Agree}}{\text{Total Agree} + \text{Total Disagree}} \_\_\%$$

Symbols	Number Observed		Same Symbol in Same Interval	
	Observer I	Reliability Observer	Agree	Disagree
As				
Ds				
(As)				
(Ds)				
Aa				
Da				
(Aa)				
(Da)				

"No Behavior Observed"_____ | | | |

Total _____ | _____

239

The *first* number recorded in the activity column indicates the number of students with whom the teacher is interacting for that time period. In most classrooms this may change constantly—the teacher may be working with an individual child, then a small group, and perhaps later conduct a class discussion. Record the exact number of students for each line of intervals.

The *second* entry should indicate the content area the teacher is pursuing with the students being instructed. The code indicates only the academic activity of the group or individual with whom the teacher is interacting; other students may be engaged in other activities. An illustrative code that has been used in elementary schools follows:

LA—Language arts	Mu—Music	F—Free time, play,
M—Mathematics	A—Art	student-selected
Sc—Science	R—Recreation	activity
SS—Social Studies	Sp—Spelling	Re—Rest
PE—Physical Educa- tion	W—Writing	L—Lunch

The *third* code uses roman numerals and indicates the specific student response that is expected:

I—Looking	V—Major Motor (jumping,
II—Minor Motor (writing)	walking)
III—Talking	VI—Resting
IV—Listening	

Categories may be expanded by multiple designations or notes in the Comments section.

Teacher observation (Form A)

Learning Activities always start with Form A. During the first interval of each time period (ten-second observing and recording intervals have been found to be most useful), the observer should observe and mentally note the ongoing behavior. Observers *do not record the behavior observed at this time.* During the second interval, the behavior observed during the first interval is recorded (marked) on the data sheet. Comments regarding general classroom inter-action and/or descriptions of behavior should also be recorded during this time. No observation of behavior occurs during the second interval as this time period is devoted to recording. Observations are continued during the third interval, but are not recorded until the fourth. The same procedure is followed with the fifth and sixth intervals. Thus behavior is observed during the first, third, and fifth intervals and is recorded during the second, fourth, and sixth. Two or more *different* behaviors may be recorded during any one ten-second interval, but, unless specific directions are given to the contrary, only one symbol of the same behavior should appear in each interval box. After observation expertise has progressed (to .80 reliability), behaviors occurring twice during the same interval can be recorded for the appropriate symbol by using numbers or additional marks. All occurrences should be checked or marked in a conspicuous manner. Colored pencils are excellent for this.

Teacher observation (Form B)

Observe and record the behaviors continuously during the first five intervals of each time line (ten-second intervals have been found effective) and record comments or rest during the last interval.

RECORDING TEACHER BEHAVIOR

Teacher behavior as well as student behavior is rated with reference to the rules of the classroom. Always attempt to know the general rules for the class and the specific rules for the activity underway.

The ratings of teacher behaviors can perhaps be best conceptualized according to the following scheme, which is essentially the same chart as on page 43 but with two contingencies (withholding approval and threat of disapproval) excluded. Ignoring is also excluded because it cannot be observed.

In demonstrating the reinforcing function of approving and disapproving teacher behavior, a brief review is advisable. Reinforcement must follow student behavior—behavior is a result of its consequences—or there will be no effect upon student behavior. Reinforcement either increases or decreases behavior. When no effect is demonstrated, then no reinforcement has occurred. For example, the attempts of most teachers to elicit student responses by using interest-provoking questions are to be commended; however, for a behavior to be reinforced, the reinforcement must follow

BEHAVIORAL CONTINGENCY INTERACTIONS: TABLE 2

TEACHER BEHAVIOR

		Approval	Disapproval
APPROPRIATE (Social & Academic)		As Aa	Ⓓⓢ Ⓓⓐ (Mistakes)
INAPPROPRIATE (Social & Academic)		Ⓐⓢ Ⓐⓐ (Mistakes)	Ds Da

(STUDENT BEHAVIOR, left margin label)

the behavior. The behavioral categories are designed to analyze teacher behaviors following responses from students.

When a teacher follows a behavior with approval, this may serve to reinforce the appropriate behavior (Box 1: When you do good things, good things happen to you). When a teacher gives approval following inappropriate behavior, this is regarded as a reinforcement mistake which may increase the rate of inappropriate behavior! This is called an *approval mistake* (Box 3: When you do bad things, good things happen to you).

Disapproval when properly used generally serves to stop or decrease the rate of the disapproved behavior (Box 4: When you do bad things; bad things happen to you). Therefore, the teacher may be making a mistake if disapproval follows appropriate behavior. This is called a disapproval mistake (Box 2: When you do good things, bad things happen to you).

Disapproval following inappropriate behavior is intended to decrease the inappropriate behavior (Box 4). But, if the student has learned an improper association, the disapproval may function in a different way, depending upon the reinforcement history of the student. Teacher attention may also be reinforcing, and students may work for whatever attention is forthcoming—even disapproval. Disapproving behavior alone without approval for appropriate behavior will often increase the very behavior that the teacher wishes to eliminate. In the lower half of Box 4, the attention serves as a payoff. The upper half of Box 4 shows occasional disapproval is strong enough to stop inappropriate behavior. (When you do bad things, bad things happen to you.) The effects of disapproval following any student behavior probably depend upon the amount of approval to appropriate behavior (Box 1) in relation to the amount of disapproval to inappropriate behavior (Box 4). When the teacher uses more approval to appropriate behavior than disapproval to inappropriate, then both are generally more effective. The contrast between approval and disapproval also serves to enhance the effect of both. When the teacher uses only approval, then students learn that no matter what one does, "good things" happen. When the teacher uses only disapproval, the students learn that no matter what they do, "bad things" happen to them.

Approving and disapproving behaviors are not confined to verbal behavior. As human beings we communicate in a variety of ways—by touch, by gesture, by facial expression. Therefore the teacher must be consistent within her/himself as well as with the rules for the particular activity. When the teacher smiles at a student and also verbally disapproves, the teacher is making either a disapproval or an approval mistake. When the teacher frowns while giving verbal approval, the teacher is also making a reinforcement mistake.

Responses available to the teacher to express approval or disapproval are classified in five categories:

1. Words (spoken or written)
2. Physical expressions (facial or bodily)
3. Closeness (nearness or touching)
4. Activities (social or individual)
5. Things (materials, food, awards, or tokens)

The observer should have these categories memorized and analyze teacher behaviors in terms of the responses available. Should the teacher dispense facial approval while hitting, shaking, or forcibly restraining a child, then all applicable categories should be checked depending upon the immediately preceding student behavior. Observers should study in detail the examples of approval and disapproval in Chapter 7.

Academic and social definitions

Approval for academic behavior is easily understood. This category includes what most teachers generally label feedback concerning the correctness of a student's academic response whether oral or written. Academic approval concerns only the correctness of the answer to curricular materials and does not include approval for "working hard" or "trying hard" or getting out materials. Of course, any behavior may be academic if the teacher's goals are to teach the behavior as subject matter. Disapproval for academic behavior involves any means, verbal or physical, of indicating to the student that his answer to the specific activity or question is in error.

Approval for social behavior involves giving approval following any aspect of the student's behavior which gets or maintains the student on-task. This category includes reinforcement for appropriate interaction patterns with either the curriculum materials or other individuals. It does not pertain to the correctness or incorrectness of an academic response.

Disapproval of inappropriate social behavior involves disapproval following a discriminated aspect of the student's behavior which either interrupts or disturbs the learning environment for himself or another person. This is off-task behavior (see Glossary).

It is possible to approve the student's attempts to complete assignments (social behavior) while at the same time disapprove an incorrect academic response—"You are working hard; six responses are not correct." The student may be helped to understand the differences among learning how to "work hard," following instructions, and attempting academic material, even though the product is not as expert as it may become with continued effort. Alternately, some students may have many correct responses but still engage in inappropriate social behavior—"Johnny, all your answers are correct, but you should learn to stay on-task and quit disrupting during seatwork."

Teacher Observation Categories

Aa   Approval for academic behavior is recorded if the teacher indicates the academic work is correct. Academic approval usually involves words, spoken or written. The observer should watch carefully to determine if physical expressions, closeness, activities, or things (see Chapter 7) are specifically paired with correct answers, indicating attention or commendation for the correct answer rather than the "working" itself. Care should be exercised in discriminating between approval directed toward academic work and approval for correct social behavior.

As   Approval for social behavior is recorded if the teacher gives any approving response paired specifically with appropriate social behavior. This category includes words, physical expressions, closeness, activities, and things directed toward any social behavior (following rules, working, cooperating, getting on-task).

Da   Disapproval for academic behavior includes any disapproval indicating that a student's response to the curriculum materials was incorrect. Disapproval in classrooms generally involves words, spoken or written (grades), but one should not overlook physical expression, closeness (hitting, grabbing, forcibly holding, putting out of group), or deprivation of activities or things.

Ds   Disapproval for social behavior given by the teacher follows any disruption of the learning environment which interferes with learning. Disapproval includes words, spoken or written, that reprimand. Disapproval may be of either high or low intensity and includes yelling, scolding, threats, and threatening comments concerning later consequences. Disapproval also includes bodily expressions such as frowning, grimacing, or shaking a fist, closeness such as hitting, slapping, paddling, or other means of corporal punishment, and deprivation of activities or things.

(Aa)   An approval mistake of reinforcement following academic behavior occurs when the teacher indicates the academic response is correct when, in fact, the answer is incorrect.

(As)   An approval mistake of reinforcement following social behavior involves giving approval to inappropriate social behavior. For example, a teacher may touch a student "gently" during or following a misbehavior (closeness)

245

or may reinforce the misbehavior through words, bodily expressions, activities, or things. An approval mistake is recorded when the teacher follows a student's breaking of classroom rules with an approval response (inconsistency). The teacher may verbally recognize a student who is walking around when he is supposed to be in his seat, or the teacher may recognize a student who blurts out an answer (whether correct or incorrect) although the student is supposed to raise his hand for recognition. An approval mistake could also occur if the teacher uses words to dispense group verbal approval (praise) when one or more of the students in the group is off-task.

(Da) A disapproval mistake of reinforcement following academic behavior is recorded when the teacher indicates the student's academic answer was incorrect when the answer was, in fact, correct.

(Ds) A disapproval mistake of reinforcement following social behavior is recorded if the teacher uses disapproval when the social behavior was indeed appropriate to the classroom situation. This occurs most frequently when the teacher gives group disapproval and one or more of the students are, in fact, on-task. A disapproval mistake may also occur when the teacher interrupts his work with one student in order to attend another student. Interruptions may lead to a disapproval mistake of reinforcement if the student behavior is disapproved in the process. Disapproval mistakes also occur when the teacher delays too long in using disapproval for inappropriate behavior. For example, a student engages in inappropriate behavior, stops the inappropriate behavior, is working appropriately, and then the teacher disapproves.

Non-reinforcement categories

Any response from the teacher that gives specific directions and requires a response from one or more students in the class is not recorded as either approval or disapproval. Academic instructions pertaining to the academic curriculum which do not require a response from the students are not considered as reinforcement.

Attempts by the teacher to stimulate behavioral responses are extremely common. Often these techniques elicit responses from students that can be reinforced. Questioning, probing, cueing, prompts, illustrations, modelling correct procedures, and so on seem to be tools of most effective teachers, yet these procedures do not necessarily reinforce behavior. While eliciting techniques may increase reinforcement possibilities for some students, elicitation techniques are less effective with students who lack experience or the ability to stay on-task. Observations concerning reinforcements focus only on behaviors which follow a student's response. The individual teacher must establish goals and ascertain the most effective strategies of presentation to elicit responses which then can be reinforced. This is true especially for those individuals whose reinforcement histories do not include enough background for the academic materials to be self-reinforcing.

Student observation (Form C and Form D)

Classroom behavioral observation focusing on the student is concerned with two major behaviors: (1) on-task or appropriate behavior and (2) off-task or inappropriate behavior. Students' behaviors can be appropriate or inappropriate only with reference to classroom rules and/or the teacher's objectives. Therefore, observers must know the rules of each classroom and differing rules for specific situations before reliable observations can be recorded. It is sometimes necessary to ask teachers what their rules are, since some teachers permit students to stand up, sit on the floor, talk during certain activities, or leave their seats without permission.

Child Categories

On-Task
+
This category includes verbal and motor behavior that follows the classroom rules and is appropriate to the learning situation. On-task behavior is defined with reference to both the rules of the classroom and the teacher-designated academic activity. If a student is working on the appropriate academic activity and is obeying the rules of the classroom, then the student's behavior is recorded as being on-task. Examples of on-task behavior might include sitting at desk while work-

ing, engaging in group games when appropriate, responding to teacher questions (whether or not the answer is correct or incorrect), walking to chalkboard when asked, demonstrating activities to others when expected, talking during class discussions, or participating actively in physical education class.

Verbal Noise

Off-task   Verbal noise is any oral response that breaks the class
  N   rules and/or interrupts the learning situation. This category may include inappropriate talking, yelling, blurting out, whistling, humming, screaming, singing, and laughing. The verbalization must be heard for it to be recorded. Simply seeing the student's lips move is not enough. If a child responds to a teacher's question or instruction, then the student is on-task. Further examples of verbal off-task behavior include blurting out an answer instead of raising hand, talking to a neighbor instead of working on materials, and singing during discussion.

Object Noise

Object noise is any audible noise resulting from any behavior on the part of the child that may cause other children to be off-task, such as slamming books, kicking furniture, or rapping a desk.

Motor

M   Motor off-task is any motor response (gross or minor) that breaks the class rules and/or interrupts the learning situation. Some motor behaviors are inappropriate during certain classroom periods but not always at others.

V or I   Should it be important to record differences between gross versus minor motor or verbal noise versus object noise, merely use a different check for each.

Gross Motor

Gross motor behaviors may include getting out of one's seat, turning around at least 90°, running, turning cartwheels, walking around the room, waving arms. Another area of inappropriate gross motor behavior includes behaviors generally labelled "aggressive"— hitting, kicking, pushing, pinching, slapping, striking another person with objects, grabbing another's property, and throwing.

Minor Motor

Minor motor behaviors are only recorded when attention is not directed toward the student's work. If the student is engaged in appropriate activities while he exhibits these small motor behaviors, then his behavior is recorded as being on-task with a check mark on "M" and mention is made of these motor activities in the comment section. Examples of minor motor behaviors include thumbsucking, fingernail biting, fiddling with hair, finger twiddling, chewing on a pencil or other object, and playing with academic materials when not appropriate.

Other or Passive Off-Task

O   The student is involved in no interaction or is doing nothing when expected to be involved. Behaviors recorded in this category include daydreaming and staring into space. The student must be engaged in no motor or verbal activity for this category to be recorded. It is important to remember that there are times when doing nothing is not inappropriate, for example, when an assignment is completed and nothing has been assigned. This is very rare as most teachers have activities for all students when one assignment is completed.

Student-teacher interactions (Form E and Form F)

Behavioral studies during the past few years have indicated that the response of the teacher to student behavior maintains a great deal both of appropriate, on-task behavior and inappropriate, off-task behavior (see Selected Bibliography).

A common question asked by teachers who refer specific children for counseling or other outside help is: How does the

FORM C: STUDENT OBSERVATION

Observer _____ Student _____
Reliability Observer_____ Teacher _____
No. in class or group_____ Grade or Subject_____Date_____
General Activity_____ Time: Start_____ End_____
Observation Interval _____ Page_____ of _____
                (seconds)   Record Interval _____
                                        (seconds)

TIME	ACTIVITY CODE	(1)	2 - RECORD	(3)	4 - RECORD	(5)	6 - RECORD	COMMENTS
1			+N M O		+N M O		+N M O	
2			+N M O		+N M O		+N M O	
3			+N M O		+N M O		+N M O	
4			+N M O		+N M O		+N M O	
5			+N M O		+N M O		+N M O	
6			+N M O		+N M O		+N M O	
7			+N M O		+N M O		+N M O	
8			+N M O		+N M O		+N M O	
9			+N M O		+N M O		+N M O	
10			+N M O		+N M O		+N M O	
11			+N M O		+N M O		+N M O	
12			+N M O		+N M O		+N M O	
13			+N M O		+N M O		+N M O	
14			+N M O		+N M O		+N M O	
15			+N M O		+N M O		+N M O	
16			+N M O		+N M O		+N M O	
17			+N M O		+N M O			

The (1), (3), (5) columns are labeled OBSERVE NOW and the record columns are labeled OBSERVE NOW (vertical).

% On - task = _____(+ %)
% Off - task = 100 – (% On - task) = _____

Intervals Observed
Totals: + = _____ - _____ = _____ %
        N= _____ - _____ = _____ %
        M= _____ - _____ = _____ %
        O= _____ - _____ = _____ %

250

FORM D: STUDENT OBSERVATION

Observer _____   Student _____
Reliability Observer _____   Teacher _____
No. in Class or Group _____   Grade or Subject _____ Date _____
General Activity _____   Time: Start _____ End _____
Observation Interval _____   Page _____ of _____
                    (seconds)   Record Interval _____
                                                     (seconds)

TIME	ACTIVITY CODE	INTERVALS					COMMENTS
		1	2	3	4	5	
1		+N M O	+N M O	+N M O	+N M O	+N M O	
2		+N M O	+N M O	+N M O	+N M O	+N M O	
3		+N M O	+N M O	+N M O	+N M O	+N M O	
4		+N M O	+N M O	+N M O	+N M O	+N M O	
5		+N M O	+N M O	+N M O	+N M O	+N M O	
6		+N M O	+N M O	+N M O	+N M O	+N M O	
7		+N M O	+N M O	+N M O	+N M O	+N M O	
8		+N M O	+N M O	+N M O	+N M O	+N M O	
9		+N M O	+N M O	+N M O	+N M O	+N M O	
10		+N M O	+N M O	+N M O	+N M O	+N M O	
11		+N M O	+N M O	+N M O	+N M O	+N M O	
12		+N M O	+N M O	+N M O	+N M O	+N M O	
13		+N M O	+N M O	+N M O	+N M O	+N M O	
14		+N M O	+N M O	+N M O	+N M O	+N M O	
15		+N M O	+N M O	+N M O	+N M O	+N M O	

% On - Task = _____ (+%)

% Off - Task = 100 − (% On - Task) = _____ %

TOTALS INTERVALS PERCENT

OBSERVED

$+$ = _____ ÷ _____ = _____ %

N = _____ ÷ _____ = _____ %

M = _____ ÷ _____ = _____ %

O = _____ ÷ _____ = _____ %

teacher respond to these particular students in the classroom? The Student-Teacher Form is designed to answer this question.

This form is a combination of Form A and the Form C given above. During each interval, the observer checks whether the student is on-task (+) or off-task (N for noise, M for motor, O for other, or Passive) and also indicates the response of the teacher to *this particular child.* Following a series of observations (we suggest at least five be completed during those class periods the teacher considers most troublesome), an analysis can be made of the teacher responses to the particular student. Should the teacher or observer desire to note the differences between the teacher's overall responses to the class and his responses to the particular student, then one mark (e.g., X) can be used for responses to other class members and a different mark (e.g., 1) for the individual in question.

Many studies have been conducted using this form in a variety of ways. It can be expanded to include more than one student by using the student's initial as the recording mark and placing the initial for each student in the appropriate squares over the symbol, using red pencils. The form may also be used to observe from two to five students by using a coded number as the recording mark and writing the actual number in each square. Additionally, the form may be used to observe one child during the first time period (three or five intervals), a second child during the next time period, and so on, then recycling across all children after all have been observed.

The basic form has also been expanded into a series of observation forms which include space for more than one student in each observation block (see Form G). On Form G, three students are observed simultaneously and the teacher's responses are also recorded. For this form, mistakes of reinforcement are recorded as approval mistakes (Am) and disapproval mistakes (Dm), with no distinction between academic as opposed to social mistakes. Should this information be required, a different mark can be used. Thus it is also possible with Form E or other adaptations of it to record precise student-teacher interactions.

FORM E: STUDENT-TEACHER

Observer _____
Reliability Observer _____
No. in class or group _____
General Activity _____
Observation Interval _____
    (seconds)

Student _____
Teacher _____
Grade or Subject _____ Date ____
Time: Start _____ End _____
Page _____ of _____
Record Interval _____
    (seconds)

TIME	NAME(S)	ACTIVITY CODE	INTERVALS						COMMENTS
			(1)	2 - RECORD	(3)	4 - RECORD	(5)	6 - RECORD	
1	Teacher		OBSERVE NOW	+ N M O Aa As Da Ds Aa As Da Ds	OBSERVE NOW	+ N M O Aa As Da Ds Aa As Da Ds	OBSERVE NOW	+ N M O Aa As Da Ds Aa As Da Ds	
2	Teacher			+ N M O Aa As Da Ds Aa As Da Ds		+ N M O Aa As Da Ds Aa As Da Ds		+ N M O Aa As Da Ds Aa As Da Ds	
3	Teacher			+ N M O Aa As Da Ds Aa As Da Ds		+ N M O Aa As Da Ds Aa As Da Ds		+ N M O Aa As Da Ds Aa As Da Ds	
4	Teacher			+ N M O Aa As Da Ds Aa As Da Ds		+ N M O Aa As Da Ds Aa As Da Ds		+ N M O Aa As Da Ds Aa As Da Ds	
5	Teacher			+ N M O Aa As Da Ds Aa As Da Ds		+ N M O Aa As Da Ds Aa As Da Ds		+ N M O Aa As Da Ds Aa As Da Ds	
6	Teacher			+ N M O Aa As Da Ds Aa As Da Ds		+ N M O Aa As Da Ds Aa As Da Ds		+ N M O Aa As Da Ds Aa As Da Ds	
7	Teacher		OBSERVE NOW	+ N M O Aa As Da Ds Aa As Da Ds	OBSERVE NOW	+ N M O Aa As Da Ds Aa As Da Ds	OBSERVE NOW	+ N M O Aa As Da Ds Aa As Da Ds	
8	Teacher			+ N M O Aa As Da Ds Aa As Da Ds		+ N M O Aa As Da Ds Aa As Da Ds		+ N M O Aa As Da Ds Aa As Da Ds	
9	Teacher			+ N M O Aa As Da Ds Aa As Da Ds		+ N M O Aa As Da Ds Aa As Da Ds		+ N M O Aa As Da Ds Aa As Da Ds	
10	Teacher			+ N M O Aa As Da Ds Aa As Da Ds		+ N M O Aa As Da Ds Aa As Da Ds		+ N M O Aa As Da Ds Aa As Da Ds	
11	Teacher			+ N M O Aa As Da Ds Aa As Da Ds		+ N M O Aa As Da Ds Aa As Da Ds		+ N M O Aa As Da Ds Aa As Da Ds	
12	Teacher		OBSERVE NOW	+ N M O Aa As Da Ds Aa As Da Ds		+ N M O Aa As Da Ds Aa As Da Ds		+ N M O Aa As Da Ds Aa As Da Ds	
13	Teacher			+ N M O Aa As Da Ds Aa As Da Ds					

Totals :

+ = _____ Aa _____ As _____
N = _____ Da _____ Ds _____
M = _____ Aa _____ As _____
O = _____ Da _____ Ds _____

253

FORM F: STUDENT–TEACHER

TIME	NAME(S)	ACTIVITY CODE	INTERVAL 1	INTERVAL 2	INTERVAL 3	INTERVAL 4	INTERVAL 5	COMMENTS
1	Teacher		+ N M O Aa As Da Ds Aa As Da Ds	+ N M O Aa As Da Ds Aa As Da Ds	+ N M O Aa As Da Ds Aa As Da Ds	+ N M O Aa As Da Ds Aa As Da Ds	+ N M O Aa As Da Ds Aa As Da Ds	
2	Teacher		+ N M O Aa As Da Ds Aa As Da Ds	+ N M O Aa As Da Ds Aa As Da Ds	+ N M O Aa As Da Ds Aa As Da Ds	+ N M O Aa As Da Ds Aa As Da Ds	+ N M O Aa As Da Ds Aa As Da Ds	
3	Teacher		+ N M O Aa As Da Ds Aa As Da Ds	+ N M O Aa As Da Ds Aa As Da Ds	+ N M O Aa As Da Ds Aa As Da Ds	+ N M O Aa As Da Ds Aa As Da Ds	+ N M O Aa As Da Ds Aa As Da Ds	
4	Teacher		+ N M O Aa As Da Ds Aa As Da Ds	+ N M O Aa As Da Ds Aa As Da Ds	+ N M O Aa As Da Ds Aa As Da Ds	+ N M O Aa As Da Ds Aa As Da Ds	+ N M O Aa As Da Ds Aa As Da Ds	
5	Teacher		+ N M O Aa As Da Ds Aa As Da Ds	+ N M O Aa As Da Ds Aa As Da Ds	+ N M O Aa As Da Ds Aa As Da Ds	+ N M O Aa As Da Ds Aa As Da Ds	+ N M O Aa As Da Ds Aa As Da Ds	
6	Teacher		+ N M O Aa As Da Ds Aa As Da Ds	+ N M O Aa As Da Ds Aa As Da Ds	+ N M O Aa As Da Ds Aa As Da Ds	+ N M O Aa As Da Ds Aa As Da Ds	+ N M O Aa As Da Ds Aa As Da Ds	
7	Teacher		+ N M O Aa As Da Ds Aa As Da Ds	+ N M O Aa As Da Ds Aa As Da Ds	+ N M O Aa As Da Ds Aa As Da Ds	+ N M O Aa As Da Ds Aa As Da Ds	+ N M O Aa As Da Ds Aa As Da Ds	
8	Teacher		+ N M O Aa As Da Ds Aa As Da Ds	+ N M O Aa As Da Ds Aa As Da Ds	+ N M O Aa As Da Ds Aa As Da Ds	+ N M O Aa As Da Ds Aa As Da Ds	+ N M O Aa As Da Ds Aa As Da Ds	
9	Teacher		+ N M O Aa As Da Ds Aa As Da Ds	+ N M O Aa As Da Ds Aa As Da Ds	+ N M O Aa As Da Ds Aa As Da Ds	+ N M O Aa As Da Ds Aa As Da Ds	+ N M O Aa As Da Ds Aa As Da Ds	
10	Teacher		+ N M O Aa As Da Ds Aa As Da Ds	+ N M O Aa As Da Ds Aa As Da Ds	+ N M O Aa As Da Ds Aa As Da Ds	+ N M O Aa As Da Ds Aa As Da Ds	+ N M O Aa As Da Ds Aa As Da Ds	

ANALYSIS FORM: STUDENT-TEACHER FORMS E AND F

Symbols	Total Number Observed		Total Intervals Observed		Percentage Intervals in which Behavior Observed
+	= _____	÷	_____	=	_____ %
N	= _____	÷	_____	=	_____ %
M	= _____	÷	_____	=	_____ %
O	= _____	÷	_____	=	_____ %

On - Task Percentage (+)_____ %

Academic Assignment _____

Teacher Academic Reinforcement

Symbols	Total Number Observed		Total Intervals Observed		Percentage Intervals in which Behavior Observed
Aa	= _____	÷	_____	=	_____ %
Da	= _____	÷	_____	=	_____ %
(Aa)	= _____	÷	_____	=	_____ %
(Da)	= _____	÷	_____	=	_____ %

Approval Ratio: $\dfrac{Aa}{Aa + Da + (Aa) + (Da)}$ = ___ ÷ ___ + ___ + ___ + ___ = _____ %
(Academic)

Social Reinforcement

Symbols	Total Number Observed		Total Intervals Observed		Percentage Intervals in which Behavior Observed
As	= _____	÷	_____	=	_____ %
Ds	= _____	÷	_____	=	_____ %
(As)	= _____	÷	_____	=	_____ %
(Ds)	= _____	÷	_____	=	_____ %

Approval Ratio = $\dfrac{As}{As + Ds + (As) + (Ds)}$ = ___ ÷ ___ + ___ + ___ + ___ = _____ %
(Social)

255

FORM G: STUDENT (S)-TEACHER

Observer _____
Reliability Observer _____
Students:
1. _____
2. _____
3. _____

Teacher _____
Date _____
Time Start _____ Time End _____
Page _____ of _____
Observation Interval _____

TIME	S	INTERVAL 1	INTERVAL 2	INTERVAL 3	INTERVAL 4	INTERVAL 5	COMMENT
1	1	X N M O Aa Da	X N M O Aa Da	X N M O Aa Da	X N M O Aa Da	X N M O Aa Da	
	2	X N M O As Ds	X N M O As Ds	X N M O As Ds	X N M O As Ds	X N M O As Ds	
	3	X N M O Am Dm	X N M O Am Dm	X N M O Am Dm	X N M O Am Dm	X N M O Am Dm	
2	1	X N M O Aa Da	X N M O Aa Da	X N M O Aa Da	X N M O Aa Da	X N M O Aa Da	
	2	X N M O As Ds	X N M O As Ds	X N M O As Ds	X N M O As Ds	X N M O As Ds	
	3	X N M O Am Dm	X N M O Am Dm	X N M O Am Dm	X N M O Am Dm	X N M O Am Dm	
3	1	X N M O Aa Da	X N M O Aa Da	X N M O Aa Da	X N M O Aa Da	X N M O Aa Da	
	2	X N M O As Ds	X N M O As Ds	X N M O As Ds	X N M O As Ds	X N M O As Ds	
	3	X N M O Am Dm	X N M O Am Dm	X N M O Am Dm	X N M O Am Dm	X N M O Am Dm	
4	1	X N M O Aa Da	X N M O Aa Da	X N M O Aa Da	X N M O Aa Da	X N M O Aa Da	
	2	X N M O As Ds	X N M O As Ds	X N M O As Ds	X N M O As Ds	X N M O As Ds	
	3	X N M O Am Dm	X N M O Am Dm	X N M O Am Dm	X N M O Am Dm	X N M O Am Dm	
5	1	X N M O Aa Da	X N M O Aa Da	X N M O Aa Da	X N M O Aa Da	X N M O Aa Da	
	2	X N M O As Ds	X N M O As Ds	X N M O As Ds	X N M O As Ds	X N M O As Ds	
	3	X N M O Am Dm	X N M O Am Dm	X N M O Am Dm	X N M O Am Dm	X N M O Am Dm	
6	1	X N M O Aa Da	X N M O Aa Da	X N M O Aa Da	X N M O Aa Da	X N M O Aa Da	
	2	X N M O As Ds	X N M O As Ds	X N M O As Ds	X N M O As Ds	X N M O As Ds	
	3	X N M O Am Dm	X N M O Am Dm	X N M O Am Dm	X N M O Am Dm	X N M O Am Dm	
7	1	X N M O Aa Da	X N M O Aa Da	X N M O Aa Da	X N M O Aa Da	X N M O Aa Da	
	2	X N M O As Ds	X N M O As Ds	X N M O As Ds	X N M O As Ds	X N M O As Ds	
	3	X N M O Am Dm	X N M O Am Dm	X N M O Am Dm	X N M O Am Dm	X N M O Am Dm	
8	1	X N M O Aa Da	X N M O Aa Da	X N M O Aa Da	X N M O Aa Da	X N M O Aa Da	
	2	X N M O As Ds	X N M O As Ds	X N M O As Ds	X N M O As Ds	X N M O As Ds	
	3	X N M O Am Dm	X N M O Am Dm	X N M O Am Dm	X N M O Am Dm	X N M O Am Dm	
9	1	X N M O Aa Da	X N M O Aa Da	X N M O Aa Da	X N M O Aa Da	X N M O Aa Da	
	2	X N M O As Ds	X N M O As Ds	X N M O As Ds	X N M O As Ds	X N M O As Ds	
	3	X N M O Am Dm	X N M O Am Dm	X N M O Am Dm	X N M O Am Dm	X N M O Am Dm	
10	1	X N M O Aa Da	X N M O Aa Da	X N M O Aa Da	X N M O Aa Da	X N M O Aa Da	
	2	X N M O As Ds	X N M O As Ds	X N M O As Ds	X N M O As Ds	X N M O As Ds	
	3	X N M O Am Dm	X N M O Am Dm	X N M O Am Dm	X N M O Am Dm	X N M O Am Dm	

Group on-task/off-task teacher response (Form H)

The average number of students off-task and on-task, expressed as a ratio of students engaged in appropriate or inappropriate behavior compared to the total number of students in the classroom or group being observed, usually is important to most classroom teachers. Form H may be used to collect these data. As with all forms, the identification section is completed so that accurate reconstruction of the observational situation is possible.

The activity for the class or group is recorded for each time period, numbered down the left hand side of the page. The observer then records the number of students in the group who are being observed. This is necessary as the ratio of off-task to on-task students will change depending upon the number being observed. Five students recorded as off-task when a group of five is being observed is 100 percent off-task (0.0 percent on-task), whereas five off-task when twenty are being observed is 25 percent off-task (75 percent on-task). Therefore it is important to record the number of students present for each time interval. Within the record boxes, the upper half is for recording the total number of students off-task and the lower portion is for recording teacher responses.

During interval number 1, the observer scans the group or class and then records the number of students off-task by writing the number in the square under No. Off-Task. In most classrooms the number off-task is less than the number on-task, but if a very disruptive class is being observed, it may be easier to record the number on-task. During the recording interval, the observer also listens carefully to the teacher and mentally notes all teacher responses to the entire class. Then, following the recording of students off-task, the observer marks the teacher symbols in the lower portion of the interval. If, for example, the teacher had given approval for appropriate social behavior, the observer would check As in the lower portion under the number of students who were recorded as off-task. Immediately following the recording of teacher behavior and prior to the next observation interval, the observer records whether any students were added or subtracted from the group being observed during the preceding interval. If any change has occurred, the observer records the number under + or − students

FORM H: GROUP ON-TASK/OFF-TASK TEACHER RESPONSE

Observer _____ Teacher _____
Reliability Observer _____ Grade or Subject _____ Date _____
No. in class or group _____ Time: Start _____ End _____
General Activity _____ Page _____ of _____
Observation Interval _____ Record Interval _____
        (seconds)   (seconds)

TIME	ACTIVITY CODE	NO. STUDENTS	(1)	2 - RECORD		(3)	4 - RECORD		(5)	6 - RECORD		OFF-TASK RATIO		
				No. Off-Task	+ or – Students		No. Off-Task	+ or – Students		No. Off-Task	+ or – Students	INTERVALS 2	4	6
1			OBSERVE NOW	As Aa Ds Da As Aa Ds Da		OBSERVE NOW	As Aa Ds Da As Aa Ds Da		OBSERVE NOW	As Aa Ds Da As Aa Ds Da				
2				As Aa Ds Da As Aa Ds Da			As Aa Ds Da As Aa Ds Da			As Aa Ds Da As Aa Ds Da				
3				As Aa Ds Da As Aa Ds Da			As Aa Ds Da As Aa Ds Da			As Aa Ds Da As Aa Ds Da				
4			OBSERVE NOW	As Aa Ds Da As Aa Ds Da		OBSERVE NOW	As Aa Ds Da As Aa Ds Da		OBSERVE NOW	As Aa Ds Da As Aa Ds Da				
5				As Aa Ds Da As Aa Ds Da			As Aa Ds Da As Aa Ds Da			As Aa Ds Da As Aa Ds Da				
6				As Aa Ds Da As Aa Ds Da			As Aa Ds Da As Aa Ds Da			As Aa Ds Da As Aa Ds Da				
7			OBSERVE NOW	As Aa Ds Da As Aa Ds Da		OBSERVE NOW	As Aa Ds Da As Aa Ds Da		OBSERVE NOW	As Aa Ds Da As Aa Ds Da				
8				As Aa Ds Da As Aa Ds Da			As Aa Ds Da As Aa Ds Da			As Aa Ds Da As Aa Ds Da				
9				As Aa Ds Da As Aa Ds Da											

TOTALS:

As _____ Aa _____ Cumulative Students Off-Task = _____(A)
Ds _____ Da _____ Cumulative Students Observed = _____(B)
As _____ Aa _____
Ds _____ Da _____ $\frac{A}{B}$ = Percent Off-Task = _____

The observer then proceeds to the next interval and repeats the observational procedure, using exactly the same procedure as during the first interval and making certain to record the number of students in the group being observed who are off-task. When total observations have been completed, the Off-Task Ratios are subsequently recorded for all observation intervals. The area above the diagonal line is used to record the number of students off-task in each observed interval and the portion below the diagonal line to record the number of all students observed during that single interval.

Analysis of the percentage of students off-task represents an average of the percentage off-task during all observed intervals. This is computed by adding each individual fraction from the off-task ratios section and completing the division. If six intervals (two time lines) were observed with the following ratios:

Second interval (No. Students = 20, 5 off-task = 5/20), 3 students left (− 3)
Fourth interval (20 − 3 = 17 Students, 4 off-task = 4/17), 10 students came in (+ 10)
Sixth interval (17 + 10 = 27 students, 8 off-task = 8/27), four students were taken out (No. Students, Line 2, 27 − 4 = 23)

Second interval (10 off-task = 10/23), number of students remained the same (± 0)
Fourth interval (23 + 0 = 23, 6 off-task = 6/23), two students came in (+ 2),
Sixth interval (23 + 2 + 25, 3 off-task = 3/25)

the average percent off-task would be computed as follows:

$$5/20 + 4/17 + 8/27 + 10/23 + 6/23 + 3/25 =$$
$$.25 + .235 + .296 + .435 + .26 + .12 = 1.596/6 =$$
$$.266 = 27 \text{ percent average off-task.}$$

Calculating on the form:

Cumulative Students Off-task (A) = 5 + 4 + 8 + 10 + 6 + 3 = 36.
Cumulative Students Observed (B) = 20 + 17 + 27 + 23 + 23 + 25 = 135.

A/B = 36/135 = .266 = 27 percent off-task.

The analysis of teacher responses takes place in exactly the same way as when using the Teacher Observation Form. The result is an indication of the average classroom off-task behavior and at the same time shows how the teacher reinforcement for both academic and social behavior may be maintaining the on- or off-task behavior. An interval by interval analysis of the data in terms of increase and decrease across specific intervals can be used in examining results with teachers who desire to become more competent in the application of reinforcement principles in the classroom.

INTERPERSONAL OBSERVATION

Interpersonal observation (Form J)

Sometimes interpersonal behaviors between students need to be observed. This is especially pertinent in newly integrated situations regardless of mode of integration: race, sex, academic ability, schools, agression, passivity, or other relationships between one, two, or any group of people.

Interpersonal behaviors are most frequently expressed by means of verbal or motor expression. Verbal behaviors include any oral response of either an approving or disapproving nature by the person being observed, directed toward any designated person(s). Verbal responses primarily include words spoken, but also comprise yelling, whistling, humming, screaming, and laughing. Verbalizations must be heard for the observer to record the behavior.

Motor behavior includes both gross and minor motor behaviors as well as bodily and facial expressions. Touching, hitting, pushing, slapping, and striking with objects are motor behaviors as well as patting and tapping. Bodily expressions such as raising hands or holding fists may also be included.

This observation form provides two basic designations for persons being observed (X and O) and a method of recording the direction of the behavior (X toward O or O toward X). These X and O symbols may designate any individual or number of individuals.

FORM J: INTERPERSONAL OBSERVATION

Person (s)_____ Teacher_____
Observed_____ Grade or Subject _____ Date _____
Observer I_____ Activity_____
Reliability Observer_____ Time Start _____ Time End_____

TIME	ACTIVITY	Interval 1				Interval 3				Interval 5				Analysis
		V	V	M	M	V	V	M	M	V	V	M	M	COMMENTS SYMBOL FREQ. %
		x	o	x	o	x	o	x	o	x	o	x	o	
		↓	↓	↓	↓	↓	↓	↓	↓	↓	↓	↓	↓	$Vx \rightarrow o_a$ ____ ___
		o	x	o	x	o	x	o	x	o	x	o	x	$Vx \rightarrow o_d$ ____ ___
1														$Vo \rightarrow x_a$ ____ ___
2														$Vo \rightarrow x_d$ ____ ___
3														$Mx \rightarrow o_a$ ____ ___
4														$Mx \rightarrow o_d$ ____ ___
5														$Mo \rightarrow x_a$ ____ ___
6														$Mo \rightarrow x_d$ ____ ___
7														
8														Reliability
9														Agree Disagree
10														$x \rightarrow o_a$ _____ _____
11														$x \rightarrow o_d$ _____ _____
12														$o \rightarrow x_a$ _____ _____
13														$o \rightarrow x_d$ _____ _____
14														Total _____ _____
15														
16														
17														Total Agree _____

Total Agree + Total Disagree = _____

REACTION _____
_____
_____
_____

Interpersonal Categories

$Vx \rightarrow o_a$ Any verbal behavior (words spoken) initiated by the student designated by the X subsymbol (white-black, male-female, friend-protagonist), directed toward the student designated by the O subsymbol, and defined as approval. (See teacher approval category.)

$Vo \rightarrow x_a$ Any verbal behavior (words spoken) initiated by the student designated by the O subsymbol, directed toward the student designated by the X subsymbol, and defined as approval. (See teacher approval category.)

$Vx \rightarrow o_d$ Any verbal behavior (words spoken) initiated by the student designated by the X subsymbol, directed toward the student designated by the O subsymbol, and defined as disapproval. (See teacher disapproval category.)

$Vo \rightarrow x_d$ Any verbal behavior (words spoken) initiated by the student designated by the O subsymbol, directed toward the student designated by the X subsymbol, and defined as disapproval. (See teacher disapproval category.)

$Mx \rightarrow o_a$ Any motor (definition of student categories) behavior (bodily expression or closeness) initiated by the student designated by the X subsymbol, directed toward the student designated by the O subsymbol, and defined as approval. (See teacher approval category.)

$Mo \rightarrow x_a$ Any motor (definition of student categories) behavior (bodily expressions or closeness) initiated by the student designated by the O subsymbol, directed toward the student designated by the X subsymbol, and defined as approval. (See teacher approval category.)

$Mx \rightarrow o_d$ Any motor (definition of student categories) behavior (bodily expressions or closeness) initiated by the student designated by the X subsymbol, directed toward the student designated by the O subsymbol, and defined as disapproval. (See teacher disapproval category.)

$Mo \rightarrow x_d$ Any motor (definition of student categories) behavior response (bodily expressions or closeness) initiated by the student designated by the O subsymbol, directed toward the student designated by the X subsymbol, and defined as disapproval. (See teacher disapproval category.)

If we assume that a teacher desires to observe the approval and disapproval behaviors directed toward a particular pupil who does not appear to respond to interpersonal contingencies, the observer could designate this child as X and all other children as O. Observations are then recorded in the appropriate squares underneath the symbols by placing either an A (approval) or D (disapproval) in the square and a number to indicate the number of children who received or dispensed the particular behavior. Suppose that three children stuck out their tongues at a retarded student. The observer would record a D in the first interval under $M_{o \rightarrow x}$ and following the D write a small "3." Should the observer desire to record the particular response the word "tongue" could be written under the comments section. Anyone analyzing the report would then know that three children engaged in motor disapproval toward the particular pupil.

It is thus possible to observe one or more students at any time. In a newly integrated high school class, for instance, the teacher wished to know the number of approving and disapproving responses directed toward members of each group by all members of the group. In this case, the X would be one group and the O would designate the other group. The observer would record the number of responses in each square as well as the symbol A or D. This particular example of recording would indicate the total number of approval or disapproval responses, whether motor or verbal or both, of an entire group in each interval. Similar procedures can be used for any number of questions involving interpersonal responses in classrooms, recreation areas, cafeterias, playgrounds, and so on.

The precise designation of persons being observed depends upon the questions of interest to the persons who are responsible for asking such questions. Should more than two groups or persons be of interest, it is necessary to attach a subsymbol to the A and D. For example, the responses of male and female faculty (two groups) toward male and female students could be of interest. In this case, the A receives a subscript. Thus X represents faculty and O represents students. Responses of an approving nature by males is recorded A_m and by females A_f. These kinds of distinctions may, of course, be expanded, but it is suggested that no more than four groups be observed at any one time as it becomes much more difficult with each additional subscript.

Interpersonal observation (Form K)

Precise observations of group interactions are possible with the use of Form K: Interpersonal Observation. Through the analysis of the categories, group totals, individual reactions, and individual or group reactions to a teacher or group leader may be analyzed.

Categories include Verbal, Contact, and Expressions of an approving nature; Verbal, Contact, and Expressions of a disapproving nature; and Neutral interactions.

It is recommended for this type of recording that one observer record each participant and indicate the direction of the recorded behavior. For example, if there were eight participants, all would be numbered and the observer watching No. 1 would record each behavior and indicate whether it was directed toward any other participant by recording the other participants' number(s) under the appropriate symbol. Recording in this manner requires a great deal more time for reliability training than the more simple observation codes (twelve to eighteen hours of training).

Should one desire to reconstruct a precise matrix of behavioral interactions, it is necessary to employ some mechanical means of keeping all observers in the same interval at the same time. A prerecorded tape may be used for this purpose. The taped voice begins by warning the observers prior to the first observation and then states "Get ready. . . . Line one. . . . Observe." This is followed by fifteen seconds of blank tape whereupon the taped voice continues, "Record." The recording interval usually constitutes five seconds of blank tape and the recorded voice then continues, "Observe," with fifteen seconds of blank tape, and "Record," with five seconds of blank tape, until four intervals have been recorded. The recorded voice will then state, "Line Two . . . Observe." The taped voice takes little time to prerecord and keeps all observers on-task while reducing unreliability when observers lose their place. Thus these time indicators given every minute allow few problems with observers and eliminate recording in the wrong interval.

FORM K: INTERPERSONAL OBSERVATION

Observer Name _____ Date _____ Time _____ End _____

Activity _____ Location _____ Reliability Observer _____ Number in Group _____

Page _____ Of _____ Subject Name _____ Subject Number _____

Observation Interval _____ Record Interval _____

	Record A									Record B									Record C									Line Totals								
	APR			NEU			DISAPR			APR			NEU			DISAPR			APR			NEU			DISAPR			APR			NEU			DISAPR		
	V	C	E	V	C	O	V	C	E	V	C	E	V	C	O	V	C	E	V	C	E	V	C	O	V	C	E	V	C	E	V	C	O	V	C	E
1																																				
2																																				
3																																				
4																																				
5																																				
6																																				
7																																				
8																																				
9																																				
10																																				

Page Totals

Behavioral Definitions

The following behavioral definitions used in analysis of a series of "encounter and personal growth groups" indicate that the categories of Approval, Disapproval, and Neutral are sufficient for almost all interpersonal interactions.

Symbol

V   Verbal: One continuous, audible, meaningful phrase or idea

Apr
V

Approving Verbal. Verbal communication which indicates either a compliment or caring, correctness, acceptance, or agreement which is unbroken by a different thought or idea

Examples: Words

yes	fantastic
good	terrific
nice	swell
great	marvelous
fascinating	exactly
charming	of course
commendable	cool
delightful	groovy
brilliant	likeable
fine	wonderful
uh-huh	outstanding
positively	exciting
go ahead	interesting
yeah	pleasant
all right	delicious
correct	fabulous
excellent	splendid
that's right	thoughtful
perfect	remarkable
satisfactory	cheerful
absolutely	friendly
keep going	elegant
beautiful	well thought out
wonderful	

Examples: Sentences

I like you.	You are very friendly.
I respect you for that.	You have a nice _____.
I agree.	That's interesting.
I approve.	Show us how.
I'm glad you're here.	You're doing better.
You make us happy.	That's very good.
That shows thought.	I'm proud of you.
How charming.	That's logical.
We think a lot of you.	You're polite, nice, cour-
You're very pleasant.	teous, etc.
You're so outgoing.	You have (a) nice eyes,
Yes, please continue.	smile, personality, etc.
A good way of putting it.	I like your clothes.

Disapr
V

Disapproving Verbal. Audible communication of disagreement, dislike, disinterest, nonacceptance, or incorrectness which is unbroken by a different thought or idea

Examples:

impractical	That's ridiculous, meaning-
Work faster	less, absurd, bad, non-
Try to understand.	sense.
Do your best.	too vague
unclear explanation	Try harder.
Don't you want to do things	That's not right.
right?	incorrect
It can't be that difficult.	You should be ashamed.
You're too slow.	That's not clear.
Stop talking.	I dislike you.
Pay attention.	I dislike that.
don't	Don't make excuses.
wrong	Listen to me.
stupid	Leave her alone.
Think for a change.	You're dull.
Use some thought.	It's hopeless for you.
No, that's not what I said.	You're worthless.
You don't understand be-	You're rude.
cause you don't listen.	Don't laugh at me.
You're gutless.	That's childish.

You'd better get on the stick.
You must be confused.
I don't see your point.
You know better than that.

That wasn't the right thing to do.
You haven't been paying attention.
People never change

Neu
V   Neutral Verbal. By exclusion, all other verbal behavior

Examples:

I went to the store today.
It sure is hot and humid outside.
It is going to rain.

I have two kids.
It sure is pretty today.
I went home yesterday.

E   Expressions: Muscular movements of the face or body, which express interpersonal meaning

Apr
E   Approving Expression. Communication by movement of caring, correctness, acceptance, or agreement directed toward some person(s).

Examples: Facial

smiling
winking
nodding
raising eyebrows,
fawning kiss
opening eyes
slowly closing eyes
laughing
chuckling

widening eyes
wrinkling nose
blinking rapidly
giggling
whistles
cheering
licking lips
smacking lips
rolling eyes

Examples: Bodily

clapping hands
raising arms
grabbing
bouncing
signaling OK.
cocking head
rubbing stomach
thumbs up
"right-on" sign

shaking head
shrugging shoulders
expansive movement of
    hands
taking a fast breath
opening hands
embracing hand or finger
    to face, hair, head

Disapr
E

Disapproving Expression. Communication by movement of dislike, disinterest, nonacceptance or incorrectness directed toward some person(s)

Examples: Expression

frowning	clicking tongue
curling lip	pointing finger
furrowing brows	putting hand behind ear
lowering eyebrows	grimacing
shaking finger or fist	sniffing
squinting eyes	tightening jaw
wrinkling forehead	sticking out tongue
puckering lips	snickering
pounding fist	turning head away
laughing at	letting out breath
shaking head	kissing
turning away	fingers in front of lips
gritting teeth	shaking head no
biting lips	showing teeth
closing eyes	pulling in bottom lip

None

Neutral Expression. Not recorded

Contact: The touching of any parts of the bodies of two or more people

Apr
C

Approving Contact: The touching of another person which expresses caring, correctness, acceptance, or agreement. Examples:

hugging	nudging
patting	holding
kissing	leaning against
touching	caressing

Disapr
C

Disapproving Contact: The touching of another person which expresses dislike, disinterest, nonacceptance, incorrectness (determined by intensity). Examples:

hitting	restraining
grabbing	kicking
pushing	shoving

Neu
O

Neutral Contact. Recorded as neutral other. Unintentional contact or passive behavior.

General Instructions: All behaviors should be recorded even if they occur simultaneously. If a person being observed makes a comment, smiles, and touches someone else, then a mark would be placed under verbal, expression, and contact. In addition, all behaviors should be recorded even if they are contradictory. A smile is always recorded as an approval. Sarcasm when it can be recorded is disapproving.

If a behavior begins prior to the record time and its meaning cannot be determined, then record the behavior as neutral. Two or more unbroken statements of the same type (either approving, neutral, or disapproving) are recorded as one unit of behavior. A broken statement is one which is interrupted; a pause is not considered as a break.

The direction of the behavior (toward another member of the group) is sometimes difficult to assess and observe correctly. If the direction of the behavior is unknown, record the behavior under the appropriate symbol by using a question mark. When the behavior is directed toward the group (four or more persons is considered as the group), a G should be used in the appropriate box.

During each observation interval, the observer should be prepared to answer the following questions with recorded data:

Did a vocalization (verbal behavior) occur? If the answer is yes, determine whether it was approving, disapproving, or neutral.

Was there an expression other than neutral? If so, then determine whether it was approving or disapproving.

Was there physical contact? If yes, then determine whether it was approving, disapproving, or neutral.

Should behaviors occur that do not fit any of the category definitions implied by the above questions during the observation interval, put an X in the Neutral Other category.

General observation (Form L)

Form L: General Observation is an overall model for record keeping. As most teachers realize, behavioral principles are of little use unless accurate records are kept. Behaviors are defined (pinpointed) in precise behavioral terms and then observed by checking occurrences of the defined behavior during the planned recording

FORM L: GENERAL OBSERVATION

PINPOINT_____ Person(s) observed_____

Observer(s)_____ Location _____

Time of observation_____ Desire that behavior increase decrease_____

I (we) will conduct_____ observations per_____ every_____for_____
               (number)   (min-hr-day)   (day-wk)   (day-wk)

before consequating takes place

Observation interval_____ Time between obs._____
           (sec-min-hr-day)   (sec-min-hr-day)

RECORD Each occurrence of Pinpoint			CONSEQUATE Consequences following occurrence of behavior					EVALUATE Each occurrence of Pinpoint		
Date	Obs. No.		Date	Obs. No.	Approval	Dis- approval	Other	Date	Obs. No.	

Total = _____   Totals = _____   _____ _____   Total = _____
No. Obs. = _____   No. Obs. = _____
Average = _____   When_____   When_____   Average = _____
                         (appropriate)   (inappropriate)

Comments _____   for_____   Then this   SUMMARY
_____   (time-times)   disapproval
_____   Then these approvals   will follow: Record total_____
_____   will follow: a._____   Evaluate total_____
_____   a._____   Record average_____
_____   b._____   Evaluate average_____
_____   c._____   Increase_____
                                                         Decrease_____

interval. Consequences are applied systematically and recorded, then the behavior is again measured (recorded) in order to evaluate the effect of the consequences.[2]

The specific behavior to be observed is determined and written on the Pinpoint line. The person or persons to be observed are indicated together with the person who is going to do the observation (teacher, students themselves, other pupils, teacher aides). The recording times for observations are determined, and whether the behavior is to be increased or decreased is noted by circling the appropriate word. Next the observer makes a contract with himself or the teacher to insure that a sufficient number of observations (baseline recording) take place prior to the application of consequences.

The Record section includes dates, observation numbers(s), and a space for checking, or marking in any way, each occurrence of the behavior observed. It is recommended that observations take place over at least a five-day period and/or that ten observations be made to insure that an accurate representative measure of the behavior has been achieved. The teacher then determines what consequences are to be applied (approval and/or disapproval) and fills in the lower portion of the Consequate section. During the Record phase, the teacher has sufficient time to determine just what potential reinforcers are to be used and when these consequences are to be applied (schedule of reinforcement). The observer records the number of approvals and/or disapprovals. A record of the pinpointed behavior is generally achieved automatically and this gives a preliminary check to see if the behavior is increasing, decreasing, or not changing. However, it is suggested that a teacher apply consequences for two weeks before taking additional observations to evaluate the effectiveness of the program.

Following the application of consequences for two weeks, the observer records in the Evaluate section using exactly the same procedure as was employed during the Record phase. The Summary indicates the effectiveness of the procedures by comparing the Record average with the Evaluate average.

Following completion of Form L, it is generally necessary to

---

[2] Extensive examples of the use of this form are included in another volume by Clifford K. Madsen and Charles H. Madsen, Jr., *Parents/Children/Discipline: A Positive Approach* (Boston: Allyn and Bacon, 1972.)

maintain the appropriate behavior through effective use of reinforcements. When the environment of the child changes, it is expected that the responses of the child will also change. Self-motivation (response to internal reinforcement) is achieved only after extensive structuring across many different situations. Continual reevaluation and application of appropriate contingencies is almost always necessary.

OBSERVATIONAL ANALYSIS

Observational information should include all necessary identification as well as a complete summary. Observational forms include an analysis section (on the back or front) which should be completed.

Frequency: All discrete observational symbols recorded (marked or written) should be counted across all intervals and the total number written on the line opposite the appropriate symbol.

Percentages: After recording the frequency of various behaviors, the relative frequency with which each rated behavior has occurred should be computed. It may be desirable to express observational findings in terms of the percentage of observational intervals in which a given behavior was recorded, rather than dealing only with frequency.

The percentage of occurrences for each discrete symbol is found by dividing the total number of times a symbol was recorded by the total number of intervals over which observation was conducted. For example, let us assume that Aa is recorded four times in a fifteen-minute observation, three ten-second observations being made each minute. The numerator in this case is four. The denominator is found by multiplying the number of minutes in the observation period (fifteen minutes) by the number of observation periods per minute (three). In this example, the denominator is forty-five. When the necessary division is made, it is found that during .088 or .09 or 9 percent of the intervals observed, an approval for academic behavior was recorded. In the same manner, percentages may be obtained for all other symbols.

Percentages for any symbol or combination of symbols may be graphed across time intervals such as subject periods, times of day, days, or weeks. Such a graph will supply information as to whether the behavior(s) being observed are increasing, decreasing, or remaining the same. Applications of specific consequences may be indicated and changes in behavior noted.

Reliability computation

Observer reliability concerns the amount of agreement/disagreement on the part of various observers when observing the same behaviors at the same time. In behavioral observation it is very important to determine the measure of agreement between two observers. This is expressed as a percentage—how often do two observers watching the same behavior record it as same behavior? In this way it is possible to check the accuracy of any classroom observation.

While it is important to assess interobserver reliability, it is also usually not practical to have two observers at all times. Reliability training can be conducted and then one may assume that reliable observation is achieved. Generally a reliability coefficient of .80 is considered a minimal average. After training, reliability should be assessed often to be certain there is not a systematic change in one or more observers. It has been determined that when reliability checks occur 20 percent of the total observation time with subsequent observer feedback, then observers remain reliable. Of course, some particular projects may require additional reliability checks.

When calculating observer reliability, each discrete symbol is listed separately. For computation, use the reliability section of the observer form and record the number of times observer 1 and the reliability observer agree for each symbol in the same time intervals. Thus if As behavior has been checked on both forms in the third interval of the second time period and the first interval of the fourth time period, then two agreements would be recorded for the As category. Similarly, if Da behavior occurred in the second interval of the first time period, the third interval of the tenth time period, and the first interval of the fifteenth time period, on both observer forms, then three agreements would be recorded for the Da symbol. To compute reliability, systematically check each symbol on both forms in every interval for agreements.

The next stage is to record the number of times both observers *disagree* for each symbol. When each observer has a different symbol checked in the same interval, disagreement is recorded under both symbols. For example, if a Ds behavior occurred on one observation sheet and a Da behavior occurred on the other sheet, both in the first interval of the third time period, then a disagreement would be recorded for each symbol (Ds and Da). This procedure is continued across the entire observation with the total number of agreements and disagreements being recorded for each symbol.

Nothing is also a category and can be recorded with a horizontal line through the interval. This category may be included in reliability calculations. However it is better that reliability approaches .80 using defined categories only.

In the final stage, sum the total number of agreements and total number of disagreements for all symbols. Next, divide the sum of the total number of agreements by the sum of total agreements plus total disagreements in order to obtain a percentage of reliability, as shown:

$$\frac{\text{Total Number Agreements}}{\text{Total Number Agreements plus Disagreements}} = \frac{\text{Percentage}}{\text{Reliability}}$$

While there are many different formulas to compute reliability, the above is both stringent and manageable enough to be used with all observers.

Observer reliability for group off-task student behavior uses the same basic rationale and is calculated as follows:

$$\frac{\dfrac{(N - [n_1 - n_2])}{N} + \cdots + \dfrac{(N - [n_1 - n_2])}{N}}{O} = \underline{\quad}\%$$

where N = total number of students under observation in each interval, and

n_1 = number of students observed off-task by the first observer.

Observational summary

Accurate recording, assessment of social behavior, and subsequent remediation seem to be the most important considerations when students are referred for inappropriate behavior. Unfortunately, when many students are referred they are taken out of the environment where the problem is occurring (the classroom) and are administered tests by a professional who only rarely observes the child in the classroom. The use of a combination of observational procedures (including tests), when analyzed properly, are generally more beneficial to teachers. However, cursory nonsystematic observation does not appear to be any better than other types of nonspecific evaluation. The environmental situation must be carefully analyzed (baseline) by rigorous observation and a specific plan designated for implementation. Discussions may then be held with appropriate personnel and procedures determined to alter the student's inappropriate responses. Diagnostic evaluation, whether by tests or observation, seems limited unless remedial steps are planned and implemented in the classroom where the maladaptive behaviors occur.

Complete analysis of a child's problem requires that the person who is to interpret the results know the implications of the results. If a teacher is told that a child who was referred for observation engages in 50 percent inappropriate behavior, what conclusion can be drawn? Obviously the conclusion must be based upon answers to some of the following questions: Were the inappropriate behaviors of a passive variety or active interference with other children? What behaviors of the teachers or peers served to maintain or reinforce the inappropriate behavior? Was the activity during which the student was observed of such a nature that the whole class was approaching 50 percent off-task behavior? What constitutes the baseline of appropriate behavior for this class during these particular activities? How many observations of other members of the class have been taken under similar circumstances? Were the behaviors of an interpersonal nature? What is the academic achievement level of the student during this activity? Is the academic material geared to the student's level? What is the level of off-task behavior in other activities with the same teacher? different teachers? What reinforcers are important to the particular student? Does the teacher use appropriate rewards for this student as well as others?

An analysis of answers to these and similar questions is generally necessary if the student is to be helped to achieve his highest potential.

CHAPTER 10

OUTLINE FOR LEARNING

The learning activities contained in this chapter were specifically developed for use in college classes and in-service workshops. Many variations of these activities are possible: media additions or supplementary activities may be used in lieu of or in addition to the live classroom observations. Five to seven hours of prerecorded videotapes are generally used by the authors for in-service or classroom sessions. In-service workshops and classes have been conducted with varying lengths of instruction lasting from two hours, to two weeks, through a complete academic term of thirty-six to fifty-two hours. Considerations of time availability and specific goals are important. Every hourly time period and attendant learning activity can be developed in a variety of ways (e.g., contingency managed discussion groups, students as aides, lectures, group work on activity, videotape feedback). Adaptations of the activities may facilitate whatever predetermined objectives are deemed important. Individual participation is paramount and actual doing as opposed to passivity cannot be overemphasized.

The following outline for learning indicates specific learning activity numbers. These numbers refer to experiences called General Learning Activities starting on page 286.

BEHAVIORAL TECHNIQUES FOR CLASSROOM USE

Objectives

General and specific objectives are intended to involve participants in learning behavioral techniques (applied behavior analysis principles) for potential classroom use. Objectives are formalized as follows:

General Objective: Participants will become familiar with behavior modification. *Specifically*, participants will:

1. Pinpoint specific social/academic behaviors
2. Develop skills in observational techniques
3. Learn how to use approval/disapproval reinforcers across time, in specific time intervals, to shape desired classroom behavior
4. Develop techniques to evaluate classroom effects following application of specific consequences

Outline of learning topics

Each topic in the following outline serves as the basis for one hour of instruction (lecture, interview, group discussion, classroom application, videotape or film viewing, observation, or in-class activity). This particular sequence of instruction and activities is a direct outgrowth of experience gained in conducting workshops and classes. However, many variations in the sequencing of specific topics and attendant learning activities are possible in any class or workshop. In addition, participants may be involved in additional readings (see books and articles listed in the Selected Bibliography) which can also serve as a basis for quizzes, discussions, and examples for additional applications.

    A. Introduction: Values and behavior modification
        1. Pre-test on behavioral principles, such as a test covering Part I to be administered the first hour: When possible an observational evaluation of classroom behavior prior to taking a course or workshop can serve to document

actual in-class behavior as a baseline from which subsequent change may be evaluated (see Chapter 8).

2. Orientation and explanation of evaluation procedures: Assignment of study guide (Learning Activity A, page 286), explanation of time logs (Learning Activity B, page 290), and assignment of outside reading

3. Definitions of behavioral terms: An overview of behavioral models dealing with teaching and learning

   a. *Pinpoint*: The behavioral objective toward greater specificity

   b. *Record*: An actual record of observed behavior

   c. *Consequate*: The teaching strategy (use of approval/disapproval reinforcers)

   d. *Evaluate*: The effect of the reinforcement (is the behavior better, same, or worse?)

4. Values and behavior modification: An understanding of the differences between teachers' (or society's) values and the techniques used to achieve these values (Learning Activity 1, page 303

5. Values/Techniques differentiation: Discussion of differential techniques to achieve similar values or the use of identical techniques to achieve opposing values (Learning Activity 2, page 305)

B. *Pinpoint*: Specifying observable behavior

   1. Attributes of a pinpoint: A pinpointed behavior must be (1) observable and (2) measurable (counted). Why are *observable* and *measurable* academic and social behaviors necessary for effective behavioral change?

   2. Translation of values/ideas into behaviors: Ideas must be translated into observable and measurable behaviors which are specific enough to be taught (Learning Activity 3, page 308

   3. Behaviors actually define ideas: Participants list all behaviors that pertain to more than one idea within Learning Activity 3.

   4. Pinpoint ranking exercise: Participants structure values into specific behaviors to increase skill in determining methods of recording observable behaviors (Learning Activity 4, page 313).

5. Discussion of ranking exercise: Small group discussion of Learning Activity 4 generally increases skills in helping participants determine behaviors that are both observable and measurable.

C. *Record*: Observational training

1. Recording classroom behavior: Recording specific behaviors of teacher-student interactions; observational instructions, definitions, and forms, based upon an introduction of the 2 × 2 Behavioral Interaction Table 2 (page 242)

2–3. Observation of teacher reinforcement: Recording of classroom behaviors involving teacher-student interaction patterns based upon Behavioral Interaction Table 2 and observational definitions. A teacher training film designed to teach observation of teacher-student reinforcement is used by the authors (available from Iowa City Schools). Videotape or simulated classroom observation may be substituted.

4–5. Observation of student behavior: Recording of student on-task and off-task behavior. The authors use film or videotape specifically developed to teach student behavior. Role-playing or other simulated classroom observation may be substituted.

D. *Record*: Actual classroom observation

1–4. Classroom observation: Participants record on observation forms (Learning Activity 5, page 315). Participants observe two teachers and two students (on-task, off-task) as well as two student-student interaction patterns and classroom off-task. Observational order:

a. Student
b. Teacher
c. Human relations: Student-student
d. Classroom off-task
e. Student
f. Human relations
g. Classroom off-task
h. Teacher

5. Observational evaluation: Participants evaluate observation techniques (Learning Activity 6, page 316).

E. *Record*: Reliability
1. Correction or observational evaluation: Group or small group discussion of Learning Activity 6.
2-3. Computation of reliability: Reliability is computed from classroom or videotape observations with discussion and feedback (see Chapter 9).
4. Inconsistency: Analysis of existing teacher/student behavioral patterns. Discussion of the effect of teacher inconsistency (mistakes of reinforcement) in the classroom (see Behavioral Interaction Tables, pp. 236 and 242). The authors use a videotape which illustrates a classroom starting with 95 percent of students on-task. Then the teacher reinforces academic behavior but makes approval mistakes for social behavior. In only nineteen minutes the class becomes 95 percent off-task. The teacher then uses contingent social approval and restores the original level of on-task behavior within five minutes.
5. Approval versus disapproval: A model is developed to illustrate specific effects of differential reinforcement in the classroom. The authors use a film which shows a teacher using high approval for ten minutes, high disapproval for ten minutes, and so on, to pinpoint the effects of approval versus disapproval.
F. *Consequate*: Cause-and-effect relationships
1. The effect of reinforcement across time: Using participants' essays (How is time important in modifying behavior? Learning Activity 7, page 321), a gambling model is constructed to illustrate the effects of partial reinforcement.
2. The effect of partial reinforcement: Discussion of gambling model followed by participants' writing four pinpoints (Learning Activity 7)
3. Reinforcement principles applied: Participants gather in small groups and read selected pinpoints from Part II (pages 57–174) and discuss cause-and-effect relationships.
4-5. Ecology and reinforcement: Human ecology and discrimination of reinforcement. What controls are avail-

able to societal agents in order to influence student behavior? (See Learning Activity 8, page 322.)

G. *Consequate*: Choice of reinforcers

1. Consequate evaluation: Participants take Consequate
   Evaluation Test, correct and discuss it within groups
   (Learning Activity 9, page 323).
2. Structuring potential reinforcers: Participants fill in
   logical consequates for the pinpointed behaviors to indicate that there are many different ways to consequate
   behaviors (Learning Activity 10, page 326).
3. Categorization of reinforcers: Participants state reasons
   for selecting specific reinforcers and categorize all reinforcers listed for the preceding pinpoints into:
   a. Words
   b. Closeness
   c. Bodily expressions
   d. Activities
   e. Things
4. Consequating personal behaviors: Participants pinpoint
   specific personal behaviors and develop a specific plan
   to consequate (Learning Activity 11, page 333).
5. Success and failure of reinforcement: Participants write
   short behavioral analysis (pinpoint model) of personal
   classroom problems and state how reinforcement principles apply (Learning Activity 12, page 336).

H. *Developing Responses*: Classroom presentations

1–5. On-site school activities: Two live twenty-minute
   presentations and four teacher observations of other
   participants, working in small groups of three (Learning Activity 13, page 338).

I. *Developing Responses*: Role-playing

1–2. Human relations: Small group discussions to separate
   values from techniques applied to teacher-teacher interactions toward more positive human relations. Compute
   positive/negative interactions—rotate record keeper
   (Learning Activity 14, page 339).
3. Structuring personal responses: Write pinpoints and
   consequate strategies for human relations problems aris-
   ing from previous small group discussion (Learning
   Activity 15, page 341).

4-5. Role-playing demonstration: Participants present six-minute role-playing illustrations of an essay from Chapters 1-5. Participants work with other class or workshop members (Learning Activity 16, page 342).

J. *Developing Responses*: Summary of techniques

1-3. On-site school activities: Each participant takes charge of a classroom for two twenty-minute mini-presentations. Participants work in groups of three and complete four teacher observations of other participants as they take over classrooms for mini-presentations.

4. Analyzing classroom observations: Compute and discuss reliability for preceding observations.

5. Summary of workshop or class: A summary of behavioral models dealing with teaching and learning—Pinpoint, Record, Consequate, Evaluate. Discussion of personal projects, and sharing of results. Evaluation of workshop or class (Learning Activity 17, page 344) is generally comprised of subjective verbal reports, although verbal reports provide only limited information. Therefore actual on-site, in-class, pre- post-observations should be conducted whenever possible.

Additional assignments

In addition to the Learning Activities described above, other assignments to supplement lectures and discussions are generally included in most classes and, of course, should be chosen to implement the specific objectives of the workshop director or class instructor. Some additional assignments that are illustrative of many which could be beneficial are listed by major scheduled topics.

A. Introduction: Values and behavior modification

1. Read or reread Chapters 1-5 and complete in detail the Study Guide in Learning Activity A.

2. Write a short one or two page essay on the question: Why is it important to pinpoint specific social and academic behaviors?

3. Maintain time logs for all activities (General Learning Activity B, page 290).

B. Pinpoint: Specifying observable behavior
1. Study in detail the examples listed in Part II.
2. Write a short essay discussing the difference between values as opposed to behaviors.
3. Complete Time Log.
C. Record: Observational training
1. Study Observational and Reliability Summary in Chapter 9 and compute category percentages.
2. Detail subjective observations of teaching techniques employed during observations.
3. Complete Time Log.
D. Record: Actual classroom observation
1. Write a one-page essay on the topic: What is the relationship between teacher behavior and student behavior?
2. Explain the necessity for using various forms for observing behavior.
3. Complete Time Log.
E. Record: Reliability
1. Explain the necessity for impartial, unbiased, reliable observations in the evaluation of teaching.
2. Write a short essay on: The effects of teacher inconsistency.
3. Complete Time Log.
F. Consequate: Cause-and-effect relationships
1. Study again selected examples in Part II, paying close attention to the notes.
2. Write an essay on the importance of analyzing cause-and-effect relationships in human interactions.
3. Complete Time Log.
G. Consequate: Choice of reinforcers
1. Explain how a teacher could get identical results using two different "methods."
2. Write a short essay on the effectiveness of using behavioral principles to consequate one's own behavior.
3. Complete Time Log.
H. Developing Responses: Classroom presentations
1. Explain why actual teaching is different from classroom discussions about teaching.

2. Write a short essay indicating how observation increases teaching effectiveness.
3. Complete Time Log.

I. Developing Responses: Role-playing
1. List how one may use reinforcement principles in developing personal responses and outline a plan for your own on-site classroom activity.
2. Write an essay on the topic: Why is it easier to analyze and explain another's behavior than one's own?
3. Complete Time Log.

J. Developing Responses: Summary of techniques
1. Prepare summary charts and graphs for your group's observations of each other from on-site classroom observations or role-playing.
2. Write a critical appraisal concerning the use of reinforcement techniques in classroom teaching. Specifically indicate how this learning will be applied in your classroom, home, or life.
3. Complete Time Log.

GENERAL LEARNING ACTIVITY A—
STUDY GUIDE FOR CHAPTERS 1–5[1]

1. What is suggested as an important variable in being an effective teacher?

*2. State the behavioral principle that we try to teach children and the "perversions" of the principle. If you disagree with this, state why.

*3. What does "discipline" involve?

4. State specifically to what discipline and motivation refer.

5. What is a general attribute?

6. Paraphrase the gist of the paragraph beginning, "When learning is defined. . . ." (See page 8).

7. How is self-control or self-discipline acquired?

*8. Why is discipline neither strictness or permissiveness but is related to cause-and-effect relationships?

*9. What is one of the most effective rewards a teacher can use?

*10. How is worry (depression) reinforced?

*11. List the three states in which children are considered to be born. Explain the teacher's role in each. What is your position?

12. Why is a traditional analysis of a child's problem behavior unproductive?

*13. Describe why some children may not *want* to learn. Explain why they are not just "born that way." Provide an explanation of what can be done.

*14. Where does this analysis put the notion of motivation? Since motivation is typically referred to as an "inner" state, explain why unmotivated behavior is not explained in this way.

---

[1] The authors gratefully acknowledge the help of Dr. Jon Bailey of Florida State University in the development of this study guide. Dr. Bailey first used a similar guide for an undergraduate course in Educational Psychology.

15. Why is the capacity for work necessary?

16. How is the capacity for work developed? Some people are industrious and some are lazy; how is this difference analyzed?

*17. What is meant by who decides who decides?

*18. What does the behavioral approach represent?

19. Why is it possible to teach different values using identical techniques?

*20. What types of behaviors are learned? Are any of these types amenable to change through behavior modification?

*21. At any given time, a person's responses may be thought of as coming from one of three explanations. List these three explanations.

*22. In what way is "making learning fun" a behavioral manipulation?

*23. What is specificity?

24. How is it possible to specify values?

*25. Be able to present the argument for specifying in detail the goals of education. Be able to analyze one of the generalities listed.

26. Why is it necessary to record behavior?

27. How might you record talking out, looking out the window, or a similar activity? (Remember, the first step is to define the behavior specifically, then to count it in some time interval such the number of occurrences per forty-five minutes, class period, hour, day.)

28. What does the traditional viewpoint stress in leading to a behavioral goal? What is wrong with this explanation?

29. How does one decide who has the problem?

30. How may non-behavioral explanations delay solutions to problems?

*31. What point is made with the example of students A, B, and C?

32. Explain why teachers should understand the analysis of students A, B, and C.

*33. Behavior may be eliminated in two ways. List them.

34. How is the choice made about what competing or inappropriate behavior is to be eliminated first?

35. What addition must be made, besides class rules?

36. What do you notice about the way that the rules are worded?

37. Be able to describe the initial procedures for gaining control and what may follow.

*38. What is vicarious reinforcement and modeling? Give an example. Why might it be used?

*39. What makes group approval-disapproval work effectively?

*40. List the rewards that teachers can use and give examples for each.

*41. How can you tell what will be rewarding? Can you predict in advance what may work?

*42. Is everybody alike?

*43. Should a teacher treat all children the same in academic and social situations? Explain.

*44. Should a child be taught that the world is unfair? Why or why not?

*45. Give an example of unfairness to an individual. Could this example be changed to make it fair to him? Is your example realistic?

*46. What is the purpose of reinforcement teaching?

*47. List the five techniques in structuring contingencies.

*48. Which three techniques should be employed most in structuring contingencies by teachers? Why?

*49. Name the two major categories under which appropriate and inappropriate student behaviors can be subsumed.

*50. Give an example of each category in which you would consider the student's behavior as appropriate.

*51. Give an example of each category in which you would consider the student's behavior as inappropriate.

*52. List a possible reaction the teacher should have to each of the four situations you have described in the preceding two questions.

*53. Why are rules important for both the students and the teacher?

*54. What is meant by contingent rewards?

*55. Why do you think consistency is the most difficult task for a teacher? Give an example.

*56. Explain why it is much easier to act your way into a new way of thinking than to think your way into a new way of acting.

57. List and describe the four steps teachers can use in modifying classroom behavior.

58. What elements contribute to independence?

59. From your school experience, analyze two new examples after reading Part II, using the same format (use approximations for records).

60. How would you teach independence behaviorally?

61–94. Using the preceding questions indicated by an asterisk (*), transfer the concept dealt with in the question to specific content area classroom teaching situations—in chorus, band, orchestra, art, physical education, social studies, language arts, special education, arithmetic, English, history, algebra, geometry, science, modern languages, forensics, dramatics, football, track, chemistry, literature.

GENERAL LEARNING ACTIVITY B—
YOUR BEHAVIOR CAN BE MEASURED

The most critical difference between a behavioral approach which pinpoints specific observable and measurable behaviors and less systematic approaches to human interactions is the keeping of behavioral records. Evaluation of any procedure instituted to induce behavioral change is virtually impossible without records. Measurement and specific records are crucial for accurate evaluation. The only difficulty regarding these classification procedures is that they take a little extra effort. Behavior always occurs in time intervals. If we are to know whether any particular behavior is getting worse, better, or staying the same, the frequency of behavioral occurrences must be recorded across time and in specific time intervals.

One important aspect of learning record keeping is for a person to develop the self-discipline necessary to keep individual records representing his own behavior. A good place to start is with the time spent on this course or workshop. Each participant is urged to maintain an individual time log indicating amounts of time spent engaged in learning activities. Each week one time log should be completed. (Academic instructors may require that the log be turned in weekly, workshop directors daily.) A model time log is provided.

The time log is divided into four mutually exclusive categories—Reading, Discussion, Writing, and Other—since two or more behaviors cannot occur at precisely the same time (although discussion and/or writing and reading may be closely interspersed). Any class preparation or learning time which is not covered in the Reading, Discussion, and Writing categories may be recorded under Other. This category includes classroom observations, supervision behaviors, or any activities assigned but for which no category exists. These should also be listed on the back of your log.

Keep accurate records and, each time you engage in an activity, log the amount of time in the upper half of each square which is diagonal (round up or down to fifteen-minute time periods). The number of hours are important in order to ascertain how much time one is spending on the course or workshop. It is critical to record time spent as immediately as possible. Few people have a good enough memory to record time spent after even a one-day interlude. After recording time spent, record a subjective rating in the lower

TIME LOG

RATING KEY

1	
	2

1 = Time in Minutes
2 = Rating

A = Very Worthwhile
B = Some Value
C = Little Value
D = Wasted Time

Class _____
Name _____
Week No. _____
Dates _____

Days									Wkly. Total	Last Cum. Total	New Cum. Total
A - Readings											
Texts											
Behavioral Articles											
Others Related											
B Discussion											
Class Attendance											
Class Members											
Other (Specify)											
C - Writing											
Learning Activities											
Summaries (Behavioral Articles or Texts)											
Other Assignments											
D- Other											
Observing											
Supervising Practicing Mini-Teaching											
Course - Related Thinking											

Comments on Back   Grand Totals ____ ____ ____ portion of the square as to the value of the particular learning experience you have just completed. These ratings make it possible for your instructor to continually receive feedback on daily activities and assignments and make appropriate changes when deemed necessary.

Academic course instructors may desire that you record the cumulative weekly totals in each major category. For example, suppose for the first week Reading = 3.50 (210 mins), Writing = 1.25 (75 mins), Discussion = 4.75 (285 mins), and Other = 0; the second week totals were: Reading = 2.75 (165 mins), Writing = 2.75 (165 mins), Discussion = 4.50 (270 mins) and Other 1.00 (60 mins). Recorded cumulative totals would be as follows for the second week: Reading = 3.50 + 2.75 = 6.25 (375 mins), Writing = 1.25 + 2.75 = 4.00 (240 mins), Discussion = 4.75 + 4.50 = 9.25 (555 mins), and Other = 0.00 + 1.00 = 1.00 (60 mins), and so on for each week. Your instructor may also desire that you graph these cumulative totals. The final week's time log will have the total number of hours (minutes) spent for the entire course.

GENERAL LEARNING ACTIVITY C—
TEST ON TEACHING/DISCIPLINE:
A POSITIVE APPROACH FOR EDUCATIONAL
DEVELOPMENT, SECOND EDITION,
MADSEN AND MADSEN.

Name_____

Please circle the answer which *best* completes the statement.

1. The foremost question regarding discipline in the classroom is one pertaining to

   a. strict relationships.
   b. strict and permissive relationships.
   c. cause-and-effect relationships.
   d. interpersonal relationships.
   e. strict versus permissive control.

2. The teacher's personal approval is a most effective reward for most children and should be given

   a. discriminately.
   b. noncontingently.
   c. approvingly.
   d. partially.
   e. all of the above.

3. To solve a student's inappropriate behavior, the teacher should

   a. know the reinforcement history of the student.
   b. do something to change the student's behavior.
   c. try to understand the behavior on the basis of previous test results.
   d. seek evaluation of the student's personality.
   e. none of the above.

4. A very simple behavioral principle used to teach children to respond appropriately is

   a. "when you do bad things, bad things happen to you."
   b. "no matter what you do, nice things happen to you."
   c. "when you do nice things, nice things happen to you."
   d. "no matter what you do, bad things happen to you."
   e. both a and c.

5. Why is the principle of specificity important in behavior modification?

   a. The teacher can only deal with specified traits.
   b. Only specified overt behaviors can be dealt with.
   c. The word discipline is a specific category.
   d. Generalized behavior is amenable to modification.
   e. After the behavior is specified, the student will improve.

6. Human behavior can be measured

   a. in time intervals.
   b. within discrete pinpointed categories.
   c. for specific academic responses.
   d. following appropriate student behavior.
   e. all of the above.

7. Partial reinforcement

   a. may refer to inconsistency in responding.
   b. often prolongs inappropriate behavior.
   c. often prolongs appropriate behavior.
   d. may refer to consistency in responding.
   e. all of the above.

8. If a teacher inadvertently gives approval to a student following an inappropriate response

   a. new contingencies may be structured immediately.
   b. it will not function as an error because it was unwitting.

c. the student will likely repeat the response.

d. the teacher should disapprove the next time.

e. both a and c.

9. Disapproval may be used effectively in modifying inappropriate behavior except when

a. its magnitude is too great.

b. it functions as a payoff for the inappropriate response.

c. it is given on a partial schedule.

d. it is used as a follow-through after a threat.

e. none of the above.

10. An issue which teachers should consider carefully is that it seems easier for one to _____ his way into a new way of _____ than to _____ his way into a new way of _____ .

a. think/acting/act/thinking

b. talk/feeling/feel/talking

c. work/studying/study/working

d. act/thinking/think/acting

e. both c and d.

11. If contingent rewards/punishments are to be effective, they should generally take place

a. immediately.

b. with a reward hierarchy in mind.

c. consistently.

d. without verbal explanation.

e. all of the above.

12. _____ is anything a person does, says, or thinks that can be observed directly and/or indirectly.

a. Data

b. Reality

c. Behavior

d. Behavior modification

e. Association

13. _____is defined as a change or modification of behavior.

    a. Contingency management

    b. Reinforcement

    c. Learning

    d. Teaching

    e. None of the above.

14. Some students may become upset if a teacher makes a class privilege contingent upon the behavior of a few students. Students who become upset are probably concerned with

    a. strictness of control.

    b. peer approval.

    c. group discipline.

    d. fairness.

    e. threat of disapproval.

15. "Making a game out of learning" may involve

    a. structuring learning material.

    b. establishing rewards.

    c. manipulating the environment.

    d. maintaining contingencies.

    e. all of the above.

16. When a teacher says, "I don't like all that structure and those behavioral techniques. I don't want my students to have to sit quietly all day," he/she is confusing

    a. facts with values.

    b. techniques with values.

    c. social with academic behavior.

    d. rules with how to enforce them.

    e. both b and d.

17. If creativity can be taught and learned, then the educator needs to be concerned with

    a. at what point further teaching might inhibit creativity.

    b. whether students can create from nothing.

c. what information and materials students need to get started.

d. the situation in which learning occurs.

e. all of the above.

18. If a teacher noncontingently reinforces all of the student's creative products because the teacher feels the child needs it, the child will probably learn

a. to love himself contingently.

b. to discriminate the quality of his classmates' products.

c. lack of social discrimination.

d. lack of discrimination concerning his work.

e. none of the above.

19. Many teachers quit the teaching profession because of

a. anxiety relating to teaching pressures.

b. lack of education in coping with special problems.

c. inability to discipline.

d. loss of motivation after initial teaching experience.

e. personality problems.

20. Motivation is

a. shaped by strict discipline.

b. taught by manipulating the external environment.

c. based on personality factors.

d. based upon student interest and background variables.

e. innate with every student.

21. Within the classroom, "being approved of" is probably controlled by

a. the teacher.

b. partial reinforcement.

c. both teacher and students.

d. self-concept.

e. the student.

22. Desire to learn is

    a. innate except for special problems.
    b. universal if students are left alone.
    c. taught but not learned.
    d. necessary in all situations.
    e. none of the above.

23. While handwriting is an appropriate learned behavior, yelling out the answer is often a(n) _____ behavior.

    a. cued
    b. more desirable
    c. innate
    d. more spontaneous
    e. inappropriate

24. Three things are necessary for learning to take place—

    a. motivation, assimilation, and reinforcement.
    b. experience, discrimination, and association.
    c. proper set, attention, and deduction.
    d. accommodation, reward, and adaption.
    e. attention, reinforcement, and discipline.

25. A behavior which results in pleasant consequences will likely be

    a. forgotten.
    b. appropriate.
    c. repeated.
    d. reinforced.
    e. assimilated.

Below are listed five examples of classroom contingencies. In the blank space after each statement indicate, by letter, the particular contingency situation.

    a. approval following appropriate behavior
    b. withholding approval
    c. disapproval following inappropriate behavior

CHAP 10   OUTLINE FOR LEARNING

    d. threat of disapproval

    e. ignoring

26. Making the student sit in a corner facing the wall because he threw spitballs at another student. _____

27. Inattention following a student's verbalizations. _____

28. Having the student continue working on arithmetic problems until he finishes them and telling him that only then may he go out to recess. _____

29. Providing special activities for every correct arithmetic problem completed. _____

30. Telling the student that he will be sent to the principal's office if he doesn't stop talking. _____

31. "You have not followed the rules today, Fred. Therefore I am sending you to the time-out room." _____

32. "You have not completed any science problems. You may go to band when you have correctly completed all the problems."____

33. "Good work, Jane. You have completed your homework assignment and handed it in on time."_____

34. "If you do not finish these problems correctly in five minutes, I am going to make you sit in the corner by yourself."_____

35. I am sorry Mary did not sit still. We will have the party later, if everyone is still. _____

What is the consequence to pinpoints found in the text (not necessarily the one that worked).

PINPOINT	CONSEQUENCE
___36. dishonesty	a. Grade assigned without explanation.
___37. nail biting	b. Teacher instituted multiple divergent token systems. Some children received paper

money which bought surprise gifts at end of day. Other children received candies on various time interval schedules. Some children accumulated points written on notebook. Reinforcers changed constantly.

____38. fear in young children

c. Negative practice—students practice inappropriate behavior at specific times (e.g., 8 A.M. for five minutes) in front of mirror. Parent or teacher delivered disapproval responses during sessions.

____39. excessive dawdling

d. Teacher ignored all children, made no eye contact, said nothing; only recognized children who raised hands at seats.

____40. bothering teacher at desk

e. Incompatible response— object or situation gradually introduced into child's presence while child engaged in fun activity. Gradual approach—child led by degrees, over number of days, to come closer and closer to activity or object made readily accessible to child while other children partici- pated enjoyably.

****

____41. children manipulating parents

a. Large punching bag dummy with red nose installed on playground.

____42. standing up walking around

b. None apply.

____43. striking other children
with objects

   c. Two-fold program to teach
all students discrimination
between possessing ability and
performing before class, and
teach entire class role-playing
to deliver approval feedback
to insecure students.

____44. aggressive hitting

   d. Mothers (1) instructed in
delivery of approval techniques, (2) taught to ignore
inappropriate behavior, and
(3) responded with praise
and affection for appropriate
behavior.

____45. embarrassment

   e. Adult assigned in vicinity;
child praised and given donut
when playing properly,
although when boy hit
someone supervisor hit him
back with same object.

****

____46. boredom

   a. School counselor developed
system with parents' cooperation. Every teacher signed
individual daily progress
report (one small sheet) after
each class. Decision of signing
for appropriate social and
academic behaviors based on
teacher's criteria. Allowance,
social engagements, car
privileges contingent upon
number of signatures earned
each day.

____47. school failure

   b. Teacher explained to class
that talking during study time
interfered with completion

of work assignments (this had been done before). Class discussed importance of rules for study, agreed something must be done, and suggested very extreme alternatives.

_____48. disruptive classroom behavior

c. If assignments not completed, no recess.

_____49. arithmetic achievement

d. Disruptive behavior ignored, appropriate behavior rewarded. Boy kept after school for extreme deviations and sent home on later bus. This put child with students he did not know and withdrew peer attention. Correct behaviors reinforced by teacher praise and peer approval (continuously in beginning, more infrequently later on). Also, job of blackboard monitor followed appropriate behavior.

_____50. disruptive social talking

e. Friday football game instituted, teams chosen, rules established points, yards, substitutions, etc. developed for correct academic responses. Game played on blackboard with losing team providing treat for winners.

LEARNING ACTIVITY 1—
VALUES-TECHNIQUES DICHOTOMY

Behavior modification represents the use of a series of techniques which have been scientifically verified in an attempt to promote more effective learning for both social and academic subject matter (see Selected Bibliography). A behavioral approach does not help the teacher decide why, what, and who is going to learn. But behavioral principles may be used to enhance learning of appropriate behavior after questions relating to values have been decided.

Study the Values-Techniques Dichotomy Chart shown below and fill in three or four of the most important values—academic, social, or both—you think should be instilled in the students you are going to teach. Do the same for values that you feel should not be taught to your students under any circumstances. In addition, your instructor may require that you write a short paragraph on how behavioral techniques could be used to teach both negative as well as positive values.

The purpose of this exercise is to demonstrate that behavioral techniques, much like any human product, may be used either to the benefit or the detriment of other human beings. These techniques can be used to isolate specific cause-and-effect relationships by affecting the consequences of behavior and thereby providing a scientific methodology for the evaluation of learning.

POSITIVE VALUES

a_____   b_____

c_____   d_____

1. Pinpoint: Observable   1. Non-Observable
2. Record: Measurable   2. Non-Measurable
                                              (Inferential)

TECHNIQUES

Behavioral _____   Non-Behavioral
Techniques   Techniques

3. Consequate: Cause- and-Effect   3. Non-Determined
                Relationships   (random chance,
                                              chaotic)
4. Evaluate: Isolate causes   4. Non-Explainable
                through specific   Complex Causes
                addition and   Unknown Consequences
                removal of
                consequences

a_____   b_____

c_____   d_____

NEGATIVE VALUES

LEARNING ACTIVITY 2—
VALUES-TECHNIQUES DIFFERENTIATION

Many values (implicit or explicit) are reinforced by teachers without a clear understanding of the difference(s) between values and techniques. The following list of values is derived from actual observations of classroom teachers. Any values may be reinforced using either approval or disapproval techniques.

1. In the blanks provided, fill in specific consequences (see example) including both approval and disapproval techniques (see pp. 64–174).
2. Circle all teacher values which you do not value (i.e., behavior inconsistent with your value system).
3. Go back and review your lists of consequences and change ten examples to consequences which you would not prefer to use (i.e., consequences inconsistent with your value system) that you have either observed or read about.

Teacher Values	Example of Specific Consequences Following Behavior	
1. Following classroom rules	A(pproval)	teacher's praise
	D(isapproval)	_____
2. Working (staying on-task)	A	_____
	D	_____
3. Academic achievement (learning to read)	A	academic grades
	D	_____
4. Working quietly	A	_____
	D	_____

5. Working well together
   (cooperation)

   A _____

   D _____

6. Respect for teacher
   (not being sassy)

   A _____

   D _____

7. Waiting quietly (patience)

   A _____

   D _____

8. Doing extra work (industry)

   A _____

   D _____

9. Effort

   A _____

   D _____

10. Raising hand to get attention

    A _____

    D _____

11. Completing assignments on
    time

    A allowed to work
       on own project

    D _____

12. Staying in seat while
    working

    A _____

    D _____

13. Following directions

    A _____

    D _____

14. Walking inside building

    A _____

    D _____

15. Taking responsibility for
    own materials

    A _____

    D _____

16. Liking school and school
    work (positive attitude)

    A _____

    D _____

LEARNING ACTIVITY 3—
TRANSLATING IDEAS (VALUES) INTO BEHAVIORS

The objective of this Learning Activity is to structure commonly used words that represent ideas (values) concerning social behavior into specific overt demonstrable behaviors. While all words may merely be symbolic representations, some words seem specific in their elicitations and, therefore, are preferred in describing empirical relationships. Thus "verbalizes facts" appears much more quantifiable than "honest."

Read the two examples under each idea and note How Observed and Counted Across. Next add two additional behaviors. Then fill in how they would be observed and the observational time intervals. Remember that the period of time a behavior might be measured across depends upon the urgency of dealing with the behavior, and the logical amount of time to determine whether or not the behavior is stable or infrequent (marriages are measured in years while eye contact would be recorded across seconds).

You may refer to actual behaviors that have been demonstrated in classrooms or to behaviors you may wish students, or even yourself, to acquire.

Idea: Honesty

Behaviors	How Observed	Counted Across
1. Returns materials	visually	A.M./P.M.
2. Verbalizes facts	visually/ aurally	days
3.		
4.		
5.		
6.		

Idea: Dishonesty

Behaviors	How Observed	Counted Across
1. Steals others' materials	visually	days, weeks
2. Fabricates experiences	aurally	days
3.		
4.		
5.		
6.		

Idea: Appreciation

Behaviors	How Observed	Counted Across
1. Says thank you	aurally	A.M./P.M.
2. Expresses positive words	aurally	hours
3.		
4.		
5.		
6.		

Idea: Democratic

Behaviors	How Observed	Counted Across
1. Votes	visually	months
2. Follows rules	visually	minutes, A.M./P.M.
3.		
4.		
5.		

Idea: Kind

Behaviors	How Observed	Counted Across
1. Helps others	visually	A.M./P.M., days
2. Interacts with others	visually	days, weeks
3.		
4.		
5.		
6.		

Idea: Communication

Behaviors	How Observed	Counted Across
1. Talks with others	visually	minutes
2. Looks into eyes	visually	seconds
3.		
4.		
5.		
6.		

Idea: Good Human Relations

Behaviors	How Observed	Counted Across
1. Touching	visually	seconds
2. Talking with others	visually	minutes, seconds
3.		
4.		
5.		
6.		

Idea: Cooperation

Behaviors	How Observed	Counted Across
1. Shares materials	visually	A.M./P.M., days
2. Asks for help	visually/ aurally	A.M./P.M.
3.		
4.		
5.		
6.		
7.		

Idea: Sensitivity

Behaviors	How Observed	Counted Across
1. Appropriate talking	aurally	seconds, minutes
2. Not talking	aurally	seconds, minutes
3. Picks up nonverbal motor cues	tactually	seconds
4.		
5.		
6.		

Idea: Creativity

Behaviors	How Observed	Counted Across
1. Writes using new word organization	visually	weeks, school term
2. Nonverbal expression in new media	visually	weeks

3. Divergent solutions to   aurally,   weeks
   school, social, or building   visually
   problems

4.

5.

6.

LEARNING ACTIVITY 4—
PINPOINT RANKING EXERCISE

A behavior is anything a person does that can be observed and measured. Ideas (values) are generally made more and more behavioral as behaviors are specified in observable and measurable terms; consider for example the following Values (Ideas)—Behaviors—Values (Goals) Chart.

Definitions lead from inferential nonbehavioral ideas (C) toward very specific observable and measurable behaviors (A).

A — Pinpoint defined in terms of specific behaviors. Behavior is both observable and measurable and therefore overtly demonstrable. It can be observed without further definition (nonambiguous).

B — Pinpoint somewhat inferential, some ambiguity involved. Additional definition or more specific delineation necessary before precise observation and recording can take place.

C — Pinpoint definitely an inference, is nonobservable, and nonmeasurable as stated.

Task 1: Assign a definitional category to the pinpoints for the 86 examples in Part II, pages 59–174, using the A, B, and C code given above, adding pluses and minuses as needed (A—, B+, B—, C+, C—). Use only the information given in each Pinpoint section of the Examples.

Task 2: After all pinpoints have been ranked using the A, B, and C code, check each pinpoint ranked lower than an A—. Go back to the appropriate page in Part II and re-read any information given in the Record section. When the new information serves to further specify the behavior involved, then re-rank the pinpoint. For Example 1, Bothering Teacher at Desk, the first ranking might be B; re-ranking after reading the Record could give it a B+.

First Ranking Totals

/86 =____% A pinpoints

/86 =____°'₀ B pinpoints

/86 =____°₀ C pinpoints

Re-Ranking Totals

/86 =____°₀ A pinpoints

/86 =____% B pinpoints

/86 =____% C pinpoints

Additional practice in specifying overt behaviors in observable and measurable pinpoints may be acquired by referring to the behaviors you have written in completing Learning Activity 3 and rewriting each pinpointed behavior that does not qualify as an A so that it can be readily observed and counted.

LEARNING ACTIVITY 5—
CLASSROOM OR ROLE-PLAYING OBSERVATIONS

The purpose of observing others is to sensitize teachers or potential teachers to the behaviors of both teacher and students in order to more effectively choose appropriate approval and disapproval techniques which are in line with personal value decisions.

Using the observational chapter, definitions of categories, and observational forms, observe for four twenty-minute (fifty time intervals) periods. Use Form A: Teacher Observation for one period, Form C: Student Observation for one period, Form G: Student(s)-Teacher for one period, and Form H for one period.

Participants (students) should be assigned observational tasks in groups of two. Following completion of each of the four observations, reliability should be computed and results discussed. Instructors may assign films, videotapes, or actual classroom observation or have some participants role-play while others observe.

Accuracy of observations is critical for appropriate discriminations to occur. Observers should remember to fill in every part of the observational forms including Feelings and Reactions in the comments section or on the back of the form. Interpretations and inferences are important for learning but should not be confused with the behavior observed in the classroom.

LEARNING ACTIVITY 6—
OBSERVATIONAL EVALUATION

Instruction:

Study carefully Chapter 9, paying special attention to the definitional categories. Complete all answers on the Observational Evaluation. Small discussion groups provide an excellent method to check the accuracy of the test responses and in addition develop a general competency in the application of observational rules prior to actual classroom observation.

Part I: For each category listed below, please put the appropriate symbol to the right of the category.

Teacher reinforcement categories

1. Approval Mistake (Social) _____

2. Disapproval (Academic) _____

3. Approval (Social) _____

4. Approval Mistake (Academic) _____

5. Disapproval Mistake (Social) _____

6. Instructions _____

Student categories

7. Verbal (Noise) Off-Task _____

8. Motor Off-Task _____

9. On-Task _____

10. Passive Off-Task _____

Part II: Below are listed the rules for Mrs. Jones' classroom. Using these rules, check the appropriate space(s) as to how the specific behaviors should be categorized.

Rules for specific activity

1. Work quietly (no talking).

2. During this period work individually on math in your seat.

3. Raise your hand to receive help.

4. You may get materials without permission.

5. Sign in and out on the list for going to the restroom without asking permission.

Part II A.   You are observing the students. Record behaviors using the observational code:

	On-Task	Off-Task N M O		None Apply
11. One student is talking to his neighbor.				
12. Student is quietly writing spelling words.				
13. Student is staring out the window while chewing on his pencil.				
14. Student is working in seat on math.				
15. Student lies on floor working on math.				
16. Student is staring out of window.				

17. Student signs list to go to restroom, but does not ask teacher's permission.

18. You can see the student talking to his neighbor, but you cannot hear him.

19. Student is turned forty-five degrees in his seat.

20. Student turns around ninety degrees and talks to his neighbor.

21. Student hits his neighbor.

22. Student calls out to teacher.

23. Student is staring at floor.

24. Teacher asks student a question and student responds with an incorrect answer.

25. Student gets up to get materials.

26. On the way back from getting materials, the student stops and talks with another student.

27. A child puts up his hand and looks around the room.

28. A student is talking to himself.

29. A student is gently drumming his desk while working on math.

30. A student is asking a fellow student about an assignment.

Part II B: Teacher Behaviors
   Record teacher behaviors using the following code:

Aa   Approval—Academic   As   Approval—Social
Da   Disapproval—Academic   Ds   Disapproval—Social
(Aa) Approval Mistake—   (As) Approval Mistake—Social
     Academic   (Ds) Disapproval Mistake—
(Da) Disapproval Mistake—   Social
     Academic   __   No Behavior Rated

If more than one code applies, use the following order of importance:
1. Mistakes of Reinforcement
2. Approval
3. Disapproval

31. "That's a correct answer but sit down while working." _____

32. "That's good you raised your hand for help." _____

33. Teacher asks student to respond. _____

34. "Sit up straight. You look sloppy." _____

35. Teacher gently places hand on student while telling him to sit down. _____

36. "The whole class is doing well." (Two students off-task) _____

37. Student blurts out answer and teacher says, "That's correct, Jimmy." _____

38. "I don't want to hear another word for the next ten minutes." _____

39. Teacher calls on student who is quiet but does not have hand up. (Student behaving appropriately except that his hand is not up.) _____

40. Student is out of his seat and taps teacher on shoulder. Teacher says, "Sit down, Johnny. I will not talk to you unless you raise your hand." _____

319

41. Student is out of seat and touches teacher. The teacher puts his arm on shoulder and says, "Sit down. I will not talk to you unless your hand is raised." _____

42. "No, Johnny. That is not the right answer." _____

43. "This class is just not working." (Two students are working.) _____

44. "Except for Linda and Jane, who are working very nicely, the rest of you are behaving abominably. Sit down and stop talking." _____

45. The teacher responds to a student's answer to a question by repeating the student's answer. _____

46. The teacher inadvertently marks a correct answer as incorrect. _____

47. "Johnny, you're always raising your hand to answer. Let someone else answer for a change." _____

48. "Johnny, stop copying Jimmy's paper." _____

49. "That's almost right." _____

50. The teacher puts her arm around a student and says, "These problems are all correct," when in fact, two are incorrect. _____

LEARNING ACTIVITY 7—
TIME AND BEHAVIOR MODIFICATION

1. Write an essay on: How is time important in modifying behavior? Make certain you concern yourself with the issues of (a) when the reinforcement is delivered, (b) increases in the success rate of material learned, (c) partial reinforcement effects, and (d) the learning of a reinforcement schedule.

2. Discuss, in groups or in writing, how gambling is an illustration of the effects of partial reinforcement.

3. Using the pinpoint model, indicate:

a. How you would reinforce someone in order that they become a constant gambler

b. How you would reinforce someone in order that he become a person who will never gamble

c. How you would teach an adult illiterate to learn to read, using the same consequences in a and b above

Read and discuss other participants' essays and indicate how you would apply the same principle to academic responses (reading, mathematics, obeying classroom rules) by substituting actual academic behaviors for the gambling activity.

LEARNING ACTIVITY 8—
HUMAN ECOLOGY AND REINFORCEMENT:
POTENTIAL SPHERES OF BEHAVIORAL INFLUENCE

1. Write or discuss what the teacher can realistically expect to accomplish based upon the following diagram. Keep in mind the question "Who has the responsibility?" for specific behaviors, and that the student is subject to many potentially contradictory sources of reinforcement, but also the student possesses abilities to learn discrimination and therefore behave differently under different conditions. Discuss your ideas with other participants.
    2. List different behaviors that adults exhibit under the following conditions: (a) sports events, (b) in church, (c) eating in a restaurant, (d) watching T.V. and, (e) playing tennis.

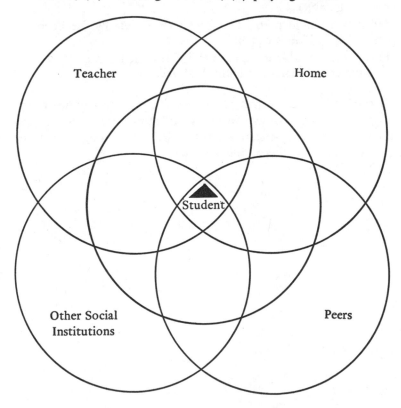

LEARNING ACTIVITY 9—
CONSEQUATE EVALUATION

Answer all questions and then check your answers by locating the appropriate pinpoint in Part II.

Correct every false answer and rewrite so that the statement becomes true. Write thirty additional true-false statements using pinpoints (Examples) not previously used in this activity.

True-False

1. Overt behaviors, such as teasing, probably elicit payoffs from classmates.

2. Behaviors that have been diminished (such as reducing activity to a more appropriate level) may be internalized to the point that they are self-reinforcing.

3. Students learn more effectively if initially taught abstract concepts rather than specifics.

4. Long-term observational feedback increases teacher effectiveness more than daily observational feedback.

5. Student repair of damaged equipment and/or financial restitution rarely stops vandalism.

6. Special activities, such as field trips, may be made contingent on appropriate classroom behavior.

7. Research indicates that teacher approval is always the best reinforcer for controlling classroom behavior.

8. Inconsistent rules are more likely to be manipulated by students.

9. Specific situational rules are made to be broken.

10. Loud reprimands often tend to increase, rather than decrease, disruptive classroom behavior.

11. The technique of removing students from a classroom as punishment is effective only when the classroom provides positive consequences for the student.

323

12. Some content areas do not lend themselves to making a game out of learning.

13. Academically related materials (pencils, crayons, paper, books, experiments) may be used as reinforcers for appropriate academic behaviors.

14. Rewards following student behavior are more meaningful when given at appropriate time intervals.

15. Children do not learn specific behavioral discrimination through negative practice.

16. Most teachers mistakenly feel that they use more approval than disapproval in the classroom.

17. Practice and/or role-playing in delivery of approval or disapproval responses is not necessary for the experienced teacher who can apply these responses intuitively.

18. If students are to learn appropriate discriminations, they must be taught to discern differences.

19. Young students, if given no instruction, are capable of establishing all of their own goals.

20. Once the behavior to be changed is pinpointed and rewards gathered, treatment must be consistent and persistent to be effective.

21. Behavior which has been reinforced in the past may persist even when the specific reinforcers used to establish the behavior are no longer given.

22. Many rewards offered by teachers and parents for appropriate behavior are ineffective because the time interval between the behavior and the reward is too long.

23. Some scientific studies apply contingencies to classroom behavior and then take them out again in an attempt to hide research results from the classroom teacher.

24. Hitting and other aggressive behaviors are to be expected from young children as these behaviors are innate.

25. Attitudes are probably learned through behavioral principles much as other behaviors are learned.

26. The ability to choose specific reinforcers is very important when interacting with older students.

27. Attention to inappropriate behavior may increase rather than decrease behavior the teacher desires to reduce.

28. Withdrawal of approval may be ineffective if the teacher uses predominantly disapproval to control inappropriate behavior.

29. Children may be taught to ignore inappropriate behavior from each other.

30. Many times, it is necessary for the teacher to remediate social behavior before the subject material can be learned.

LEARNING ACTIVITY 10—
CHOICE OF REINFORCERS

1. For all of the following pinpoints (actual classroom incidents), determine three different procedures (logical consequences) that could be tried by the classroom teacher for increasing or decreasing the pinpointed behavior. Be as specific as possible and use at least one approval and one disapproval technique for each pinpoint. (Instructors and/or students may choose to make up their own pinpoints.)

2. State one good reason for the selection of each consequence. Indicate whether the consequence is (a) approval, (b) withdrawal of approval, (c) disapproval, (d) threat of disapproval, or (e) ignoring.

3. When all pinpoints have been consequated and designations as to approval/disapproval completed, next categorize the specific reinforcers used for each separate consequate using the following categories:

a. Words
b. Closeness
c. Bodily expressions
d. Activities
e. Things

1. Pinpoint: Refusal to go outdoors for recess (Seven-year-old girl)

Record: Child refuses to go outside during morning or afternoon recess.

Consequate: 1. _____

2. _____

3. _____

2. Pinpoint:

School phobia (Seven-year-old boy)

   Record:

Child refuses to go to school; protests with disruptive behavior (crying, screaming).

   Consequate:

1._____

2._____

3._____

3. Pinpoint:

Blanket bringing behavior (Six-year-old)

   Record:

Child insists on bringing "security" blanket to school at the beginning of the second school year. The behavior was not observed during the first year of school.

   Consequate:

1._____

2._____

3._____

4. Pinpoint:

Headaches (Second-grade girl)

   Record:

Girl complains of headaches during language arts period a total of twelve times in five sessions.

   Consequate:

1._____

2._____

3._____

5. Pinpoint:

Teasing handicapped child (Third and fourth graders)

   Record:

Several boys and girls make fun of handicapped younger child every recess period.

Consequate: 1._____

       2._____

       3._____

6. Pinpoint: Pants wetting (Kindergarten)

  Record: Teacher noticed wet dress of child seven times during one week.

  Consequate: 1._____

       2._____

       3._____

7. Pinpoint: Tattling (Elementary grades)

  Record: Child observed to "tell" on others in class twenty-three times in one week.

  Consequate: 1._____

       2._____

       3._____

8. Pinpoint: Book stealing from library

  Record: Ten books missing during the first week of school.

  Consequate: 1._____

       2._____

       3._____

9. Pinpoint: Damaged musical instruments.

   Record: Fourteen instruments damaged in one week.

   Consequate: 1. _____

                    2. _____

                    3. _____

10. Pinpoint: Damage to teachers' automobiles

    Record: Eight tires slashed, four radio antennas bent, and eighteen windows broken during one week of school.

    Consequate: 1. _____

                    2. _____

                    3. _____

11. Pinpoint: Book slamming (Ninth-grade boys, English class)

    Record: Six boys slam books down on desk upon entering English class, a total of thirty-two times in one week.

    Consequate: 1. _____

                    2. _____

                    3. _____

12. Pinpoint: Lunch stealing (Seventh-grade boys)

    Record: Three seventh-grade boys are observed stealing fifth graders' lunches every day for one week.

Consequate: 1. _____

2. _____

3. _____

13. Pinpoint: Kissing in halls

Record: Seven couples observed kissing in the hall
during lunch period two consecutive days.

Consequate: 1. _____

2. _____

3. _____

14. Pinpoint: Turning in assignments late

Record: Teacher notes student delinquent in turning
in math homework nine times in one month.

Consequate: 1. _____

2. _____

3. _____

15. Pinpoint: Graffiti

Record: Writing noted on the boys' restroom walls
after each cleaning.

Consequate: 1. _____

2. _____

3. _____

16. Pinpoint: Teacher mimicry (Sixteen-year-old boy, math class)

    Record: Student mimics fifteen sentences of female math teacher during three math classes.

    Consequate: 1. _____

                       2. _____

                       3. _____

17. Pinpoint: Teacher threats (Eighteen-year-old male student, English class)

    Record: Student threatens to "get even" with teacher if she fails him.

    Consequate: 1. _____

                       2. _____

                       3. _____

18. Pinpoint: Book tearing

    Record: Four male students have ten page-tearing "accidents" in literature class during one week.

    Consequate: 1. _____

                       2. _____

                       3. _____

19. Pinpoint: Glue sniffing

    Record: Four high school seniors caught sniffing glue
                       in the boys' restroom.

    Consequate: 1. _____

                       2. _____

                       3. _____

20. Pinpoint: Profane language

    Record: Female social studies teacher records forty-
                       five outbursts of profanity during her lec-
                       tures in a two-week period.

    Consequate: 1. _____

                       2. _____

                       3. _____

21. Pinpoint: Abuse of privileges

    Record: Two girls use Honor Society work as an
                       excuse to leave chemistry class six times in
                       one month.

    Consequate: 1. _____

                       2. _____

                       3. _____

LEARNING ACTIVITY 11—
SELF-MODIFICATION

Principles are generally more useful after one has used them on oneself. Therefore, include all four aspects of the teaching principles (Pinpoint, Record, Consequate, and Evaluate) and develop some specific procedures to change one of your own behaviors:

1. An inappropriate behavior you choose to decrease in yourself

2. An appropriate behavior you choose to increase in yourself

3. A behavior either appropriate or inappropriate you desire to change in another person: child, supervisor, spouse, roommate, fiance (It is assumed that any attempt to change behaviors of others will be discussed with the person involved and his consent obtained prior to beginning any program.)

Remember to pinpoint the precise behavior(s) that will be recorded and set up an observational recording system with specific time intervals and specific times of the day when recording will take place. Record the occurrence of the behavioral pinpoint for at least five observational periods (in some instances more than one can occur on the same day) so adequate recording (baseline data) can take place prior to the instituting of the consequences. Consequences should be honestly applied and recorded for at least five days or longer before evaluation takes place. If the behavior does not change in the desired direction with the contingencies as applied, then you should "Try, try again" and implement additional consequences immediately.

The Behavioral Assessment Form may be used as a guide to analyze and graph the behavior. This Form has been used by professional behavioral therapists, marriage and family counselors, school psychologists, teachers, and parents. It may be used both to record separate contacts and to summarize a series of contacts and replace lengthy case summaries.

BEHAVIORAL ASSESSMENT FORM

Date _____ (Beginning)   Consequator _____

Date _____ (Present)   Subject _____
                                              (Name)

Page _____ of _____

A.   Pinpoint Analysis   1. _____

             or

                            2. _____

             or

                            3. _____

B.   Record Analysis   _____
     (Increase, Decrease,
     or Stable)   _____

     Recording Problems?   _____

C.   Consequate   1. _____
     (Strategies,
     Plans, Rein-   or
     forcement,   2. _____
     Contingencies)
                    or
                            3. _____

D.   Evaluate   1. _____
     (Present time) or
                            2. _____

                    or
                            3. _____

E.   Additional Notes   _____

     Techniques   _____

     Special Notes,   _____
     Inferences, Information
     from Others or for Others

     Assessment   _____
     (Test Scores,
     Results, Implications)   _____

                               _____

Comments: _____

_____

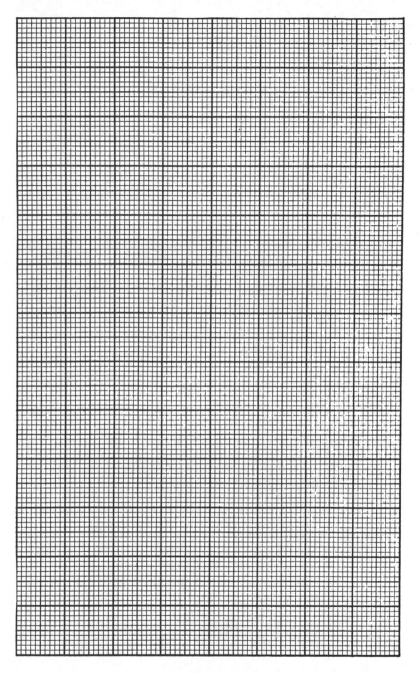

The Behavioral Assessment Form, page 2, is used to graph the changes in behavior recorded on page 1.

LEARNING ACTIVITY 12— CONCEPTUAL BEHAVIORAL ANALYSIS

Instructions:

1. Experienced teachers

   a. Choose from your experience a personal example that you consider an unqualified success. Pinpoint the behaviors involved and analyze your solution in terms of consequences applied. Include some indication of the frequency of the behavior prior to your intervention (Record) and also following (Evaluate).

   b. Choose an example from your prior teaching experience which you consider a failure. Pinpoint the behaviors which were part of the problem, indicate the frequency of the behavior (Record), analyze your consequence(s) in behavioral terms, and discuss the reasons for the failure and what procedures you would now apply to the same case.

2. Prospective teachers

   a. Pinpoint the following problems in behavioral terms.

   b. Indicate potential strategies for short-term and long-term intervention (Consequates).

   (1) Shy, withdrawn girl, non-communicative, dresses in a manner considered weird by her peers

   (2) Twelve-year-old boy recently returned from a state detention center for delinquent youths, fights with others, has chip on shoulder, lives with foster parents who say they don't care

   (3) Six-year-old who dominates entire house by screaming, yelling, throwing severe tantrums; parents are at wits end

   (4) Sixteen-year-old, tenth-grade boy who states he wants to get out of school, failed all classes preceding term

(5) Active "hyperactive" student who is continually engaged in minor and major motor behavior as well as humming, whistling, cracking joints, tapping feet

(6) Student who tests high on achievement scores but fails to complete any assignments to be turned in within the class

LEARNING ACTIVITY 13—
MINI-LESSONS AND OBSERVATIONS

Prepare a short presentation (twenty minutes of teaching the class either social or academic behavior) for actual classroom use in the school to which you have been assigned or to be modeled in front of peers. Work in groups of three with your assigned partners. Two partners will observe, using the teaching observation forms, while one presents until all three have had the opportunity to teach. If you are in front of a regular classroom, remember to coordinate your presentation with the regular classroom teacher and with each other as regards content area.

Analyze the observations in groups of three and graph the teacher approval ratios for both social and academic behavior (see Chapter 9 for instructions and procedures).

LEARNING ACTIVITY 14—
INTERACTION ANALYSIS FOR GROUPS

Participants should be separated into small groups of approximately four to six and will discuss human relations problems while keeping records of group interactions.[2] Prior to discussion, the group should determine the period of time that each record keeper will maintain the record, list each participant's name on the form, decide upon topics to discuss, set the timer, and begin discussions. Following each discussion period, the record keeper should tally the number of positive and negative comments and approving and disapproving bodily expressions and report totals for all group members prior to beginning the next discussion session. The same procedure should be repeated either until the time is used or until all members of the group have had the opportunity to be recorders.

The following form is an indication of how the record will look after each recording session.

Note: An extension of this activity has proved to be very effective in reducing negative comments in teachers' lounges, principals' offices, homes, and work areas. Construct a large chart with the name of each person written down the side of the chart and whenever any other person in the vicinity hears either a positive or negative word or comment from any other member of the group that person goes to the chart and puts a mark under either the positive or negative half of the sheet. This procedure has increased approving statements and decreased disapproving statements.

---

[2] Rotate record keeper approximately every five minutes. A kitchen timer with a bell is most effective as it reminds the group to stay on-task as well as indicates the time to change record keepers.

INTERACTION ANALYSIS FOR GROUP DISCUSSIONS

Date _3/5_

General Topic _School Lunchroom_ Time: Start _3:40 P.M._ End _5:03 PM_

Number in Group _4_ Observation Interval _10 minutes each_

Names of Participants	APPROVAL		DISAPPROVAL	
	Words*	Expressions**	Words‡	Expressions‡‡
Bob Complainer			⊮ ⊮ /	⊮ ///
Jane Ambivalent	⊮ /	///	⊮ /	///
Sam Kindly	⊮ ⊮ ⊮ ⊮	⊮ ⊮ ////		
Suzy Average	////	/	⊮ /	//

* Words - Approval are positive comments, defined as specified solutions to specific problems

** Expressions - Approval are bodily or facial expressions of an approving nature

‡ Words - Disapproval are negative comments, defined as the statement of problems with no specified solutions

‡‡ Expressions - Disapproval are bodily or facial expressions of a disproving nature

LEARNING ACTIVITY 15—
INTERPERSONAL EXTENSIONS

1. Pinpoint fifteen specific problem behaviors discussed in class, small group sessions, or from your own experiences that relate to interpersonal behaviors. Develop and outline sequential consequences based upon behavioral principles which would alleviate, remediate, or prevent additional or similar problems in the future.

2. Discuss solutions in small groups with continued recording and reporting of positive and negative comments.

LEARNING ACTIVITY 16—
ROLE-PLAYING ESSAYS FROM PART I

Participants work in groups of four to six and produce a skit to be presented to other participants which demonstrates principles covered in a single essay from Chapters 1 through 5. Each group is assigned one essay, such as "Is the World Fair?" pages 39–41, or "Who has the Responsibility?" pages 16–17, and other participants are not told which essay was assigned to another group. Thirty minutes preparation time should be sufficient to outline the skit, assign responsibility for props, decide who is going to play what roles, and practice.

Groups present skits and the others, those not presenting, use the form on page 343, recording the name, date, and presentation number, and rate the presentation on all categories. Following the presentation, they attempt to determine which essay was being presented.

Following all presentations, the results of ratings should be given to participants.

INDIVIDUAL PRESENTATION RATING

Observer Name_____

Date_____

Group_____

Presenter No._____

Essay _____	1 Fair	2 Below Average	3 Aver- age	4 Above Aver- age	5 Excel- lent
A. Model					
Specificity of behavior (pinpoint)					
Recording possibilities					
Consequences (logical?)					
Evaluation possibilities					
B. How points got across					
Communication of principles					
Organization					
Presentation (gestures, voice)					
C. Potential for consequences in classroom extensions					
Approval					
Disapproval					
D. Overall rating					
E. Comments					

LEARNING ACTIVITY 17—
SUBJECTIVE VERBAL REPORT

Complete the following Evaluation Form. Attempt to be as objective as possible.

Instructor(s)_____ Course or Workshop Name_____

Date_____   _____

The following statements are designed to allow you to help evaluate your experiences. Please answer each item honestly. *Do not put your name on this paper.*

Read each statement and indicate your agreement or disagreement by writing the appropriate number from the scale in the blank provided at the right.

Answer Scale

1	2	3	4	5	6	7
Disagree Strongly	Disagree	Disagree Slightly	Undecided	Agree Slightly	Agree	Agree Strongly

1. The general objective was accomplished.   1._____

2. Each specific objective was accomplished.   2._____

3. A schedule of specific topics and activities was provided.   3._____

4. There was at least one activity for each specific objective.   4._____

5. Activities were appropriate for   5._____
   the specific objectives.

6. Materials were supplied to   6._____
   implement activities.

7. Instructor(s) stimulated appro-   7._____
   priate participation.

8. Instructor(s) know(s) the   8._____
   subject.

9. Feedback to participants was di-   9._____
   rected toward specific objectives.

10. I intend that my teaching will   10._____
    improve as a result of this course.

11. I intend to try new methods and   11._____
    techniques in the classroom.

12. Other participants have profited   12._____
    by this experience.

13. I would recommend that most   13._____
    other teachers or prospective
    teachers take this course.

The amount of new material I learned from this experience (Circle appropriate choice) was: (a) 0–20%; (b) 21–40%; (c) 41–60%; (d) 61–80%; (e) 81–100%.

Comments:

What did you like about this course or workshop?

What did you dislike about this course or workshop?

GLOSSARY OF BEHAVIORAL
TERMINOLOGY

AN INTRODUCTION TO BEHAVIORAL
TERMINOLOGY

This glossary of terminology is included to serve as a transition from the present volume to the published research found within scientific journals dealing with aspects of behavior modification. Indeed, the entire growth of behavior modification represents a scientific approach to the control and/or modification of behavior.

Behavior refers to the way people react to their environment and what they do to their environment. The behavior modifier generally classifies behavior as operant and respondent. *Respondent behavior* refers to behavior which is involuntary, elicited, or automatic; for example, the eyeblink, sneezing, coughing, and so on. *Operant behavior* refers to behavior which is voluntary and purposeful. Most human behaviors and behaviors labeled as "doing" are considered as operant, e.g., walking, talking, driving. Operant behavior or responses are often a function of more than one stimulus (anything that activates the organism). These responses are modified primarily through their environmental consequences, that is, what happens in the external environment after the behavior occurs. All that is needed to bring about respondent behavior is the proper stimulus. For instance, the touch of a hot iron causes one to jerk the hand away. Behavior modification concerns itself *only* with the external aspects of these behaviors—the observable and the measurable.

The goal of behavior modification is to predict and influence the behavior of an individual organism through scientific laws and procedures. *Laws* are statements concerning the empirical scientific relationship between independent and dependent variables. The *de-*

pendent variable—the response—is the behavior the scientist is interested in controlling. The *independent variable(s)* represents events or occurrences within the environment, or things which will effect change in *dependent variables*. This is the variable which is manipulated or treated with consequent changes on the dependent variable noted. The relationship between these two represents the cause-and-effect relationship in behavioral science. Thus, behavior modification functions on a scientific basis. The cause-and-effect relationship constitutes the primary realm of concern for the behavioral technician. In essence, behavior modifiers maintain that behavior is a result of its consequences. Therefore, if the independent variable (cause) is known and its effect on the dependent variable is known, the behavior modifier is in a more certain position to control and predict behavior.

Behavior modification employs a variety of techniques to change maladaptive behaviors. Some selected principles underlying the use of these techniques and a glossary of key terms follow. A synthesis of techniques used in behavior therapy is given as a means of familiarizing the layman with the approaches, procedures, and principles of several of the most widely used techniques.

The first technique is used primarily to manipulate respondent behavior. Respondent behavior is often accompanied by an emotion of fear which represents a conditioned response to pain. When the emotional component becomes paired with the respondent behavior, *respondent conditioning* is said to have occurred. Technicians employing this technique view many psychological disturbances (maladaptive behavior) as a result of this type of learning. The basic principle of respondent conditioning may be summarized as follows:

> After a *neutral stimulus* (which will not normally bring a specific response, eg., a tone does not cause one to blink the eye) has been paired with an *unconditioned stimulus* which elicits an *unconditioned response*, then the neutral stimulus will also elicit that response or a part of that response. The neutral stimulus now becomes known as the *conditioned stimulus*. For example, a tone is paired with a puff of air near the eye, an eye blink occurs. After several pairings, the tone alone will elicit an eye blink (*conditioned response*).
>
> Related to this principle is the concept of *stimulus generalization* which plays a role in conditioned emotional reactions. Stimulus generalization refers to the fact that stimuli similar to a conditioned stimulus will also elicit the *conditioned response*. The conditioned response is the response which is brought

about by the conditioned stimulus (CS) alone. If the CS was a tone in "C", a tone of A or E might also bring about the conditioned response (CR).

The respondent conditioning paradigm is a model for the development of most learned emotions, the learned guilts, and angers which bring individuals to clinics or to other sources for treatment. According to basic learning principles, conditioned respondents can be eliminated through two processes, extinction and counterconditioning.

Extinction occurs when the conditioned stimulus is presented over and over again without further pairing with the unconditioned stimulus. The conditioned response begins to diminish and finally· ceases to occur at all. When the conditioned response no longer occurs, extinction has taken place. Just as the process of conditioned respondents follows the laws of stimulus generalization, so does the principle of extinction. *Generalization of extinction* is the process wherein, once extinction has occurred, simular stimuli also will not elicit the conditioned response.

A second approach to the modification of maladaptive behaviors employs the principle of *counterconditioning*: there are certain responses that do not "go together," that are incompatible; if one occurs, the other will not. For example, one cannot experience intense "hate" and "love," or excitement and tranquility, at precisely the same time. The concept of structuring an incompatible response is employed by many behavior modifiers in treating conditioned respondents. In essence, counterconditioning is accomplished by selecting a response incompatible with fear, usually something pleasurable to the individual, and gradually introducing some aspect of the conditioned stimuli that no longer evokes the fear reaction. If both techniques are used, the combined forces of reconditioning and extinction at each step will eventually result in the elicitation of a pleasurable response, in place of fear, when the conditioned stimulus is presented.

Desensitization, aligned with counterconditioning, is a very popular technique employed by behavior modifiers. Desensitization is probably successful because of the principle of incompatible behavior, i.e., if a response which prevents anxiety can be made to occur in the presence of the anxiety-evoking stimuli, new responses will then be learned. In systematic desensitization, the response which prevents anxiety is usually complete relaxation, and the "anxiety-evoking stimuli" are the fears and phobias which represent a part of or the essence of the maladaptive behaviors of the individual.

Desensitization consists of eliminating the fears and phobias through extinction, as well as reconditioning the former anxiety-stimuli to the response associated with complete relaxation. This process generally involves three basic operations: (1) training muscle relaxation; (2) the construction of anxiety hierarchies (specific stimuli arranged from least to most anxiety provoking); and (3) counterposing relaxation and anxiety-evoking stimuli from the hierarchies.

The modification of operant behaviors is also based on scientific principles. In order to more clearly understand how operant maladaptive behaviors are modified, a brief overview of how operant behaviors are acquired and maintained is necessary. *Positive reinforcement* (any stimulus which, when it follows a response, will increase the strength or maintain the occurrence of that response) is perhaps the most important aspect of operant modification.

When an operant response is strengthened after it has been succeeded by a positive reinforcer, *operant conditioning* has taken place. Examples of positive reinforcers (*primary* which are necessary for survival and *secondary* which have been learned) are food, water, rest, elimination, sex, attention, praise, money, and so on (see Part III). Operant conditioning occurs when a reinforcing stimulus is made contingent upon a response. For example, one works for a week and then receives a paycheck, one does an assignment and then receives a grade. A conditioned operant response is eliminated by terminating the contingency between that response and the reinforcing stimulus. This process is called *operant extinction*. When the response-reinforcement contingency is no longer in effect, the rate of the response gradually declines and finally ceases. The concepts of *shaping* and *schedule of reinforcement* are important aspects of operant conditioning. The process of *shaping* refers to the reinforcing of successive approximations to a desired behavior until a specific behavior is performed. Schedule of reinforcement simply refers to the temporal arrangement of reinforcement.

Positive reinforcement is of primary importance in effective modification of maladaptive behavior, but there are many situations in which ascertaining an effective reinforcer is not immediately feasible. This poses a problem; however, the use of the *Premack Principle* is one way to overcome this impasse. It has been asserted that, if some specific behavior is more probable than another, then the more probable behavior may be used to reinforce and strengthen the less probable behavior. A contingency is established between the more highly probable behavior and the less probable one (for example, if you finish your math, then you may go to recess).

Operant behaviors are also modified through the use of aversive stimuli. An *aversive stimulus* refers to any stimulus which an organism will escape from, avoid, or terminate; a stimulus causing pain or discomfort. Responses to aversive stimulus may take three possible forms: (1) *Escape behavior* occurs when the individual does something to terminate or actually remove the aversive stimulus. (2) *Avoidance behavior* takes place when the individual does something to postpone or prevent pending aversity. (3) *Punishment* occurs when an aversive stimulus is received as a consequence of a response.

Negative reinforcement is the process whereby the response which is immediately followed by the termination of an aversive stimulus becomes conditioned. In other words, a response which terminates aversity will increase in frequency or strength. The stimulus used in negative reinforcement must be "naturally" aversive to the individual, such as electric shock, or aversive as a result of conditioning.

Maladaptive operant behaviors are modified through the use of punishment, another type of aversive stimulus. The operation of punishment is constituted by either of two events: (1) the individual receives an aversive stimulus as the consequence of a response; or (2) a positive reinforcer is withheld or withdrawn as a consequence of an individual's response. Both of these events result in the suppression or decrease in the probability of the response that produced punishment. This suppression enables the behavior modifier to condition other responses, which are viewed as potentially more "desirable," to the individual's behavior repertoire. Usually these more desirable responses are incompatible with the punished responses, hopefully increasing the probability that they will be emitted on future occasions.

Remaining variables in the control of operant behavior concern *deprivation satiation* and the function of *discriminative stimuli*. The strength or probability of an organism's behavior can be increased or decreased either by depriving the individual of an appropriate stimulus, or by satiating the subject with the reinforcing stimulus. A discriminative stimulus is defined as a stimulus that sets the occasion for reinforced responding: a signal indicating that after the response reinforcement may follow. Thus the probability of the occurrence of an operant response can be made functionally dependent upon the presence or absence of this discriminative stimulus.

In summary, perhaps the most important contribution of the behavior modification movement is its emphasis on an operationally defined, readily observed, and easily measured dependent variable: behavior.

GLOSSARY OF BEHAVIORAL TERMINOLOGY

ABSCISSA: The horizontal reference axis on a graph (chart). In behavior modification the abscissa is usually labeled with a scale that represents the passage of time in some form such as minutes, days, observations, or trials.

ACCOUNTABILITY: Providing an objective demonstration in measurable terms of the effectiveness of given programs. Ex: An increase in reading scores following the introduction of contingency contracting with students.

ADAPTATION: The gradual reduction of responses or responsiveness as an organism adjusts to the introduction of new stimuli into the environment. Ex: Sensory adaptation to a bright light; students tuning out a teacher's loud (or soft) commands when there is no contrast.

ADAPTATION PERIOD: The phase (time period) in any behavioral program during which the subject (or subjects) adjusts to any novel stimuli that have been introduced into the environment. Ex: The time necessary for a class to adapt to observers prior to collection of baseline data.

ADAPTIVE BEHAVIOR: Behavior which serves to insure survival or is considered appropriate in specified societal contexts such as school.

ADDICTION: A condition in which cessation of reinforcement (usually physiological) produces physical or psychological problems of abstinence.

APPLIED RESEARCH: Research that is directed toward an analysis of variables that can be effective in improving behavior under study. Applied research is often conducted in natural settings.

APPROVAL: Any observable endorsement of behavior.

AVERSIVE CONTROL: The withdrawal or presentation of an aversive stimulus which then maintains or increases the frequency of a response. Three types of aversive control exist.

1. Escape, in which the organism terminates the aversive stimulus after it has begun.
2. Avoidance, in which the organism postpones the beginning of aversive stimuli.
3. Punishment, in which responses are followed by an aversive stimulus.

AVERSIVE STIMULUS: Any stimulus which an organism will escape from, avoid, or terminate.

BACK-UP REINFORCER: An object or event that has already demonstrated its reinforcing effect on an individual which is received in exchange for a specific number of tokens, points, or other more generalized reinforcers.

BASELINE: A stable, usually recoverable, performance (five or more observations) upon which the effects of experimental variables can be assessed. (Record phase.)

BEHAVIOR: Any act of an organism, either internal or external, that can be observed and/or measured. Any behavior may have one of four relationships to the environment.

1. Dependent, when the event *must*, by nature of the situation, occur following the behavior. Ex: Because the water must cease running from the faucet when the handle is turned, the subsequent cessation of the flow of water is said to be dependent upon behavior of turning the handle.
2. Contingent, when the event does follow the behavior but *need not* do so. Reinforcement is generally contingent upon behavior. After reinforcement has occurred a contingency is said to have been established. Ex: If one is asked to turn off the water and does so, the behavior is said to be contingent.
3. Superstitious, because behavior has nothing to do with the reinforcer. Ex: The fondling of a "good luck piece" does not cause "good luck" but is occasionally reinforced with chance good fortune.
4. Random, when the behavior has no logical relationship to the environment and all stimuli are neutral. Ex: Tuneless whistling while daydreaming.

BEHAVIOR MODIFICATION: The changing of behavior (increasing or decreasing frequency of occurrence) using a combination (schedule) of reinforcement (positive and/or negative) and/or nonreinforcement. Generally represents the programmed use of techniques based on scientifically derived principles of learning to produce observable changes in behavior.

BEHAVIOR THERAPY: The application of learning theory techniques for the purpose of changing maladaptive behavior.

BEHAVIORAL APPROACH: An approach in which values and/or ideas, in order to be considered, are operationally defined into directly observable and measurable behaviors. The assumption is made that most behavior, including behavior defined as abnormal, is learned.

BEHAVIORAL CONTRAST: A phenomenon that may occur if a behavior is placed on one reinforcement schedule under one stimulus condition and on another schedule under a different stimulus condition. In such a situation a decrease in the rate of the behavior under one stimulus-correlated condition may be accompanied by an increase in the rate under the other stimulus-correlated condition.

BEHAVIORAL DIMENSIONS: Measurable descriptive characteristics of behavior such as frequency, intensity, duration, and topography.

BEHAVIORAL GOAL: The specification of the set of responses to be emitted by the subject at the completion of a given behavior modification program. Usually the criteria for achievement of the goals and conditions under which the responses are to be emitted are also specified. When limited to academic instruction, this is often referred to as the behavioral objective.

CHAINING: A series of two or more responses joined together into a complex behavioral sequence by stimuli which act as both discriminative stimuli and conditioned reinforcers. For instance, discriminative stimulus—response—reinforcement—response to reinforcement—reinforcement for last response—etc. Therefore one operant response leads to another in a linking of the three-term paradigm (discriminative stimulus, response, reinforcement) which permits the development of a series of operants of indefinite length. Ex: Child is offered candy—takes candy and says "Thank you"—Child given a smile and "You're welcome"—Child engages in eye contact and smiles—Child is given a hug.

CONDITIONED AVERSIVE STIMULUS (See Conditioned Stimulus.)

CONDITIONED REFLEX: A reflex which is elicited by a formerly neutral stimulus which has been paired with the naturally eliciting stimulus.

CONDITIONED REINFORCER: Some stimuli acquire the power to reinforce (strengthen or maintain) behavior through being paired with the delivery of primary, or stronger conditioned reinforcers, within the experience of the organism. These are called secondary or conditioned reinforcers. Ex: Money is useless, unless one can exchange it for goods. To many people, however, money is a *conditioned reinforcer* because *it* has become the reward.

CONDITIONED STIMULUS: A formerly neutral stimulus which has been paired with an unconditioned stimulus or a reinforcing stimulus (either positively or negatively) and has taken on the reinforcing properties of the stimulus with which it has been paired.

CONDITIONING: A neutral stimulus may acquire reinforcing properties through temporal association with another reinforcer. This process is called conditioning. (See Operant Conditioning and Respondent Conditioning.)

CONFOUNDING VARIABLES: Variables that are operating in an experimental study, which make the effects of the experimental manipulation on the independent variable difficult to evaluate precisely.

CONSEQUATE: To apply consequences (reinforcement) following the occurrence of behavior.

CONTINGENCY: The relationship between the behavior of an organism and environmental events (generally reinforcing) which follow the behavior and either increase or decrease the probability of similar behavior in the future.

CONTINGENCY CONTRACT: A written contract specifying subsequent behavioral contingencies between persons involved. Ex: Completion of school assignments will result in money and special privileges from parents and free time in school.

CONTINGENCY CONTROL: The ability to manipulate the environmental consequences of a given behavior in order to achieve a specific behavioral goal.

CONTINGENT: The relationship between a specific response and environmental consequence is said to be contingent if the consequence follows the behavior and subsequently has the effect of increasing, maintaining, decreasing, or eliminating behavior. (See Contingency.)

CONTINUOUS FIELD: A continuum of stimuli.

CONTINUOUS RESPONSE: A response that does not have a clearly discriminable beginning or end.

CRITERION: Specification of a predetermined level of behavioral performance that is to be achieved. Criteria are used to specify goals and to evaluate the success of behavioral programs.

CUE: A stimulus used to help an individual remember to produce any specified response which may then be reinforced. (See Discriminative Stimulus.)

DEPENDENT VARIABLE: A phenomenon that varies in any way (appears, disappears, or changes) as a function of any application, removal, or variation in other variables (independent). A dependent variable is usually monitored or measured in behavior modification studies.

DEPRIVATION: The removal of the occurrence of a stimulus.

DIFFERENTIAL PUNISHMENT: The extinguishing of certain behaviors while others are being reinforced. (See also Differential Reinforcement.)

DIFFERENTIAL REINFORCEMENT: The strengthening of certain behaviors while others are being extinguished. A programmed contingency whereby specified responses are reinforced while others are not. (See also Differential Punishment.)

DIFFERENTIAL REINFORCEMENT OF HIGH RATES (DRH):   A schedule that involves the selective contingent reinforcement of a grouping of responses which occur in rapid succession. High rates are differentially reinforced while low rates are not.

DIFFERENTIAL REINFORCEMENT OF LOW RATES (DRL):   A schedule in which responses that are spaced relatively far apart in time are selectively reinforced. Low rates are differentially reinforced while high rates are not.

DIFFERENTIAL REINFORCEMENT OF OTHER BEHAVIORS (DRO):   A procedure in which a reinforcer follows any response an individual makes, except for one particular response. Thus, the individual receives scheduled reinforcement except when he engages in a particular specified behavior. This procedure results in a decrease of the specified behavior.

DISAPPROVAL: Any observable consequence to behavior defined negatively by the organism receiving it.

DISCRETE STIMULI: Separate presentation of stimuli.

DISCRIMINATIVE STIMULUS (S^d):   An environmental event which sets the occasion for responses which are followed by reinforcement. The probability of the response is high only when certain environmental events (discriminative stimuli) are present. Whenever the discriminative stimulus (S^d) is present, specific responses may then be reinforced. (See Stimulus Control.)

ELICITING STIMULI: Environmental events which regularly precede responses. They elicit relatively fixed and stereotyped responses. Ex: The bell in Pavlov's classic dog experiment.

EMOTION: A complex response elicited and occasioned by environmental conditions and composed of both operants and respondents. Ex: Love or sadness.

ENVIRONMENT: The sum total of an organism's surroundings (stimuli).

ERRORLESS DISCRIMINATION PROCEDURE: Teaching the acquisition of a discrimination by carefully arranging a sequence of discriminative stimuli so that only correct responses are occasioned.

Event Sampling: An observational procedure in which the frequency or duration of a specific discrete behavior, such as times tardy or number of pages completed, is recorded over a specific extended period of time. The specific time interval may be, for instance, a classroom period or day.

Extinction: A procedure in which the reinforcement for a previously reinforced behavior is discontinued. The process whereby a conditioned response is reduced to its preconditioned level or strength, often approaching or reaching zero magnitude or frequency. The process of extinction in the case of respondents involves continuing presentation of the conditioned stimulus without any further pairing with the unconditioned stimulus. With operant responses, extinction results when responding is no longer followed by reinforcement.

Fading: The gradual removal of discriminative stimuli such as cues and prompts.

Fixed Interval Reinforcement   (See Schedules of Reinforcement.)

Fixed Ratio Reinforcement   (See Schedules of Reinforcement.)

Frequency: The number of occurrences per given time period.

Functional Analysis: The determination of the external variables of which behavior is a function. (See also Functional Relation.)

Functional Relation: A relation in which the occurrence of event B consistently follows the occurrence of event A or is dependent upon the previous occurrence of event A.

Functional Relationship: A lawful relationship between two variables. In behavior modification, a dependent variable and a given procedure are functionally related if the behavior systematically varies as a function of the application of the procedure.

Generalization: Responding to two or more discriminatively different stimuli as if they were the same. Generalization involves the following components:

1. Stimulus Generalization—the spread of the effects of reinforcement (or of other operations) in the presence of one stimulus to other stimuli that differ from the original stimulus along one or more dimensions.
2. Response Generalization (induction)—the spread of effects of reinforcement to responses outside of a specific response may be accompanied by other responses that are similar

but not identical to the reinforced response.
3. Generalization Training—a procedure designed to facilitate the occurrence of generalization.

GENERALIZED REINFORCER: A conditioned reinforcer that is effective over a wide range of deprivation conditions as a result of having been paired with a variety of previously established reinforcers.

HABITUATION: A gradual decline in the magnitude of a respondent over repeated occurrences. Ex: A nurse's aversion to the sight of blood decreases as she is exposed to repeated viewings of open wounds.

IMITATION: Matching the behavior of a model

INCOMPATIBLE BEHAVIOR: Any two or more behaviors which, by the very nature of one, cannot exist with the other. Sometimes the term is used to include not only behavior that cannot occur simultaneously with another, but also behavior that interferes with other behavior. Ex: Speaking and being quiet.

INCOMPATIBLE RESPONSE: A response whose occurrence precludes the simultaneous occurrence of another response. Ex: A musician cannot be both flat and sharp at the same time.

INCONSISTENCY: Not applying the previously specified consequences to the occurrences of a behavior, applying the consequences when the behavior has not occurred, applying inappropriate consequences (approval following inappropriate behavior or disapproval for appropriate behavior), or applying appropriate and inappropriate consequences simultaneously.

INDEPENDENT VARIABLE: The factor purposely manipulated in a behavior modification program to ascertain its relationship with the dependent variable. Sometimes thought of as the "cause" of the "effect" on the dependent measure.

INTERMITTENT REINFORCEMENT (See Schedules of Reinforcement.)

INTERRESPONSE REINFORCEMENT: The amount of time which passes between two responses.

INTERVAL REINFORCEMENT ·(See Schedules of Reinforcement.)

LATENCY: The time between the occurrence of the stimulus and the occurrence of the response.

LEARNING HISTORY: The sum of an individual's behaviors that have been conditioned or modified as a result of environmental events.

LINK: Each unit of a chain, composed of a discriminative stimulus, response, and a reinforcer.

MODELING: A technique whereby the behavior which is to be taught is demonstrated for the learner and any semblance of the goal behavior is initially rewarded. The criterion for reinforcement is then gradually increased until the goal behavior is obtained. Sometimes no shaping is required.

MULTIPLE BASELINE DESIGN: An experimental design (usually single-subject) that involves:

1. Obtaining base rates on several dependent behaviors

2. Applying the independent variable to one of the dependent behaviors until it is substantially changed while the other dependent behaviors are left free to vary

3. Applying the independent variable to a second dependent variable as in No. 2 above. This procedure is continued until it is demonstrated that each behavior systematically changes when the independent variable is applied to it.

NEGATIVE REINFORCER: A stimulus whose removal, if paired with the occurrence of a behavior, will increase the probability of occurrence of the behavior. Many times the term aversive stimulus is used in place of negative reinforcer. (See also Aversive Control.)

NEGATIVE TRANSFER (See Transfer.)

NEUTRAL STIMULI: All those environmental events which, at any given moment, do not elicit any behavior change, whether they precede, accompany, or follow responses.

OFF-TASK: Any behavior that interferes or is incompatible with previously defined situational expectations.

ON-TASK: Behavior consistent with definitional classes of behavior previously defined.

OPERANT: A behavior emitted by an organism that operates on or changes the environment in a very particular way.

OPERANT BEHAVIOR: Operants have the potential to produce stimulus events which alter the behavior's future occurrence. Operant behavior is behavior that is controlled by consequences. Operant behavior is mediated by the central nervous system and involves, primarily, the skeletal musculature. Operant responses act on, and interact with, the environment and are controlled and modified by the principles of operant conditioning. Operant responding includes not only the gross motor movements of the organism but also its verbal behavior. Most of the daily, ongoing behavior of the individual as he interacts with his environment and other people is operant in nature.

OPERANT CONDITIONING: The changing of the frequency of an occurrence of a behavior by modifying the consequences of that behavior.

OPERANT LEVEL: The strength of an operant before any known reinforcement; the unconditioned level of an operant (response), or the rate at which responses occur before they have been reinforced. Generally, baseline or base rate recording is a record of the operant level.

OPERANT REINFORCEMENT: The potential of operants to produce events which will strengthen their future occurrence; following operant behavior with consequences of a reinforcing nature.

ORDINATE: The vertical reference axis on a graph. In behavior modification, the ordinate is usually labeled with a scale that measures the dependent behavior, for example, frequency, percentage of responses, or rate.

OSCILLATION: Alternation of emotional responses usually found during the process of extinction.

PAIRING: The act of associating one stimulus with another.

PAVLOVIAN CONDITIONING (See Respondent Conditioning.)

PAY-OFF: That which rewards the occurrence of a behavior.

POSITIVE REINFORCEMENT: A stimulus that, when presented as a consequence of a response, results in an increase or maintenance of that response.

PREMACK PRINCIPLE: The principle that contingent access to high frequency behaviors serves as a reinforcer for the performance of low frequency behaviors.

PRIMARY REINFORCERS: Reinforcing stimuli that have the effect of maintaining or perpetuating life, such as food, water, elimination, and warmth.

PROBE: A phase in a behavior modification experiment designed to test the effect of a given procedure. A reversal is a probe since it removes the behavioral procedure for a brief period of time to test the procedure's effects. (See also Reversal Procedure.)

PROGRAMMED INSTRUCTION: The selection and arrangement of educational content based upon principles of human learning.

PROMPT: An auxiliary discriminative stimulus that is applied to help occasion a given response. Prompts are usually faded before the terminal goal is judged as having been achieved.

PUNISHING STIMULUS: A contingent stimulus that, when presented, results in a reduction in the occurrence of the dependent behavior.

PUNISHMENT: The potential of all operants to produce events which will *weaken* their future occurrence. There are two broad types of punishment:
1. Positive punishment—those events which will weaken an operant's future occurrence by the *presentation* of stimuli; and
2. Negative punishment—those events which will weaken an operant's future occurrence by the *removal* of stimuli.

RATE OF RESPONDING: The number of occurrences per unit time of the response.

RATIO REINFORCEMENT   (See Schedules of Reinforcement.)

REFLEX: A physical response (behavior) mediated by the autonomic nervous system.

REINFORCEMENT: The contingent use of a stimulus resulting in an increase or maintenance of behavior. All operants have the potential to produce events that will strengthen their future occurrence. There are two broad types of reinforcement:
1. Positive reinforcement—those events which will strengthen an operant's future occurrence by the *presentation* of stimuli; and
2. Negative reinforcement—those events which will strengthen an operant's future occurrence by the *removal* of stimuli.

REINFORCEMENT DENSITY: Frequency or rate with which responses are reinforced. The lower the ratio or shorter the interval required by a given reinforcement schedule, the denser the reinforcement.

REINFORCEMENT HISTORY: The sum total of an organism's past.

REINFORCER: A stimulus, the contingent use of which results in the increase or maintenance of the dependent behavior. The stimulus will increase the probability of the response which precedes it (see Approval, Disapproval, and Reinforcement).

REINFORCING INCOMPATIBLE BEHAVIOR: A behavioral procedure that increases the occurrence of a behavior or behaviors that cannot coexist with another, usually "undesired," behavior.

RELIABILITY: Refers to consistency of measurement. It is usually calculated by comparing how well two or more independent observers agree among themselves. It is often calculated and reported in percentages by dividing the number of agreements by the number of agreements plus disagreements and then multiplying the fraction by one hundred. Reliability measures should be reported for each phase of a single-subject design.

REPLICATE: To repeat an experimental procedure or finding.

RESPONDENT: A regular response from all normal organisms of the same species to the same eliciting stimulus. Ex: Salivation.

RESPONDENT BEHAVIOR: All respondents are a function (elicited or maintained) of antecedent stimulus events.

RESPONDENT CONDITIONING (Classical or Pavlovian Conditioning): The process whereby eliciting stimuli increase the frequency of respondents (usually a physiological change). A neutral stimulus, when associated repeatedly with an unconditioned stimulus which reliably elicits a specific response, comes to elicit a "new" response, which is similar in some respect to that produced originally by the unconditioned stimulus.

RESPONSE: A physical reaction in time and space to an environmental event, generally synonymous with behavior and, in behavioral research, both observable and measurable (fines, etc.).

RESPONSE COST: A procedure in which there is contingent withdrawal of specified amounts of available reinforcers.

RESPONSE DIFFERENTIATION: The process whereby reinforcement alters some specific property of an operant such as its duration, intensity, or topography; a procedure that reinforces a subset of specific behavior, conforming to specified behavioral dimensions.

REVERSAL PROCEDURE: A technique that involves the removal of the procedure in order to test the effectiveness of the procedure. For instance, one frequently utilized experimental design involves: (1) obtaining a base rate of the dependent variable; (2) applying the independent variable until a substantial change in the dependent variable is recorded; (3) the reversal, a discontinuation of the independent variable and a reintroduction of the conditions in effect during the baseline period, until a substantial reversal in the value of the dependent variable is obtained; and (4) a reapplication of the independent variable to reinstate the change. (Often abbreviated as ABAB design.) Such a procedure is used to demonstrate a *functional relationship* between the *independent* and *dependent* variables.

SATIATION: The process whereby a reinforcer temporarily ceases to strengthen an operant. A reduction in performance occurs generally after a large amount of reinforcement.

362

SCALLOP: A pattern on a response record that is characterized by a sequence of positively accelerating curves.

SCHEDULE OF REINFORCEMENT: The rule followed by the environment in determining which among the many occurrences of a response will be reinforced. Schedules include three general types—ratio, interval, and mixed.

1. RATIO SCHEDULE OF REINFORCEMENT: A schedule in which reinforcement is made contingent upon the emission of a number of responses before one response is reinforced. One version is the Fixed Ratio (FR) schedule, when a specific number of responses must occur prior to the reinforced response. For example, an FR-3 schedule indicates that each third response is contingently reinforced. The other type is the Variable Ratio (VR) schedule, when a variable number of responses must occur prior to the reinforced response. The number of responses usually varies about a specified average. For example, a VR-6 means that six performances on the average are required prior to each reinforcement.

2. INTERVAL SCHEDULE OF REINFORCEMENT: A schedule in which reinforcement is made contingent upon the passage of time before the response is reinforced. It could be a Fixed Interval (FI) schedule, when a particular response is scheduled for reinforcement following the passage of a specific amount of time, and that time is held constant. For example, an FI-3 indicates that reinforcement follows the first occurrence of the primed response after three minutes have passed. Or one might establish a Variable Interval (VI) Schedule in which a variable time interval must occur prior to the reinforced response. The time interval usually varies within a specified average. For example, a VI-6 indicates that an average of six minutes passes before the primed response receives contingent reinforcement.

3. MIXED SCHEDULES OF REINFORCEMENT: Combinations of interval and ratio schedules. Most school and home reinforcement of necessity is mixed.

SHAPING: Taking the behaviors that the organism already has in his repertoire and reinforcing those that are similiar to the goal behavior, gradually requiring that the organism's behavior be more and more similar to the goal behavior to be reinforced. This is continued until the goal behavior is obtained. New behaviors may be developed by systematic reinforcement of successive approximations toward a specified goal. (See also Successive Approximations.)

SINGLE-SUBJECT EXPERIMENTAL DESIGNS: Research designs developed for evaluating the effects of one or more independent variable(s) on the behavior of a single organism.

SOCIAL REINFORCER: A conditioned reinforcing stimulus mediated by another individual within a social context.

SPONTANEOUS RECOVERY: The reappearance of a response—previously eliminated by means of an extinction procedure—following a time interval without any intervening reinforced responses.

STIMULUS: An environmental event.

STIMULUS CHANGE: A behavioral procedure that employs discriminative stimuli, or stimuli that occasion or inhibit specific behaviors.

STIMULUS CONTROL: After an operant has been reinforced in the presence of a particular stimulus a number of times, that stimulus comes to control the operant. Control of this sort is achieved when responses are reinforced in the presence of a specified stimulus and not others and the stimulus controls the probability that the response will be emitted.

STIMULUS DELTA (S^Δ): A stimulus in the presence of which a given response is not reinforced. This kind of discriminative stimulus, like S^d, is said to be established when, after several pairings with the occurrence or nonoccurrence of reinforcement, its presence or absence is accompanied by reliable changes in response.

STIMULUS DEPRIVATION: The process whereby the reinforcing power of a stimulus is restored by depriving the organism of it for a period of time.

STIMULUS DISCRIMINATION: Responding to similar stimuli which approximate the original stimulus.

STIMULUS GENERALIZATION: An increase in the frequency of responding which is dependent upon the stimulus.

STIMULUS OVERLOAD: When a response decreases in frequency because of too large a frequency or magnitude of reinforcement, stimulus overload has occurred.

SUBJECT CONFOUNDING VARIABLES: Subject characteristics (demographic, previous learning history, and present behaviors) that have not been controlled in an experiment but may effect changes in the occurrences of the dependent variable. Single-subject designs control for subject confounding variables by comparing the subject's performance under one condition with his performance under other conditions.

SUBSET OF BEHAVIOR: The group of simple response components that compose a more complex behavior.

SUCCESSIVE APPROXIMATIONS: Behavioral elements or subsets, each of which more and more closely resembles the specified terminal behavior. (See Shaping.)

SUPERSTITIOUS BEHAVIOR: Behavior that is not based on contingencies that are actually in existence but is reinforced by chance. Ex: A child might wish on a star for a bicycle and believe that his wish caused him to get it for his birthday.

SUPPLEMENTARY REINFORCERS: Reinforcers used in addition to the major contingent reinforcer.

TARGET BEHAVIOR: A behavioral goal.

TERMINAL BEHAVIOR: The behavior that is achieved at the end of a behavior modification program. The terminal behavior is described according to all its relevant behavioral dimensions and is usually assigned a criterion by which an acceptable level of performance is to be judged.

TIC: An habitual spasmodic movement of particular muscles.

TIME SAMPLING: A direct observational procedure in which the observer records the presence or absence of the behaviors to be changed, within uniform time intervals. For example, an observer may observe for 10 seconds and record during the following 5 seconds the occurrence or nonoccurrence of the subject's behavior. This procedure may continue for a specified 30 minutes each day. Observers may sample any predetermined time periods.

TIME OUT: Time out from positive reinforcement is a procedure in which access to the sources of various forms of reinforcement are removed for a particular period, contingent upon the emission of a response. The opportunity to receive reinforcement is contingently removed for a specified time. Either the behaving individual is contingently removed from the reinforcing environment or the reinforcing environment is contingently removed from him for some stipulated duration.

TIME OUT ROOM, TIME OUT BOOTH: A facility that is arranged in such a manner that the individual placed therein has little likelihood of receiving reinforcement from the environment. The place in which time out from positive reinforcement occurs.

TOKEN REINFORCER: An object that can be exchanged at a later time for another reinforcing item or activity. The extent to which tokens are reinforcing or take on the properties of a generalized reinforcer is dependent on the individual's experience and on what back-up items are available.

TOPOGRAPHY: The physical nature of the responses which compose the operant. Ex: How hard the lever was pushed, by which hand, and how long a time it stayed depressed, the movement of the body during observed motor off-task.

TRANSFER: The effect that learning a task has on the learning of another task. If having learned the first task facilitates learning the second task, it is called *positive* transfer; if learning the first task interferes with learning the second task, then it is called *negative* transfer.

UNCONDITIONED REINFORCER: When a stimulus can reinforce a behavior without the organism having had any previous experience, the reinforcer is said to be a primary or unconditioned reinforcer. Ex: The smell of food produces salivation.

UNCONDITIONED RESPONSE: A response which nearly inevitably follows a specific stimulus. This is the *unconditioned* stimulus of that response.

UNCONDITIONED STIMULUS (See Unconditioned Response.)

VARIABLE INTERVAL REINFORCEMENT (See Schedules of Reinforcement.)

VARIABLE RATIO REINFORCEMENT (See Schedules of Reinforcement.)

SELECTED BIBLIOGRAPHY

BOOKS

Ackerman, J. M. *Operant Conditioning Techniques for the Classroom Teacher.* Glenview, Ill.: Scott, Foresman & Co., 1971.

Ayllon, T., and Azrin, N. H. *The Token Economy: A Motivational System for Therapy and Rehabilitation.* Appleton-Century-Crofts, 1969.

Bandura, A. *Principles of Behavior Modification.* New York: Holt, Rinehart and Winston, 1969.

Bandura, A., and Walters, R. H. *Social Learning and Personality Development.* New York: Holt, Rinehart and Winston, 1963.

Becker, W. C. *An Empirical Basis for Change in Education.* Chicago: Science Research Associates, 1971.

―――. *Parents are Teachers: A Child Management Program.* Champaign, Ill.: Research Press, 1971.

Becker, W. C., Engelmann, S., and Thomas, D. R. *Teaching: A Course in Applied Psychology.* Chicago: Science Research Associates, 1971.

Benson, A. M. (ed.) *Modifying Deviant Social Behaviors in Various Classroom Settings.* Eugene, Ore.: Department of Special Education, University of Oregon, 1969.

Bereiter, C., and Engelmann, S. *Teaching Disadvantaged Children in the Preschool.* Englewood Cliffs, N.J.: Prentice-Hall, 1966.

Bijou, S. W., and Baer, D. M. *Child Development.* Vol. I: *A Systematic and Empirical Theory.* New York: Appleton-Century-Crofts, 1961.

―――. *Child Development.* Vol. II: *Universal Stage of Infancy.* New York: Appleton-Century-Crofts, 1965.

―――. *Child Development: Readings in Experimental Analysis.* New York: Appleton-Century-Crofts, 1967.

Blackham, G., and Silberman, A. *Modification of Child Behavior: Principles and Procedures.* Belmont, Calif.: Wadsworth Publishing Co., Inc., 1970.

Bradfield, R. W. *Behavior Modification: The Human Effort.* San Rafael, Calif.: Dimensions Publishing Co., 1970.

Browning, R. M., and Stover, D. O. *Behavior Modification in Child Treatment: An Experimental and Clinical Approach.* Chicago: Aldine Publishing Co., 1970.

Buckley, N. K., and Walker, H. M. *Modifying Classroom Behavior: A Manual of Procedures for Classroom Teachers.* Champaign, Ill.: Research Press, 1971.

Burgess, R. L., and Bushell, D., Jr. *Behavioral Sociology.* New York: Columbia University Press, 1969.

Bushell, D., Jr. *Classroom Behavior: A Little Book for Teachers.* Englewood Cliffs, N.J.: Prentice-Hall, Inc. 1973.

Catania, C. A. (ed.) *Contemporary Research in Operant Behavior.* Glenview, Ill.: Scott, Foresman & Co., 1968.

Deibert, A. N., and Harmon, A. J. *New Tools for Changing Behavior.* Champaign, Ill.: Research Press, 1970.

Eysenck, H. J., and Rachman, S. (eds.) *The Causes and Cures of Neurosis.* San Diego, Calif.: Robert R. Knapp, 1965.

Fargo, G., Behrns, C., and Nolan, P. *Behavior Modification in the Classroom.* Belmont, Calif.: Wadsworth Publishing Co., Inc., 1970.

Ferster, C. B., and Perrott, M. D. *Behavior Principles.* New York: Meredith Corp., 1968, 69–137.

Fielding, L. T. *The Modification of Human Behavior.* Minneapolis: 1970.

Franks, C. M. (ed.) *Behavior Therapy: Appraisal and Status.* New York: McGraw-Hill, 1969.

Gardner, W. I. *Behavior Modification: Applications in Mental Retardation.* Chicago: Aldine-Atherton, 1971.

Gelfand, D. M. *Social Learning in Childhood.* Belmont, Calif.: Brooks/Cole, 1969.

Guerney, B. F., Jr. (ed.) *Psychotherapeutic Agents: New Roles for Nonprofessionals, Parents, and Teachers.* New York: Holt, Rinehart and Winston, 1969.

Hall, R. V. *Managing Behavior.* Part I: *Behavior Modification-The Measurement of Behavior.* Part II: *Behavior Modification-Basic Principles.* Part III: *Behavior Modification-Application in School and Home.* Lawrence, Kan.: H & H Enterprises, 1971.

Harris, M. B. *Classroom Uses of Behavior Modification*. Columbus, O.: Charles E. Merrill, 1972.

Hewett, F. *The Emotionally Disturbed Child in the Classroom*. Boston: Allyn & Bacon, Inc., 1968.

Holland, J. G., and Skinner, B. F. *The Analysis of Behavior*. New York: McGraw-Hill, 1961.

Homme, L. E., Casanyi, A. P., Gonzales, M. A., and Rechs, J. R. *How to Use Contingency Contracting in the Classroom*. Champaign, Ill.: Research Press, 1969.

Honig, W. K. *Operant Behavior: Areas of Research and Application*. New York: Appleton-Century-Crofts, 1966.

Hunter, M. *Reinforcement, Theory into Practice*. El Segundo, Calif.: TIP Publications, 1967.

Johnson, L. V., and Bany, M. A. *Classroom Management*. New York: Macmillan, 1970.

Kanfer, F. H., and Phillips, J. S. *Learning Foundations of Behavior Therapy*. New York: Wiley and Sons, 1970.

Krasner, L., and Ullmann, L. P. *Behavior Influence and Personality*. New York: Holt, Rinehart and Winston, 1973.

———. (eds.) *Research in Behavior Modification*. New York: Holt, Rinehart and Winston, 1965.

Krumboltz, J. D., and Krumboltz, H. B. *Changing Children's Behavior*. Englewood Cliffs, N.J.: Prentice-Hall Inc., 1972.

Krumboltz, J. D., and Thoresen, C. E. *Behavioral Counseling: Cases and Techniques*. New York: Holt, Rinehart and Winston, 1969.

Kunzelmann, H. P. (ed.) *Precision Teaching: An Initial Training Sequence*. Seattle, Wash.: Special Child Publications, Inc., 1970.

Lovibond, S. H. *Conditioning and Enuresis*. Oxford, England: Pergamon Press, Ltd., 1964.

McGinnies, E., & Ferster, C. B. *The Reinforcement of Social Behavior*. Boston: Houghton Mifflin Co., 1971.

McIntire, R. W. *For Love of Children: Behavioral Psychology for Parents*. Del Mar, Calif.: CRM Books, 1970.

Madsen, C. K., Greer, R. D., and Madsen, C. H., Jr. *Research in Music Behavior: Modifying Music Behavior in the Classroom*. New York: Teachers College Press, 1974.

Madsen, C. H., Jr., and Madsen, C. K. *Teaching/Discipline: Behavioral Principles Toward a Positive Approach*. Boston: Allyn & Bacon, Inc., 1970.

Malott, R. W., and Whaley, D. L. *Elementary Principles of Be-*

havior, Vols. I and II. Kalamazoo, Mich.: Department of Psychology, Western Michigan University, 1968.

Meacham, M. L., and Wiesen, A. E. *Changing Classroom Behavior: A Manual for Precision Teaching*. Scranton, Pa., International Textbook Co., 1969.

Mehrabian, A. *Tactics of Social Influence*. Englewood Cliffs, N.J. Prentice-Hall, Inc., 1970.

Mertens, G., Luker, A., and Boltuck, C. *Behavioral Science Behaviorally Taught*. Minneapolis: Burgess Publishing Co., 1968.

Mink, O. G. *The Behavior Change Process*. New York: Harper & Row, 1970.

Neisworth, J. T., Deno, S. L., and Jenkins, J. R. *Student Motivation and Classroom Management*. Philadelphia, Pa.: Behavior Techniques, Inc., 1969.

Neuringer, C., and Michael, J. L. (eds.) *Behavior Modification in Clinical Psychology*. New York: Appleton-Century-Crofts, 1970.

Nolan, P. *Behavior Modification in the Classroom*. Belmont, Calif.: Wadsworth Publishing Co., 1970.

O'Leary, K. D., and O'Leary, S. G. *Classroom Management: The Successful Use of Behavior Modification*. New York: Pergamon Press, 1972.

Patterson, G. R., and Guillion, M. E. *Living with Children: New Methods for Parents and Teachers*. Champaign, Ill.: Research Press, 1968.

Quay, H. C., and Werry, J. S. (eds.) *Behavior Disorders of Children*. New York: Wiley, 1972.

Reese, E. P. *The Analysis of Human Operant Behavior*. Dubuque, Iowa: W. C. Brown, Co., 1966.

Reynolds, G. S. *A Primer of Operant Conditioning*. Chicago: Scott, Foresman and Co., 1968.

Rickard, H. C. *Behavioral Intervention in Human Problems*. New York: Pergamon Press, 1971.

Schaeffer, H. H., and Martin, P. L. *Behavioral Therapy*. New York: McGraw-Hill, 1969.

Skinner, B. F. *Beyond Freedom and Dignity*. New York: Knopf, Inc., 1971.

———. *Science and Human Behavior*. New York: The Macmillan Co., 1953.

———. *The Technology of Teaching*. New York: Appleton-Century-Crofts, 1968.

Sloan, H., and MacAulay, B. (eds.) *Operant Procedures in Remedial*

Speech and Language Training. Boston: Houghton Mifflin, 1968.

Smith, J. M., and Smith, D. E. P. *Child Management: A Program for Parents.* Ann Arbor, Mich.: Ann Arbor Publishers, 1966.

Staats, A. W. *Child Learning, Intelligence, and Personality. Principles of a Behavioral Interaction Approach.* New York: Harper & Row, 1971.

Sulzer, B., and Mayer, G. R. *Behavior Modification Procedures for School Personnel.* Chicago: Dryden Press, 1972.

Tharp, R. G., and Wetzel, R. J. *Behavior Modification in the Natural Environment.* New York: Academic Press, 1969.

Thomas, E. J. (ed.) *The Socio-behavioral Approach and Applications to Social Work.* New York: Council on Social Work Education, 1967.

Ullmann, L. P., and Krasner, L. (eds.) *Case Studies in Behavior Modification.* New York: Holt, Rinehart and Winston, 1965.

————. *A Psychological Approach to Abnormal Behavior.* Englewood Cliffs, N.J.: Prentice-Hall, Inc., 1969.

Ulrich, R., Stachnik, T., and Mabry, J. (eds.) *Control of Human Behavior.* Vol. I. Chicago: Scott, Foresman and Co., 1966.

————. *Control of Human Behavior.* Vol. II: *From Cure to Prevention.* Chicago: Scott, Foresman and Co., 1970.

Wenrich, W. W. *A Primer of Behavior Modification.* Belmont, Calif.: Brooks/Cole Publishing Co., 1970.

Whaley, D. L., and Malott, R. W. *Elementary Principles of Behavior.* New York: Appleton-Century-Crofts, 1971.

Wittes, G., and Radin, N. *The Reinforcement Approach: Helping Your Child to Learn.* San Rafael, Calif.: Dimensions Publishing Co., 1969.

Wolpe, J., and Lazarus, A. A. *Behavioral Therapy Techniques.* New York: Pergamon Press, 1966.

ARTICLES

Adams, G. R. "Classroom Aggression: Determinants, Controlling Mechanisms, and Guideline for the Implementation of a Behavior Modification Program," *Psychology in the Schools,* X (1973), 155–67.

Addison, R., and Homme, L. "The Reinforcing Event (R.E.)

Menu," *National Society for Programmed Instructional Journal,* IV, No. 1 (1966).

Adelman, H. S. "Reinforcing Effects of Adult Nonreaction on Expectancy of Underachieving Boys," *Child Development,* XL (1969), 111–16.

Allen, K. E., and Harris, F. R. "Elimination of a Child's Excessive Scratching by Training the Mother in Reinforcement Procedures," *Behavior Research and Therapy,* IV (1966), 79–84.

Allen, K. E., Hart, B. M., Buell, J. S., Harris, F. R., and Wolf, M. M. "Effects of Social Reinforcement of Isolated Behavior of a Nursery School Child," *Child Development,* XXXV (1964), 511–18. (Example 43)

Allen, K. E., Henke, L. B., Harris, F. R., Baer, D. M., and Reynolds, N. "Control of Hyperactivity by Social Reinforcement of Attending Behavior," *Journal of Educational Psychology,* LVIII (1967), 231–37.

Allen, K. E., Turner, F. R., and Everett, P. M. "A Behavior Modification Classroom for Headstart Children with Behavior Problems," *Exceptional Children,* XXXVII (1970), 119–29.

Anastasio, M. "Developing Appropriate Classroom Behaviors in a Severely Disturbed Group of Institutionalized Kindergarten-Primary Children Utilizing a Behavior Modification Model," *American Journal of Orthopsychiatry,* XXXVII (1967), 313–14.

Anderson, H., Jr., White, W. F., and Wash, J. A. "Generalized Effects of Praise and Reproof," *Journal of Educational Psychology,* LVII (1966), 169–73.

Andrews, J. K. "The Results of a Pilot Program to Train Teachers in the Classroom Application of Behavior Modification Techniques," *Journal of School Psychology,* VIII (1970), 37–42.

Ascare, D., and Axelrod, S. "Use of a Behavior Modification Procedure in Four Open Classrooms," *Psychology in the Schools,* X (1973), 243–48.

Axelrod, S. "Comparison of Individual and Group Contingencies in Two Special Classes," *Behavior Therapy,* IV (1973), 83–90.

Ayllon, T., Smith, D., and Rogers, M. "Behavioral Management of School Phobia," *Journal of Behavior Therapy and Experimental Psychiatry,* I (1970), 125–38.

Baer, D. M. "Laboratory Control of Thumbsucking by Withdrawal and Representation of Reinforcement," *Journal of the Experimental Analysis of Behavior,* V (1962), 525–28.

Baer, D. M., Peterson, R. F., and Sherman, J. A. "The Development of Imitation by Reinforcing Behavioral Similarity to a Model," *Journal of the Experimental Analysis of Behavior*, X (1967), 405–16.

Baer, D. M., and Sherman, J. A. "Reinforcement Control of Generalized Initiation in Young Children," *Journal of Experimental Child Psychology*, I (1964), 37–49.

Baer, D. M., and Wolf, M. M. "The Reinforcement Contingency in Pre-school and Remedial Education," *Early Education*, eds. R. D. Hess and R. M. Bear, Chicago, Ill.: Aldine Publishers, 1968, 119–29.

Baer, D. M., Wolf, M. M., and Risley, T. R. "Some Current Dimensions of Applied Behavior Analysis," *Journal of Applied Behavior Analysis*, I (1968), 90–97.

Baer, P. E., "Effects of Withdrawal of Positive Reinforcement on an Extinguishing Response in Young Children," *Child Development*, XXXII (1961), 67–74.

———. "Escape and Avoidance Response of Preschool Children to Two Schedules of Reinforcement Withdrawal," *Journal of the Experimental Analysis of Behavior*, II (1969), 155–60.

Baer, P. E., and Goldfarb, G. E. "A Developmental Study of Verbal Conditioning in Children," *Psychological Reports*, X (1962), 175–81.
(Example 12)

Bailey, J. S., and Meyerson, L. "Vibration as a Reinforcer with a Profoundly Retarded Child," *Journal of Applied Behavior Analysis*, II (1969), 133–35.

Bailey, J. S., Wolf, M. M., and Phillips, E. L. "Home-based Reinforcement and the Modification of Pre-delinquent Classroom Behavior," *Journal of Applied Behavior Analysis*, III (1970), 223–33.
(Example 47)

Baker, G. S. " 'I can learn to take care of myself'—the case of Robert," *Childhood Education*, XXV (1949), 227–30.

Bandura, A. "Behavioral psychotherapy," *Scientific American*, CCXVI (1967), 78–86.

———. "Influence of Model's Reinforcement Contingencies on the Acquisition of Imitative Responses." *Journal of Personality Social Psychology*, I (1965), 589–95.

Bandura, A., Grusec, J. E., and Menlove, F. L. "Vicarious Extinction of Avoidance Behavior," *Journal of Personality and Social Psychology*, V (1967), 16–23.

Bandura, A., and McDonald, F. J. "Influence of Social Reinforcement in the Behavior of Models in Shaping Children's Moral Judgments," *Journal of Abnormal Social Psychology*, LXVII (1963), 274–81.

Bandura, A., and Perloff, B. "Relative Efficacy of Self-monitored and Externally Imposed Reinforcement Systems," *Journal of Personality and Social Psychology*, VII (1967), 111–16.

Bandura, A., Ross, D., and Ross, S. "Vicarious Reinforcement and Imitation Learning," *Journal of Abnormal Social Psychology*, XVII (1963), 601–7.

Bank, S. P. "Behavior Therapy with a Boy who had Never Learned to Walk," *Psychotherapy: Theory, Research and Practice*, V (1968), 150–53.

Barclay, J. R. "Effecting Behavior Change in the Elementary Classroom: An Exploratory Study," *Journal of Counseling Psychology*, XIV (1967), 240–47.

Barrett, B. H. "Acquisition of Operant Differentiation and Discrimination in Institutionalized Retarded Children," *American Journal of Orthopsychiatry*, XXXV (1965), 862–85.

Barrish, H. M., Saunders, M., and Wolf, M. M. "Group Behavior Game: Effects of Individual Contingencies for Group Consequences on Disruptive Behavior in a Classroom," *Journal of Applied Behavior Analysis*, II (1969), 119–24.

Barton, E. S., Guess, D., Garcia, E., and Baer, D. M. "Improvement of Retardates' Mealtime Behaviors by Time Out Procedures Using Multiple Baseline Techniques," *Journal of Applied Behavior Analysis*, III (1970), 77–84.

Becker, W. C., Madsen, C. H., Jr., Arnold, C. R., and Thomas, D. R. "The Contingent Use of Teacher Attention and Praise in Reducing Classroom Behavior Problems," *Journal of Special Education*, I (1967), 287–307. (Example 9)

Bergan, J. R., and Caldwell, T. "Operant Techniques in School Psychology, *Psychology in the Schools*, IV (1967), 136–41.

Bernal, M. E. "Training Parents in Child Management," *Behavioral Modification of Learning Disabilities*, ed. R. H. Bradfield, San Rafael, Calif.: Academic Therapy Publications, 1971.

Bernal, M. E., Duryee, J. S., Pruett, H. L., and Burns, B. J. "Behavior Modification and the Brat Syndrome," *Journal of Consulting and Clinical Psychology*, XXXII (1968), 447–55.

Bensberg, G. J., Colwell, C. N., and Cassel, R. H. "Teaching the Profoundly Retarded Self-help Activities by Shaping Behavior Techniques," *American Journal of Mental Deficiency*, LXIX (1965), 674–79.

Bijou, S. W. "A Behavioral Theory of Mental Retardation," *Psychology Today*, II (1968), 47–51.

———. "Child Behavior and Development: A Behavioral Analysis," *International Journal of Psychology*, III (1968), 221–38.

———. "An Empirical Concept of Reinforcement and a Functional Analysis of Child Behavior," *Journal of Genetic Psychology*, CIV (1964), 215–23.

———. "Experimental Studies of Child Behavior, Normal and Deviant," *Research in Behavior Modification: New Developments and Implications*, eds. L. P. Ullmann and L. Krasner, New York: Holt, Rinehart and Winston, 1965, 56–81.

———. "Implications of Behavioral Science for Counseling and Guidance," *Revolution in Counseling*, ed. J. D. Krumboltz, Boston: Houghton Mifflin Co., 1966, 27–48.

———. "Methodology for an Experimental Analysis of Child Behavior," *Psychological Reports*, III (1957), 243–50.

———. "Operant Extinction After Fixed-interval Schedules with Young Children," *Journal of the Experimental Analysis of Behavior*, I (1958), 25–29.

———. "Patterns of Reinforcement and Resistance to Extinction in Young Children," *Child Development*, XXVIII (1957), 47–54.

———. "Studies in the Experimental Development of Left-right Concepts in Retarded Children Using Fading Techniques," *International Review of Research in Mental Retardation*: Vol. III, ed. N. R. Ellis, Academic Press, 1968.

———. "What Psychology Has to Offer Education—Now," *Journal of Applied Behavior Analysis*, III (1970), 65–71.

Bijou, S. W., and Baer, D. M. "Operant Methods in Child Behavior and Development," *Operant Behavior: Areas of Research and Application*, ed. W. K. Honig, New York: Appleton-Century-Crofts, 1966.

Bijou, S. W., Birnbrauer, J. S., Kidder, J. D., and Tague, C. "Programmed Instruction or an Approach of Reading, Writing, and Arithmetic to Retarded Children," *The Psychological Record*, XVI (1966), 505–22.

Bijou, S. W., Peterson, R. F., and Ault, M. "A Method to Integrate Descriptive and Experimental Field Studies at the Level of Data and Empirical Concepts," *Journal of Applied Behavior Analysis*, III (1969), 175–91.

Bijou, S. W., Peterson, R. F., Harris, F. R., Allen, K. E., and Johnston, M. S. "Methodology for Experimental Studies of Young Children in Natural Settings," *Psychological Record*, XIX (1969), 177–210.

Bijou, S. W., and Sloane, H. N. "Therapeutic Techniques with Children," *An Introduction to Clinical Psychology* (3rd Rev.), eds. L. A. Pennington and I. A. Berg, New York: Ronald Press, 1966.

Bijou, S. W., and Sturgess, P. T. "Positive Reinforcers for Experimental Studies with Children—Consumables and Manipulatables," *Child Development*, XXX (1959), 151–70.

Birnbrauer, J. S., Bijou, S., Wolf, M. M., and Kidder, J. "Programmed Instruction in the Classroom," eds. L. Ullmann and L. Krasner, *Case Studies in Behavior Modifications*, New York: Holt, Rinehart and Winston, (1965), 358–63.

Birnbrauer, J. S., and Lawler, J. "Token Reinforcement for Learning," *Mental Retardation*, II (1964), 275–79.

Birnbrauer, J. S., Wolf, M. M., Kidder, J. D., and Tague, C. "Classroom Behavior of Retarded Pupils with Token Reinforcement," *Journal of Experimental Child Psychology*, II (1965), 219–35.

Bisett, B. M., and Reiber, M. "The Effects of Age and Incentive Value on Discrimination and Learning," *Journal of Experimental Child Psychology*, III (1966), 199–206.

Blain, I. J., and Harirez, R. "Increasing Sociometric Rank, Meaningfulness and Discriminability of Children's Names through Reinforcement and Interaction," *Child Development*, XXXIX (1968), 949–55.

Blake, P., and Moss, T. "The Development of Socialization Skills in an Electively Mute Child," *Behavior Research and Therapy*, V (1967), 349–56.

Blau, B., and Rafferty, J. "Changes in Friendship Status as a Function of Reinforcement," *Child Development*, XXXXI (1970), 113–21.

Blom, G. E. "Psycho-educational Aspects of Classroom Management," *Journal of Exceptional Children*, XXXII (1966), 377–83.

Boardman, W. K. "Rusty: A Brief Behavior Disorder," *Journal of Consulting Psychology*, XXVI (1962), 293–97.

Bostow, D. E., and Bailey, J. S. "Modification of Severe Disruptive and Aggressive Behavior Using Brief Time-out and Reinforcement Procedures," *Journal of Applied Behavior Analysis*, II (1969), 31–37.

Brackbill, Y. "Extinction of the Smiling Response in Infants as a Function of Reinforcement Schedule," *Child Development*, XXIX (1958), 115–24.

Brawley, B. R., Harris, F. R., Allen, E. K., Fleming, R. S., and

Peterson, R. F. "Behavior Modification of an Autistic Child," *Behavioral Science*, XIV (1969), 87–97.

Brigham, T. A., and Sherman, J. A. "An Experimental Analysis of Verbal Imitation in Preschool Children," *Journal of Applied Behavior Analysis*, I (1968), 151–58.

Briskin, A. S., and Gardner, W. I. "Social Reinforcement in Reducing Inappropriate Behavior," *Young Children*, XXIV (1968), 84–89.

Brison, D. W. "A Non-talking Child in Kindergarten: An Application of Behavior Therapy," *Journal of School Psychology*, IV (1966), 65–69.

Broden, M. Hall, R. V., Dunlap, A., and Clark, R. "Effects of Teacher Attention and a Token Reinforcement in a Junior High School Special Education Class," *Exceptional Children*, XXXVI (1970), 341–50.

Brown, G. D., and Tyler, V. O., Jr. "Time-out from Reinforcement: A Technique for Dethroning the 'Duke' of an Institutionalized Delinquent Group," *Journal of Child Psychology and Psychiatry*, IX (1968), 203–11.

Brown, J. C., Montgomery, R., and Barclay, J. R. "An example of Psychologist Management of Teacher Reinforcement Procedures in the Elementary Classroom," *Psychology in the Schools*, VI (1969), 336–40.

Brown, L., and Pearce, E. "Increasing the Production Rates of Trainable Retarded Students in a Public School Simulated Workshop," *Education and Training of the Mentally Retarded*, V (1970), 15–22.

Brown, R., and Elliott, R. "Control of Aggression in a Nursery School Class," *Journal of Experimental Child Psychology*, II (1965), 103–7.
(Example 36)

Brown, R. A., Pace, Z., Becker, S., and Becker, W. C. "Treatment of Extreme Negativism and Autistic Behavior in a 6-Year-Old Boy," *Exceptional Children*, XXXVI (1969), 155–72

Bryan, J. H. "How Adults Teach Hypocrisy," *Psychology Today*, III (1969), 50–52.

Buehler, R. E., Patterson, G. R., and Furniss, J. M. "The Reinforcement of Behavior in Institutional Settings," *Behaviour Research and Therapy*, IV (1966), 157–67.

Buell, J., Stoddard, P., Harris, F. R., and Baer, D. M. "Collateral Social Development Accompanying Reinforcement of Outdoor Play in a Preschool Child," *Journal of Applied Behavior Analysis*, I (1968), 167–73.

Burgess, R. L., Clark, R. N., and Hendee, J. C. "An Experimental Analysis of Anti-litter Procedures," *Journal of Applied Behavior Analysis*, IV (1971), 71–75.

Bushell, D., Jr., Wrobel, P. A., and Michaelis, M. L. "Applying Group Contingencies to the Classroom Study Behavior of Preschool Children," *Journal of Applied Behavior Analysis*, I (1968), 55–61.

Cantrell, R. P., Cantrell, M. L., Huddleston, C. M., and Wooldridge, R. L. "Contingency Contracting with School Problems," *Journal of Applied Behavior Analysis*, II (1969), 215–20.

Carlson, C., Arnold, C., Becker, W. C., and Madsen, C. H., Jr. "The Elimination of Tantrum Behavior of a Child in an Elementary Classroom," *Behavior Research and Therapy*, VI (1968) 117–19.

Carlson, R. M. "Behavior Modification: Educational Implications," *Journal of Learning Disabilities*, I (1968), 515–19.

Cautela, J. R. "Covert Reinforcement," *Behavior Therapy*, I (1970), 33–50.

Chadwick, B. A., and Day, R. C. "Systematic Reinforcement: Academic Performance of Under-achieving Students," *Journal of Applied Behavior Analysis*, IV (1971), 311–19. (Example 81)

Chan, A., Chiu, A., and Mueller, D. J. "An Integrated Approach to the Modification of Classroom Failure and Disruption: A Case Study," *Journal of School Psychology*, VIII (1970), 114–21.

Charlesworth, R., and Hartup, W. "Positive Social Reinforcement in the Nursery School Peer Group," *Child Development*, XXXVIII, No. 4 (1967), 993–1002.

Cieutat, V. C. "Surreptitious Modification of Verbal Behavior During Class Discussion," *Psychological Reports*, V (1959), 648.

Clark, M., Lechowicz, J., and Wolf, M. M. "A Pilot Basic Education Program for School Dropouts Incorporating a Token Reinforcement System," *Behavior Research and Therapy*, VI (1968), 183–88.

Clark, O. A., and Walberg, H. J. "The Use of Secondary Reinforcement in Teaching Inner-city School Children," *Journal of Special Education*, III (1969), 177–85.

Clarizo, H. F., and Yelon, S. L. "Learning Theory Approaches to Classroom Management: Rationale and Intervention Techniques," *Journal of Special Education*, I (1967), 267–74.

Clement, P. W., and Milne, D. C. "Group Play Therapy and Tangible Reinforcers Used to Modify the Behavior of 8-Year-Old Boys," *Behavior Research and Therapy*, V (1967), 301–12.

Cohen, H. L. "Model: Motivationally Oriented Designs for an Ecology of Learning," *Training Professionals in Procedure for the Establishment of Educational Environments*, eds. H. L. Cohen, I. Goldiamond, J. Filipazek, and R. Pooley, Silver Springs, Md.: Educational Facility Press, IBR, 1968.

Cohen, J., Filipczak, J. A., and Bis, J. S. "Case Project: Contingencies Applicable to Special Education," *Research in Psychotherapy*, ed. J. Shlien, Washington, D.C.: American Psychological Association, 1968.

Coleman, R. "A Conditioning Technique Applicable to Elementary School Classrooms," *Journal of Applied Behavior Analysis*, III (1970), 293–97.

Cook, C., and Adams, H. E. "Modification of Verbal Behavior in Speech Deficient Children," *Behavior Research and Therapy*, IV (1966), 265–71.

Cooper, M. L., Thomson, C. L., and Baer, D. M. "The Experimental Modification of Teacher Attending Behavior," *Journal of Applied Behavior Analysis*, III (1970), 153–57.

Cossairt, A., Hall, R. V., and Hopkins, B. L. "The Effects of Experimenter's Instructions, Feedback, and Praise on Teacher Praise and Student Attending Behavior," *Journal of Applied Behavior Analysis*, VI (1973), 89–100.

Costello, C. G. "Behavior Modification Procedures with Children," *Canadian Psychologist*, VIII, No. 2 (1967), 73–75.

Cotler, S. "The Effects of Positive and Negative Reinforcement and Test Anxiety on the Reading Performance of Male Elementary School Children," *Genetic Psychology Monographs*, LXXX (1969), 29–50.

Cotter, V. "A Procedure to Determine the Musical Preference of the Mentally Retarded," *Journal of Music Therapy*, CCCXII (1966), 56–63.

Coyle, P. J. "The Systematic Desensitization of Reading Anxiety, a Case Study," *Psychology in the Schools*, V (1968), 140–41.

Craig, H. B., and Holland, A. L. "Reinforcement of Visual Attending in Classrooms for Deaf Children," *Journal of Applied Behavior Analysis*, III (1970), 97–109.

Crighton, J., and Jehu, D. "Treatment of Examination Anxiety by Systematic Desensitization of Psychotherapy in Groups," *Behavior Research and Therapy*, VII (1969), 245–48.

Davison, G. C. "Self-control through 'Imaginal Aversive Contingency' and 'One-downmanship' Enabling the Powerless to Accommodate Unreasonableness," *Behavioral Counseling: Cases and Techniques*, eds. J. D. Krumboltz and C. E. Thoresen, New York: Holt, Rinehart and Winston, 1969, 319–27. (Example 68)

Davison, G. C. "The Training of Undergraduates as Social Reinforcers for Autistic Children," *Case Studies in Behavior Modification*, eds. L. Ullmann and L. Krasner, New York: Holt, Rinehart and Winston, 1965, 146–48.

Dickinson, D. J. "Changing Behavior with Behavioral Techniques," *Journal of School Psychology*, VI (1968), 278–83. (Example 17)

Donner, L., and Guerney, B. G., Jr. "Automated Group Desensitization for Test-anxiety," *Behavior Research and Therapy*, VII (1969), 1–14.

Doubros, S. G., and Daniels, G. J. "An Experimental Approach to the Reduction of Overactive Behavior," *Behavior Research and Therapy*, IV (1966), 251–58. (Example 4)

Dredge, K. "Modification of Disruptive Behavior of Two Young Children and Follow-up One Year Later," *Journal of School Psychology*, VIII (1970) 60–63.

Dunn-Rankin, P., Shimizu, M., and King, F. J. "Reward Preference Patterns in Elementary School Children," *International Journal of Educational Science*, III (1969), 1–10.

Dyer, V. "An Example: Reinforcement Principles in a Classroom for Emotionally Disturbed Children," *Exceptional Children*, XXXIV (1968), 597–99.

Edlund, C. V. "The Effect on the Behavior of Children, as Reflected in the IQ Scores, when Reinforced after each Correct Response," *Journal of Applied Behavior Analysis*, V (1972), 317–19.

Eklund, S. J. "A Comparison of Behavioral Modification and Traditional Evocative Therapies, with Special Reference to the Treatment of School Phobia," *Peabody Papers*, V, No. 2 (1967), 1–19.

Ellison, D. G., Barber, L., Engle, T. L., and Kampwerth, L. "Programmed Tutoring: A Teaching Aid and Research Tool," *Reading Research Quarterly*, I (1965), 77–127. (Example 56)

Engeln, R., Knutson, Jr., Laughy, L., and Garlington, W. "Behavior Modification Techniques Applied to a Family Unit: A Case Study," *Journal of Child Psychology and Psychiatry and Allied Disciplines*, IX (1968), 245–52.

Etzel, B. C., and Gewirtz, J. L. "Experimental Modification of Caretaker Maintained High-rate Operant Crying in a 6- and 20-month old-infant (Infant Tyrannateurus): Extinction of Crying with Reinforcement of Eye Contact and Smiling," *Journal of Experimental Child Psychology*, I (1967), 303–17.

Evans, G. W., and Oswalt, G. L. "Acceleration of Academic Progress through the Manipulation of Peer Influence," *Behavior Research and Therapy*, VI (1968), 189–95.

Eysenck, H. J. "New Ways in Psychotherapy," *Psychology Today*, I, No. 2 (1967), 39–47.

Ferritor, D. E., Buckholdt, D., Hamblin, R. L., and Smith, L. "The Non-effects of Contingent Reinforcement for Attending Behavior on Work Accomplished," *Journal of Applied Behavior Analysis*, V (1972), 7–17.
(Example 84)

Ferster, C. B. "Arithmetic Behavior in Chimpanzees," *Scientific American*, CCX (1964), 98–106.
(Example 8)

———. "Classification of Behavioral Pathology," *Research in Behavior Modification*, eds. L. Krasner and L. Ullmann, New York: Holt, Rinehart and Winston, 1965, 6–26.

———. "Reinforcement and Punishment in the Control of Human Behavior by Social Agencies," *Psychiatry Research Report*, X (1958), 101–18.

Fessant, J. M. "Application of Programmed Learning for Deaf Children to Industrial Arts," *American Annals of the Deaf*, CVIII (1963), 241–44.

Festbach, S. "The Reinforcing Effect of Witnessing Aggression," *Journal of Experimental Research in Personality*, V (1967) 97–106.

Fine, M. J. "Some Qualifying Notes on the Development and Implementation of Behavior Modification Programs," *Journal of School Psychology*, VIII (1970), 301–5.

Fineman, K. R. "An Operant Conditioning Program in a Juvenile Detention Facility," *Psychological Reports*, XXII, No. 3 (1968), 1119–20.

Flanagan, B., Goldiamond, I., and Azrin, N. "Operant Stuttering: The Control of Stuttering Behavior through Response-contingent Consequences," *Journal of the Experimental Analysis of Behavior*, I (1958), 173–78.

Forehand, R. T., Mulhern, T., and Richard, H. C. "Effects of Token Reinforcement in a Therapeutic Camp," *Psychological Reports*, XXV (1969), 349–50.

Fox, L. "Effecting the Use of Efficient Study Habits," *Journal of Mathematics*, I (1962), 75–86.

Franks, C. M., and Susskind, D. J. "Behavior Modification with Children: Rationale and Technique," *Journal of School Psychology*, VI (1968), 75–88.

Friedman, D. "Treatment of a Case of Dog Phobia in a Deaf Mute by Behavior Therapy," *Behavior Research and Therapy*, IV (1966), 141.

Furriman, A. J. "Structuring for Academic Success," *Behavioral Counseling: Cases and Techniques*, eds. J. D. Krumboltz and C. E. Thoresen, New York: Holt, Rinehart and Winston, 1969.

Gardner, J. M. "Behavior Modification in Mental Retardation: A Search for an Adequate Paradigm," *Journal of Mental Deficiency*, LXXIII (1969), 844–51.

Garvey, W. P., and Hegrenes, J. R. "Desensitization Techniques in the Treatment of School Phobia," *American Journal of Orthopsychiatry*, XXXVI (1966), 147–52.

Gelfand, D. M. "Behavior Therapy with Children: A Review and Evaluation of Research Methodology," *Psychological Bulletin*, LXIX (1968), 204–15.

Gewirtz, J. L., and Baer, D. M. "Deprivation and Satiation of Social Reinforcers as Drive Conditions," *Journal of Abnormal and Social Psychology*, LVII (1958), 165–72.

———. "The Effect of Brief Social Deprivation on Behaviors for a Social Reinforcer," *Journal of Abnormal and Social Psychology*, LVI (1958), 49–56.

Giles, D. K., and Wolf, M. M. "Toilet Training Institutionalized Severe Retardates: An Application of Operant Behavior Modification Techniques," *American Journal of Mental Deficiency*, LXX (1966), 766–80.

Girardeau, F. L., and Spradlin, J. E. "Token Rewards in a Cottage Program," *Mental Retardation*, II (1964), 345–51.

Glynn, E. L. "Classroom Applications of Self-determined Reinforcement," *Journal of Applied Behavior Analysis*, III (1970), 123–32.

Glynn, E. L., Thomas, J. D., and Shee, S. M. "Behavioral Self-control of On-task Behavior in an Elementary Classroom," *Journal of Applied Behavior Analysis*, V (1973) 105–13.

Goldiamond, I. "Justified and Unjustified Alarm over Behavioral Control," *Behavior Disorders: Perspectives and Trends*, ed. O. Milton, Philadelphia: Lippincott, 1965.

Goodlet, G. R., Goodlet, M. M., and Dredge, K. "Modification of

Disruptive Behavior of Two Young Children and Follow-up One Year Later," *Journal of School Psychology*, VIII (1970), 60–63.

Gordon, S. M., and Thomas, A. "Children's Behavioral Style and the Teacher's Approval of their Intelligence," *Journal of School Psychology*, V, No. 4 (1967), 292–300.

Gorton, C. E., and Hollis, J. H. "Redesigning a Cottage Unit for Better Programming and Research for the Severely Retarded," *Mental Retardation*, III (1965), 16–21.

Grandy, G. S., Madsen, C. H., Jr., and DeMersseman, L. M. "Effects of Individual and Interdependent Contingencies on Inappropriate Classroom Behavior," *Psychology in the Schools*, X (1973), 488–93.
(Example 74)

Graubard, P. S. "Utilizing the Group in Teaching Disturbed Delinquents to Learn," *Exceptional Children*, XXXVI (1969), 267–72.

Gray, B. B., and Fygetakis, L. "The Development of Language as a Function of Programmed Conditioning: Experiment II," *Behavior Research and Therapy*, VI (1968), 455–60.

———. "Mediated Language for Dysphasic Children," *Behavior Research and Therapy*, VI (1968), 263–80.

Green, R. L., and Stachnik, R. J. "Money, Motivation and Academic Achievement," *Phi Delta Kappan*, (December, 1968), 228–30.

Greene, R. J., and Hoats, D. L., "Reinforcing Capabilities of Television Distortion," *Journal of Applied Behavior Analysis*, II (1969), 139–41.

Grieger, R. M., II. "Behavior Modification with a Total Class, A Case Report," *Journal of School Psychology*, VIII (1970), 103–6.

Guerney, B. G., and Flumer, A. B. "Teachers as Psychotherapeutic Agents for Withdrawn Children," *Journal of School Psychology*, VIII (1970), 107–13.

Halcomb, C. G., and Blackwell, P. "Motivation and the Human Monitor: 1. The Effect of Contingent Credit," *Perceptual and Motor Skills*, XXVIII (1969), 623–29.

Hall, R. V., Cristler, C., Cranston, S. S., and Tucker, B. "Teachers and Parents as Researchers using Multiple Baseline Designs," *Journal of Applied Behavior Analysis*, III (1970), 247–55.
(Example 79)

Hall, R. V., Fox, R., Willard, D., Goldsmith, L., Emerson, M.,

Owen, M., Davis, F., and Porcia, E. "The Teacher as Observer and Experimenter in the Modification of Disputing and Talking-out Behaviors," *Journal of Applied Behavior Analysis*, IV (1971), 141–49.

Hall, R. V., Lund, D., and Jackson, D. "Effects of Teacher Attention on Study Behavior," *Journal of Applied Behavior Analysis*, I (1968), 1–12.
(Example 32)

Hall, R. V., Panyan, M., Rabon, D., and Broden, M. "Instructing Beginning Teachers in Reinforcement Procedures which Improve Classroom Control," *Journal of Applied Behavior Analysis*, I (1968), 315–28.
(Example 64; Example 70)

Hampe, E., and Kennedy, W. "Modification of Dominant Behavior in School Children: An Attempted Replication," *Psychological Reports*, XXIII (1968), 743–50.

Hanley, E. M. "Review of Research Involving Applied Behavior Analysis in the Classroom," *Review of Educational Research*, XL (1970), 597–625.

Haring, N. G., Hayden, A. H., and Nolen, P. A. "Accelerating Appropriate Behavior of Children in a Head Start Program," *Exceptional Children*, XXXV (1969), 773–84.

Haring, N. G., and Lovitt, T. C. "Operant Methodology and Educational Technology in Special Education," *Methods in Special Education*, eds. N. G. Haring and R. L. Schiefelbusch, New York: McGraw-Hill, 1972, 12–48.

Harleys, W. W. "Friendship Status and the Effectiveness of Peers as Reinforcing Agents," *Journal of Experimental Child Psychology*, I (1964), 154–62.

Harris, F. R., Johnston, M. K., Kelly, C. S., and Wolf, M. M. "Effects of Positive Social Reinforcement on Regressed Crawling of a Nursery School Child," *Journal of Educational Psychology*, LV (1964), 35–41.
(Example 33)

Harris, F. R., Wolf, M. M., and Baer, D. M. "Effects of Adult Social Reinforcement on Child Behavior," *Young Children*, XX (1964), 8–17.
(Example 25)

Hart, B., Allen, K. E., Buell, J. S., Harris, F. R., and Wolf, M. M. "Effects of Social Reinforcement in Operant Crying," *Journal of Experimental Child Psychology*, I (1964), 145–53.

Hart, B. M., Reynolds, M., Baer, D. M., Brawley, E., and Harris, F. R. "Effects of Contingent and Non-contingent Social Reinforcement on Cooperative Play of a Pre-school Child," *Journal of Applied Behavior Analysis*, I (1968), 73–76.

Hart, B., and Risley, T. "Establishing Use of Descriptive Adjectives in the Spontaneous Speech of Disadvantaged Preschool Children," *Journal of Applied Behavior Analysis*, I (1968), 109–20.

Harter, S., and Zigler, E. "Effectiveness of Adult and Peer Reinforcement on the Performance of Institutionalized and Noninstitutionalized Retardates," *Journal of Abnormal Psychology*, LXXIII (1968), 144–49.

Hartup, W. W. "Friendship Status and the Effectiveness of Peers as Reinforcing Agents," *Journal of Experimental Psychology*, I (1964), 154–62.

Hawkins, R. P., Peterson, R. F., Schweid, E., and Bijou, S. W. "Behavior Therapy in the Home: Amelioration of Problem Parent-child Relations with the Parent in a Therapeutic Role," *Journal of Experimental Child Psychology*, IV (1966), 99–107. (Example 61)

Headrick, M. W. "Operant Conditioning in Mental Deficiency," *American Journal of Mental Deficiency*, LXVII (1963), 924–29.

Heitzman, A. J. "Effects of a Token Reinforcement System on the Reading and Arithmetic Learnings of Migrant Primary School Pupils," *Journal of Educational Research*, X (1970), 455–58.

Herman, S. H., and Tramontana, J. "Instructions and Group Versus Individual Reinforcement in Modifying Disruptive Group Behavior," *Journal of Applied Behavior Analysis*, IV (1971), 113–19.

Hersen, M. "Behavior Modification Approach to a School-phobia Case," *Journal of Clinical Psychology*, XXVI (1970), 128–32.

Hewett, F. M. "Educational Engineering with Emotionally Disturbed Children," *Exceptional Children*, (March, 1967), 459–68.

Hewett, F. M., Taylor, F. D., and Artuso, A. A. "Santa Monica Project. Evaluation of an Engineered Classroom Design with Emotionally Disturbed Children," *Exceptional Children*, XXXV (1969), 523–32.

Hinds, W. C., and Roehlke, H. J. "A Learning Theory Approach to Group Counseling with Elementary School Children," *Journal of Counseling Psychology*, XVII (1970), 49–55.

Holbrook, A., and Crawford, G. H. "Modification of Vocal Frequency and Intensity in the Speech of the Deaf," *The Volta Review*, LXXII (1970), 492–97.

Holbrook, A., and Meador, M. M. "A Device for Automatic Modification of Vocal Frequency and Intensity," *The Southern Speech Journal*, XXXV, No. 3 (1969), 154–62.

Holland, A. L. "Some Applications of Behavioral Principles to Clinical Speech Problems," *Journal of Speech and Hearing Disorders*, XXXII (1967), 11–17.

Holland, C. J. "Elimination of Fire-setting Behavior in a Seven-Year-Old Boy," *Behavior Research and Therapy*, VII (1969), 135–37.

————. "An Interview Guide for Behavioral Counseling with Parents," *Behavior Therapy*, I (1970), 70–79.

Holms, D. S. "The Application of Learning Theory to the Treatment of a School Behavior Problem: A Case Study," *Psychology in the Schools*, III (1966), 355–58. (Example 13)

Homme, L. E. "Contiguity Theory and Contingency Management," *The Psychological Record*, XVI (1966), 233–41.

————. "Control of Coverants, the Operants of the Mind," *The Psychological Record*, XV (1965), 501–11.

Homme, L., Homme, A., Cide Baca, P., and Cottingham, L. "What Behavioral Engineering Is," *The Psychological Record*, XVIII (1968), 425–34.

Hopkins, B. L., Schutte, R. C., and Garton, K. L. "The Effects of Access to a Playroom on the Rate and Quality of Printing and Writing of First and Second-grade Students," *Journal of Applied Behavior Analysis*, IV (1971), 77–87.

Hudson, E., and DeMyer, M. "Food as a Reinforcer in Educational Therapy of Autistic Children," *Behavior Research and Therapy*, VI (1968), 37–43.

Jacobson, J. M., Bushell, D., Jr., and Risley, T. "Switching Requirements in a Head Start Classroom," *Journal of Applied Behavior Analysis*, II (1969), 43–47.

Jersild, A. T., and Holmes, F. B. "Methods of Overcoming Children's Fears," *Journal of Psychology*, I (1935), 75–104. (Example 23)

Johnson, S. M., and Brown, R. A. "Producing Behavior Change in Parents of Disturbed Children," *Journal of Child Psychology and Psychiatry*, X (1969), 107–21.

Kazdin, A. E. "The Effect of Vicarious Reinforcement on Attentive Behavior in the Classroom," *Journal of Applied Behavior Analysis*, VI (1973), 71–78.

Keller, F. S. "Goodbye, Teacher," *Journal of Applied Behavior Analysis*, I (1968), 79–89.

Kennedy, D., and Thompson, I. "Use of Reinforcement Technique with a First Grade Boy," *Personnel and Guidance Journal*, XLVI (1967), 366–70.

Kennedy, W. A. "School Phobia: Rapid Treatment of Fifty Cases," *Journal of Abnormal Psychology*, LXX (1965), 285–89. (Example 24)

Kennedy, W. A., and Willcutt, H. C. "Praise and Blame as Incentives," *Psychological Bulletin*, LXII (1964), 323–32.

Kerr, N., Meyerson, L., and Michael, J. "A Procedure for Shaping Vocalizations in a Mute Child," *Case Studies in Behavior Modification*, eds. L. P. Ullmann and L. Krasner, New York: Holt, Rinehart and Winston, 1965, 366–70.

Kimbrell, D. L., Luckey, R. E., Barbuto, P. F., and Love, J. G. "Operation Dry Pants: An Intensive Habit-training Program for Severely and Profoundly Retarded," *Mental Retardation*, II (1966), 32–36.

Kirby, F. D., and Shields, F. "Modification of Arithmetic Response Rate and Attending Behavior in a Seventh-grade Student," *Journal of Applied Behavior Analysis*, V (1972), 79–84. (Example 76)

Kirby, F. D., and Toler, H. C., Jr. "Modification of Preschool Isolate Behavior: A Case Study," *Journal of Applied Behavior Analysis*, III (1970), 309–14.

Knowles, P. L., Prutsman, T. D., and Raduege, V. "Behavior Modification of Simple Hyperkinetic Behavior and Letter Discrimination in a Hyperactive Child," *Journal of School Psychology*, VI (1968), 157–60.

Kobasigawa, A. "Inhibitory and Disinhibitory Effects of Models on Sex-appropriate Behavior in Children," *Psychologia*, XI (1968), 86–96. (Example 57)

Kolb, D. A., and Schwitzgebel, R. "Introducing Behavior Change in Adolescent Delinquents," *Behavior Research and Therapy*, I, No. 4 (1964), 297–304.

Kondas, O. "The Treatment of Stammering in Children by the

Shadowing Method," *Behavior Research and Therapy*, V (1967), 325–29.

Krasner, L. "The Behavioral Scientist and Social Responsibility: No Place to Hide," *Journal of Social Issues*, XXI, No. 2 (1965), 9–30.

Kroth, R. L., Whelan, R. J., and Stables, J. M., "Teacher Application of Behavior Principles in Home and Classroom Environments," *Focus on Exceptional Children*, I (1970), 1–12.

Krumboltz, J. D. "Behavioral Counseling: Rationale and Research," *Personnel Guidance*, XLIV (1965), 383–87.

————. "Parable of the Good Counselor," *Personnel Guidance*, XLIII (1964), 118–23.

————. "Prompting Adaptive Behavior: New Answers to Familiar Questions," *Revolution in Counseling*, ed. J. D. Krumboltz, Boston: Houghton Mifflin Company, 1966, 3–26.

Krumboltz, J. D., and Thoreson, C. E. "The Effect of Behavioral Counseling in Group and Individual Settings on Information-seeking Behavior," *Journal of Counseling Psychology*, XL (1964), 324–33.

Kuypers, D. S., Becker, W. C., and O'Leary, K. D. "How to Make a Token System Fail," *Exceptional Children*, XXXV (1968), 101–9.

Lahey, B. B. "Modification of the Frequency of Descriptive Adjectives in the Speech of Head Start Children through Modelling Without Reinforcement," *Journal of Applied Behavior Analysis*, IV (1971), 19–22.

Lahey, B. B., McNees, M. P., and McNees, M. C. "Control of an Obscene 'Verbal Tic' through Timeout in an Elementary School Classroom," *Journal of Applied Behavior Analysis*, VI (1973), 101–4.

Larimer, G. "Some Effects of Monetary Reward and Knowledge of Results on Judgment," *Journal of Experimental Psychology*, LXVII, No. 1 (1964), 27–32.

Lattal, K. A. "Contingency Management of Tooth-brushing Behavior in a Summer Camp for Children," *Journal of Applied Behavior Analysis*, II (1969), 195–98.

Lazarus, A. A., Davison, G. C., and Polefka, D. A. "Classical and Operant Factors in the Treatment of a School Phobia," *Journal of Abnormal Psychology*, LXX (1965), 225–29.

Leith, G. O. M., and Davis, T. N. "The Influence of Social Reinforcement on Achievement," *Educational Research*, XI (1969), 132–37.

Lewis, M. "Social Isolation, A Parametric Study of its Effects on Social Behavior," *Journal of Experimental Child Psychology*, II (1965), 205–17.

Liberman, R. "A View of Behavior Modification Projects in California," *Behaviour Research and Therapy*, VI (1968), 331–41.

Liebert, R. M., and Fernandez, L. E. "Effects of Vicarious Consequences on Imitative Performance," *Journal of Child Development*, XLI (1970), 847–52.

Lindsley, O. R. "An Experiment with Parents Handling Behavior at Home," *Johnstone Bulletin*, IX (1966), 27–36. (Johnstone Training Center, Bordertown, N.J.).

———. "Experimental Analysis of Cooperation and Competition," *The Experimental Analysis of Behavior: Selected Readings*, ed. T. Verhave, New York: Appleton-Century-Crofts, 1966, 470–501.

Lipe, D., and Jung, S. M. "Manipulating Incentives to Enhance School Learning," *Review of Educational Research*, IV (1971), 249–84.

Lounin, J. S., Friesen, W. V., and Norton, A. E. "Managing Emotionally Disturbed Children in Regular Classrooms," *Journal of Educational Psychology*, LVII (1966), 1–13.

Lovaas, O. I. "The Control of Food Intake in Children by Reinforcement of Relevant Verbal Behavior," *Journal of Abnormal and Social Psychology*, LXVIII (1965), 672–78.

———. "Cue Properties of Words: The Control of Operant Responding by Rate and Content of Verbal Operants," *Child Development*, XXXV (1964), 245–56.

———. "Effects of Exposure to Symbolic Aggression on Aggressive Behavior," *Child Development*, XXXII (1961), 37–44.

———. "A Program for the Establishment of Speech in Psychotic Children," *Early Childhood Autism: Clinical Educational and Social Aspects*, ed. J. K. King, London: Pergamon Press, 1966, 115–44.

Lovaas, O. I., Freitag, G., Kinder, M. I., Ribenstein, B. D., Schaeffer, G., and Simmons, J. Q. "Establishment of Social Reinforcers in Schizophrenic Children Using Food," *Journal of Experimental Child Psychology*, IV (1966), 109–25.

Lovaas, I. O., and Simmons, J. Q. "Manipulation of Self-destruction in Three Retarded Children," *Journal of Applied Behavior Analysis*, II (1969), 143–57.

Lovitt, T. C., and Curtiss, K. A. "Academic Response Rate as a

Function of Teacher and Self-imposed Contingencies," *Journal of Applied Behavior Analysis*, III (1969), 49–53.

———. "Effects of Manipulating an Antecedent Event on Mathematics Response Rate," *Journal of Applied Behavior Analysis*, I (1968), 329–33.

Lovitt, T. C., Guppy, T. E., and Blattner, J. E. "The Use of a Free Time Contingency with Fourth Graders to Increase Spelling Accuracy," *Behavior Research and Therapy*, VII, No. 2 (1969), 151–56.

McAllister, L. W., Stachowiak, J. G., Baer, D. M., and Conderman, L. "The Application of Operant Conditioning Techniques in a Secondary School Classroom," *Journal of Applied Behavior Analysis*, II (1969), 277–85.

McClain, W. A. "The Modification of Aggressive Classroom Behavior through Reinforcement, Inhibition, and Relationship Therapy," *Training School Bulletin*, LXV (1969), 122–25.

MacDonald, W. S., Gallomore, R., and MacDonald, G. "Contingency Counseling by School Personnel: An Economic Model of Intervention," *Journal of Applied Behavior Analysis*, III (1970), 175–92.

McIntire, R. W. "Spare the Rod, Use Behavior Mod," *Psychology Today*, IV (1970), 42–44.

McKenzie, H. S., Clark, M., Wolf, M., Kothera, R., and Benson, C. "Behavior Modification of Children with Learning Disabilities Using Grades as Tokens and Allowances as Back-up Reinforcers," *Exceptional Children*, XXXV (1968), 745–53.

McKerracher, D. W. "Alleviation of Reading Difficulties by a Simple Operant Conditioning Technique," *Journal of Child Psychology and Psychiatry*, XVIII (1967), 51–56.

McLaughlin, T. F., and Malaby, J. "Intrinsic Reinforcers in a Classroom Token Economy," *Journal of Applied Behavior Analysis*, V (1972), 263–70.

McMains, M. J. "Children's Adoption of Self-rewarding Patterns: Verbalizations and Modeling," *Perceptual and Motor Skills*, XXVIII (1969), 515–18.

McManus, M. "Group Desensitization of Test Anxiety," *Behavior Research and Therapy*, IX (1971), 51–56.

MacMichael, J. S., and Corey, J. R., "Contingency Management in an Introductory Psychology Course Produces Better Learning," *Journal of Applied Behavior Analysis*, II (1969) 79–84.

McNamara, J. R. "Behavior Therapy in the Classroom: A Case Report," *Journal of School Psychology*, VII (1968–69), 48–51.

McReynolds, L. V. "Application of Timeout from Positive Reinforcement for Increasing the Efficiency of Speech Training," *Journal of Applied Behavior Analysis*, II (1969), 199–205.

Madsen, C. H., Jr. "Nurturance and Modeling in Preschoolers," *Child Development*, XXXIX (1968), 221–36.

———. "Positive Reinforcement in the Toilet Training in a Normal Child: A Case Report," *Case Studies in Behavior Modification*, eds. L. P. Ullmann and L. Krasner, New York: Holt, Rinehart and Winston, Inc., 1965, 305–7.

Madsen, C. H., Jr., Becker, W. C., and Thomas, D. R. "Rules, Praise and Ignoring: Elements of Elementary Classroom Control," *Journal of Applied Behavior Analysis*, I (1968), 139–50. (Example 71)

Madsen, C. H., Jr., Becker, W. C., Thomas, D. R., Koser, L., and Plager, E. "An Analysis of the Reinforcing Function of Sitdown Commands," *Readings in Educational Psychology*, ed. R. K. Parker, Boston: Allyn & Bacon, Inc., 1968. (Example 49)

Madsen, C. K., and Forsythe, J. L. "The Effect of Contingent Music Listening on Increases of Mathematical Responses," *Research in Music Behavior*, eds. C. K. Madsen, R. D. Greer and C. H. Madsen, Jr., New York: Teachers College Press, 1974. (Example 38)

Madsen, C. K., and Madsen, C. H., Jr. "Music as a Behavior Modification Technique with a Juvenile Delinquent," *Journal of Music Therapy*, V (1968), 72–76. (Example 83)

Magdison, A. T. "A Token from the Teacher," *Trans-Action*, VI, No. 3 (1969), 26–31.

Malott, R. W., and Svinicki, J. G. "Contingency Management in an Introductory Psychology Course for One Thousand Students," *Psychological Record*, XIX (1969), 545–56.

Mandelker, A. V., Brigham, T. A., and Bushell, D., Jr. "The Effects of Token Procedures on a Teacher's Social Contacts with her Students," *Journal of Applied Behavior Analysis*, III (1970), 169–74.

Marlowe, R., and Madsen, C. H., Jr. "Teacher Approval vs. Group Counseling Techniques for Junior High School Behavioral Problems," Paper presented at the meeting of the Florida Psychological Association, Daytona Beach, Fla., April, 1972. (Example 85)

Marshall, H. H. "The Effects of Punishment on Children: A Review of the Literature and a Suggested Hypothesis," *The Journal of Genetic Psychology*, CVI (1965), 23–33.

Martin, G. L., England, G., Kaprowy, E., Kilgour, K., and Pilek, V. "Operant Conditioning of Kindergarten-class Behavior in Autistic Children," *Behavior Research and Therapy*, VI (1968), 281–94.

Martin, M., Burkholder, R., Rosenthal, T., Tharp, R. G., and Thorne, G. L. "Programming Behavioral Change and Reintegration into School Milieux of Extreme Adolescent Deviates," *Behavior Research and Therapy*, VI (1968), 371–83.

Martin, N., Schwyhart, K., and Wetzel, R. "Teaching Motivation in a High School Reading Program," *Journal of Reading*, IX (1967), 111–21.

Martin, R. R., and Siegel, G. M. "The Effects of Response Contingent Shock on Stuttering," *Journal of Speech and Hearing Research*, IX (1966), 340–52. (Example 46)

Masling, J., and Stern, G. "Effect of the Observer in the Classroom," *Journal of Educational Psychology*, LX (1969), 351–54.

Mawhinney, V. T., Bostow, D. E., Laws, D. R., Blumenfeld, G. J., and Hopkins, B. L. "A Comparison of Students Studying Behavior Produced by Daily, Weekly, and Three-week Testing Schedules," *Journal of Applied Behavior Analysis*, IV (1971), 257–64.

Meachan, M. L. "Reinforcement Theory as a Basis for Clinical School Psychology," *Psychology in the Schools*, IV (1968), 114–17.

Medland, M. B., and Stachnik, T. J. "Good-behavior Game: A Replication and Systematic Analysis," *Journal of Applied Behavior Analysis*, V (1972), 45–51.

Meichenbaum, D., Bowers, K., and Ross, R. "Modification of Classroom Behavior of Institutionalized Female Adolescent Offenders," *Behavior Research and Therapy*, VI (1968), 343–53.

Meyer, J. B., Strowig, W., and Hosford, R. E. "Behavioral-reinforcement Counseling with Rural High School Youth," *Journal of Counseling Psychology*, XVII (1970), 127–32.

Michael, J. "Contingency Management in an Introductory Psychology Course Produces Bitter Learning," *Journal of Applied Behavior Analysis*, II (1969), 79–83.

Michael, J., and Meyerson, L. "A Behavioral Approach to Counseling and Guidance," *Harvard Educational Review*, XXXII (1962), 382–402.

Miller, L. K. "A Note on the Control of Study Behavior," *Journal of Experimental Child Psychology*, I (1965), 108–10. (Example 34)

Miller, L. K., and Schneider, R. "The Use of Token System in Project Head Start," *Journal of Applied Behavior Analysis*, III (1970), 213–20.

Mira, M. "Results of a Behavior Modification Training Program for Parents and Teachers," *Behavior Research and Therapy*, VIII (1970), 309–11.

Mithaug, D. E., and Burgess, R. L. "The Effects of Different Reinforcement Contingencies in the Development of Social Cooperation," *Journal of Experimental Child Psychology*, VI (1968), 402–26.

———. "Effects of Different Reinforcement Procedures in the Establishment of a Group Response, Experiments I, II, and III," *Journal of Experimental Child Psychology*, V (1967), 441–54.

Montgomery, J., and Burney, R. D. "Problems and Pitfalls of Establishing an Operant Conditioning-Token Economy Program," *Mental Hygiene*, LIV (1970), 382–87.

Morice, H. O. "The School Psychologist as a Behavioral Consultant: A Project in Behavior Modification in a Public School Setting," *Psychology in the Schools*, V (1968), 253–61.

Muller, S. D., and Madsen, C. H., Jr. "Group Desensitization for 'Anxious' Children with Reading Problems," *Psychology in the Schools*, VII (1970), 184–89.

Murdock, E. E., and Della-Piana, G. M. "Contingent Stimuli in the Classroom," *NSPI Journal*, IX (1970), 6–9.

Myers, K. E., Travers, R. M., and Sanford, M. E. "Learning and Reinforcement in Student Pairs," *Journal of Educational Psychology*, LVI (1965), 67–72.

Nawas, M. M., Fishman, S. T., and Pucel, J. "A Standardized Desensitization Program Applicable to Group and Individual Treatments," *Behavior Research and Therapy*, VIII (1970), 49–56.

Nolen, P., Kunzelman, H., and Haring, N. G. "Behavioral Modification in a Junior High Learning Disabilities Classroom," *Exceptional Children*, XXXIV (1967), 163–68.

O'Connor, R. D. "Modification of Social Withdrawal Through Symbolic Modeling," *Journal of Applied Behavior Analysis*, II (1969), 15–22.

O'Leary, K. D. "Diagnosis of Children's Behavior Problems," *Be-

havior Disorders of Children, eds. H. C. Quay and J. S. Werry, New York: Wiley, 1972.

O'Leary, K. D., and Becker, W. C. "Behavior Modification of an Adjustment Class: A Token Reinforcement Program," *Exceptional Children*, IX (1967), 637–42. (Example 45)

————. "The Effects of the Intensity of a Teacher's Reprimands on Children's Behavior," *Journal of School Psychology*, VII (1968), 8–11. (Example 51)

O'Leary, K. D., Becker, W. C., Evans, M. B., and Saudargas, R. A. "A Token Reinforcement Program in a Public School: A Replication and Systematic Analysis," *Journal of Applied Behavior Analysis*, II (1969), 3–14.

O'Leary, K. D., and Drabman, R. "Token Reinforcement Programs in the Classroom: A Review," *Psychological Bulletin*, VI (1971), 379–98.

O'Leary, K. D., Kaufman, K. F., Kass, R. E., Drabman, D. S. "The Effects of Loud and Soft Reprimands on the Behavior of Disruptive Students," *Exceptional Children*, XXXVIII (1970), 145–55.

O'Leary, K. D., O'Leary, S., and Becker, W. C. "Modification of a Deviant Sibling Interaction Pattern in the Home," *Behavior Research and Therapy*, V (1967), 113–20.

Orlando, R. "Shaping Multiple Schedule Performances in Retardates; Establishment of Baselines by Systematic and Special Procedures," *Journal of Experimental Child Psychology*, II (1965), 135–53.

Orlando, R., Schoelkoph, A. M., and Tobias, L. "Tokens as Reinforcers: Classroom Applications by Teachers of the Retarded," *Institute on Mental Retardation and Intellectual Development*, IV (1967), *Papers and Reports* No. 14.

Osborne, J. G. "Free-time as a Reinforcer in the Management of Classroom Behavior," *Journal of Applied Behavior Analysis*, II (1969), 113–18.

Packard, R. G. "The Control of 'Classroom Attention': A Group Contingency for Complex Behavior," *Journal of Applied Behavior Analysis*, III (1970), 13–28.

Panyan, M., Boozer, H., and Morris, N. "Feedback to Attendants for Applying Operant Techniques," *Journal of Applied Behavior Analysis*, III (1970), 1–4.

Parke, R. D. "Some Effects of Punishment on Children's Behavior," *Young Children*, XXIV (1969), 225–55.

Patterson, G. R. "An Application of Conditioning Techniques to the Control of a Hyperactive Child," *Case Studies in Behavior Modification*, eds. L. P. Ullmann and L. Krasner, New York: Holt, Rinehart and Winston, 1965, 370–75. (Example 54)

———. "A Community Mental Health Program for Children," *Behavior Modification and Ideal Mental Health Services*, eds. L. A. Hammerlynck, P. O. Davidson, and L. E. Acker, University of Calgary, Calgary, Alberta, Canada, 1969, 130–79.

———. "A Learning Theory Approach to the Treatment of School Phobia in Child," *Case Studies in Behavior Modification*, eds. L. P. Ullmann, and L. Krasner, New York: Holt, Rinehart and Winston, 1965, 279–85.

Patterson, G. R., and Anderson, D. "Peers as Social Reinforcers," *Child Development*, XXXV (1964), 951–60.

Patterson, G. R., Jones, R., Whittier, J., and Wright, A. "A Behavior Modification Technique for the Hyperactive Child," *Behavior Research and Therapy*, II (1965), 217–26.

Patterson, G. R., Littman, R. E., and Hinsey, W. C. "Parental Effectiveness as Reinforcers in the Laboratory and its Relation to Child Rearing Practices and Child Adjustment in the Classroom," *Journal of Personality*, XXXII (1964), 180–99.

Patterson, G. R., McNeal, S., Hawkins, N., and Phelps, R. "Programming the Social Environment," *Journal of Child Psychology and Psychiatry*, VIII (1967), 181–95.

Patterson, G. R., Ray, R. S., and Shaw, D. A. "Direct Intervention in Families of Deviant Children," *Handbook of Psychotherapy and Behavior Change*, eds. A. E. Bergin, and S. L. Garfield, New York: Wiley, 1971,

Patterson, R., and Shige, M. "Token Reinforcement in the Shaping of Children's Mealtime Behavior," *Canadian Psychologist*, IX (1968), 22–27.

Perline, I. H., and Levinsky, D. "Controlling Maladaptive Classroom Behavior in the Severely Retarded," *American Journal of Mental Deficiency*, LXXIII (1968), 74–78.

Peterson, D. R., and London, P. "Neobehavioristic Psychotherapy: Quasihypnotic Suggestion and Multiple Reinforcement in the Treatment of a Case of Post-infantile Dyscopresis," *Psychological Record*, XIV (1964), 469–74.

————. "A Role for Cognition in the Behavioral Treatment of a Child's Eliminative Disturbance," *Case Studies in Behavior Modification*, eds. L. P. Ullmann, and L. Krasner, New York: Holt, Rinehart and Winston, Inc., 1965, 289–95.

Peterson, L. W. "Operant Approach to Observation and Recording," *Nursing Outlook*, XV, 1967.

Peterson, R. F., and Peterson, L. R. "The Use of Positive Reinforcement in the Control of Self-destructive Behavior in a Retarded Boy," *Journal of Experimental Child Psychology*, VI (1968), 351–60.

Phillips, E. L. "Achievement Place: Token Reinforcement Procedure in a Home-style Rehabilitation Setting for Pre-delinquent Boys," *Journal of Applied Behavior Analysis*, I (1968), 213–23.

Phillips, E. L., Phillips, E. A., Fixsen, D. L., and Wolf, M. M. "Achievement Place: Modification of the Behaviors of Predelinquent Boys within a Token Economy," *Journal of Applied Behavior Analysis*, IV (1971), 45–59.

Pinkston, E. M., Reese, N. M., LeBlanc, J. M., and Baer, D. M. "Independent Control of a Preschool Child's Aggression and Peer Interaction by Contingent Teacher Attention," *Journal of Applied Behavior Analysis*, VI (1973), 115–24.

Pumroy, D. K., and Pumroy, S. S. "Systematic Observation and Reinforcement Techniques in Toilet Training," *Psychological Reports*, XVI (1965), 467–71.

Quay, H. C., Sprague, R. L., Werry, J. S., and McQueen, M. "Conditioning Visual Orientation of Conduct Problem Children in the Classroom," *Journal of Experimental Child Psychology*, V (1967), 512–17.

Quay, H., Werry, J., McQueen, M., and Sprague, R. "Remediation of the Conduct Problem Child in the Special Class Setting," *Exceptional Children*, XXXII (1966), 509–15.

Rabb, E., and Hewett, F. M. "Developing Appropriate Classroom Behaviors in a Severely Disturbed Group of Institutionalized Kindergarten-Primary Children Utilizing a Behavior Modification Model," *American Journal of Orthopsychiatry*, XXXVII (1967), 313–14.

Ray, R. S., Shaw, D. A., and Cobb, J. A. "The Work Box: An Innovation in Teaching Attentional Behavioral," *The School Counselor*, XVIII (1970), 15–35.

Resnick, J. H. "The Control of Smoking Behavior by Stimulus Satiation," *Behavior Research and Therapy*, VI (1968), 113–14.

Reynold, N. J., and Risley, T. R. "The Role of Social and Material

Reinforcers in Increasing Talking of a Disadvantaged Preschool Child," *Journal of Applied Behavior Analysis,* I (1968), 253–62.
(Example 31)

Rickard, H. C., Dignam, P. J., and Horner, R. F. "Verbal Manipulation in a Psycho-therapeutic Relationship," *Journal of Clinical Psychology,* XVI (1960), 364–67.

Rickard, H. C., and Dinoff, M. "Behavior Change in a Therapeutic Summer Camp: A Follow-up Study," *Journal of Genetic Psychology,* I, No. 10 (1967), 181–83.

Risley, T. R. "The Effects and Side Effects of Punishing the Autistic Behaviors of a Deviant Child," *Journal of Applied Behavior Analysis,* I (1968), 21–34.

———. "Generalization Gradients Following Two-response Discrimination Training," *Journal of Experimental Analysis of Behavior,* VII (1964), 199–204.

Risley, T. R., and Hart, B. "Developing Correspondence Between the Nonverbal and Verbal Behaviors of Preschool Children," *Journal of Applied Behavior Analysis,* I (1968), 267–81.

Risley, T. R., and Lee, J. "Learning and Lollipops," *Psychology Today,* VIII (1968), 28–31.

Risley, T. R. and Wolf, M. M. "Establishing Functional Speech in Echolaic Children," *Behavior Research and Therapy,* V (1967), 73–88.

———. "Experimental Manipulation of Autistic Behaviors and Generalization into the Home," *Child Development: Readings in Experimental Analysis,* eds. S. W. Bijou, and D. M. Baer, New York: Appleton-Century-Crofts, 1967.

Rosenthal, T. L., Underwood, B., Martin, M. "Assessing Classroom Incentive Practices," *Journal of Educational Psychology,* LX (1969), 370–76.

Rouse, S. T. "Effects of a Training Program on the Productive Thinking of Educable Mental Retardates," *American Journal of Mental Deficiency,* LXIX (1965), 666–73.

Russell, J. C., Clark, A. N., and Van Sommers, P. "Treatment of Stammering by Reinforcement of Fluent Speech," *Behavior Research and Therapy,* VI (1968), 447–53.

Ryback, D., and Staats, A. W. "Parents as Behavior Therapy Technicians in Treating Reading Deficits (Dyslexia)," *Journal of Behavior Therapy and Experimental Psychiatry,* I (1970), 109–19.

Sailor, W. S., Guess, D., Rutherford, G., and Baer, D. M. "Control of Tantrum Behavior During Experimental Verbal Training," *Journal of Applied Behavior Analysis*, I (1968), 237–43.

Sanders, R. M., and Hanson, P. J. "A Note on a Simple Procedure for Redistributing a Teacher's Student Contacts," *Journal of Applied Behavior Analysis*, IV (1971), 157–61.

Saper, B. "The Application of Behavior Modification Techniques to Programs for Mentally Disordered Patients," *Psychiatric Quarterly*, Part II (1966), 1–14.

Sassenrath, J. M. "Effects of Differential Feedback from Exam on Retention and Transfer," *Journal of Educational Psychology*, LVI (1965), 259–63.

Schein, E. H. "The Student Image of the Teacher," *Journal of Applied Behavioral Science*, XIII, No. 3 (1967), 3–5, 337.

Schmidt, G. L., and Ulrich, R. E. "Effects of Group Contingent Events Upon Classroom Noise," *Journal of Applied Behavior Analysis*, II (1969), 171–79.

Schmitt, D. R., and Marwell, G. "Stimulus Control in the Experimental Study of Cooperation," *Journal of Experimental Analysis of Behavior*, XI (1968), 571–74.

Schutte, R. C., and Hopkins, B. L. "The Effects of Teacher Attention on Following Instructions in a Kindergarten Class," *Journal of Applied Behavior Analysis*, III (1970), 117–22. (Example 72)

Schwarz, M. L., and Hawkins, R. P. "Application of Delayed Reinforcement Procedures to the Behavior of an Elementary School Child," *Journal of Applied Behavior Analysis*, III (1970), 85–96.

Schwitzgebel, R. L., and Kolb, D. A. "Inducing Behavior Change in Adolescent Delinquents," *Behavior Research and Therapy*, I (1964), 297–304. (Example 77)

Scott, W. A. "Attitude Change through the Reward of Verbal Behavior," *Journal of Abnormal and Social Psychology*, LV (1957), 72–75.

Shapiro, D. "The Reinforcement of Disagreement in a Small Group," *Behavior Research and Therapy*, I (1964), 267–72.

Sibley, S., Abbott, M. S., and Cooper, B. P. "Modification of the Classroom Behavior of a Disadvantaged Kindergarten Boy by Social Reinforcement and Isolation," *Journal of Experimental Child Psychology*, VII (1969), 203–19.

Sidman, M. "Normal Sources for Pathological Behavior," ed. R.

Ulrich, *Control of Human Behavior*, Glenview, Ill.: Scott, Foresman, and Co., 1966, 42–52.

Sidman, M. and Stoddard, L. T. "The Effectiveness of Fading in Programming a Simultaneous Form Discrimination for Retarded Children," *Journal of the Experimental Analysis of Behavior*, X (1967), 3–15.

Simkins, L., Kingery, M., and Bradley, P. "Modification of Cluttered Speech in an Emotionally Disturbed Child," *The Journal of Special Education*, IV (1970), 81–88.

Skiba, E. A., Pettigrew, L. E., and Alden, S. E. "A Behavioral Approach to the Control of Thumbsucking in the Classroom," *Journal of Applied Behavior Analysis*, IV (1971), 121–25.

Skinner, B. F. "Freedom and the Control of Man," *American Scholar*, XXV (1955), 47–65. (Reprinted in *Cumulative Record*)

Sloane, H. N., Johnston, M. K., and Bijou, S. W. "Successive Modification of Aggressive Behavior and Aggressive Fantasy Play by Management of Contingencies," *Journal of Child Psychology and Psychiatry*, VIII (1967), 217–26.

Spradlin, J. E. "Effects of Reinforcement Schedules on Extinction in Several Mentally Retarded Children," *American Journal of Mental Deficiency*, LXVI (1962), 634–40.

Spradlin, J. E., Girardeau, F. L., and Corts, E. N. "Fixed Ratio and Fixed Interval Behavior of Severely and Profoundly Retarded Subjects," *Journal of Experimental Child Psychology*, II (1965), 340–53.

Staats, A. W. "A General Apparatus for the Investigation of Complex Learning in Children," *Behavior Research and Therapy*, VI (1968), 45–50.

Staats, A. W., and Butterfield, W. H. "Treatment of Nonreading in a Culturally-deprived Juvenile Delinquent; An Application of Reinforcement Principles," *Child Development*, XXXVI (1965), 925–42.

Staats, A. W., Linley, J. R., Linke, K. A., and Wolf, M. M. "Reinforcement Variables in the Control of Unit Reading Responses," *Journal of the Experimental Analysis of Behavior*, VII (1964), 139–49.

Staats, A. W., Minke, K. A., Goodwin, W., and Landeen, J. "Cognitive Behavior Modification: 'Motivated Learning' Reading Treatment with Subprofessional Therapy-technician," *Behavior Research and Therapy*, V (1967), 283–99.

Staats, A. W., Staats, C. K., Schutz, R. E., and Wolf, M. "The

Conditioning of Textual Responses using 'Extrinsic Reinforcers,'" *Journal of the Experimental Analysis of Behavior*, V (1962), 33–40.

Steele, A. L. "Effects of Social Reinforcement on the Musical Preference of Mentally Retarded Children," *Journal of Music Therapy*, IQ 92 (1967), 57–62.

Stein, A. H. "The Influence of Social Reinforcement on the Achievement Behavior of Fourth-grade Boys and Girls," *Child Development*, XL (1969), 727–36.

Steinman, W. M. "The Social Control of Generalized Imitation," *Journal of Applied Behavior Analysis*, III (1970), 159–67.

Stephens, T. M. "Psychological Consultation to Teachers of Learning and Behaviorally Handicapped Children using a Behavioral Model," *Journal of School Psychology*, VIII (1970), 13–18.

Stimbert, V. E., Frazuerm, J. R., Keller, H. R., and King, F. J. "The Effect of Tangible Reinforcement on the Learning and Retention of Programmed Material in Academically Retarded Children," *Journal of School Psychology*, VI (1968), 246–49.

Straughan, J. H. "Treatment with Child and Mother in the Playroom," *Behavior Research and Therapy*, II (1964), 37–41.

Stuart, R. B. "Behavioral Control of Overeating," *Behavior Research and Therapy*, V (1967), 357–65.

Sullivan, W. J., Baker, R. L., and Schutz, R. E. "Effects of Intrinsic and Extrinsic Reinforcement Contingencies on Learner Performance," *Journal of Educational Psychology*, LVIII (1967), 165–69.

Surratt, P. R., Ulrich, R. E., and Hawkins, R. P. "An Elementary Student as a Behavioral Engineer," *Journal of Applied Behavior Analysis*, II (1969), 85–92.

Tate, B. F., and Baroff, G. S. "Aversive Control of Self-injurious Behavior in a Psychotic Boy," *Behavior Research and Therapy*, IV (1966), 281–87.

Thelen, M. H., and Soltz, W. "The Effect of Vicarious Reinforcement on Imitation in Two Social-Racial Groups," *Child Development*, XL (1969), 879–87.

Thomas, D. R., Becker, W. C., and Armstrong, M. "Production and Elimination of Disruptive Classroom Behavior by Systematically Varying Teacher's Behavior," *Journal of Applied Behavior Analysis*, I (1968), 35–45.

Thoreson, C., and Krumboltz, J. D. "Relationship of Counselor

Reinforcement of Selected Responses to External Behavior," *Journal of Counseling Psychology*, XIV (1967), 140–44.

Tramontana, J. A. "Review of Research on Behavior Modification in the Home and School," *Educational Technology*, XI (1971), 61–69.

Tyler, V. O., and Brown, G. D. "The Use of Swift Brief Isolation as a Group Control Device for Institutionalized Delinquents," *Behavior Research and Therapy*, V (1967), 1–9.

Tyler, V. O., and Brown, G. D. "Token Reinforcement of Academic Performance and Institutional Delinquent Boys," *Journal of Educational Psychology*, LIX (1968), 164–68.

Ulrich, R. E., Louisell, S. E., and Wolf, M. "The Learning Village: A Behavioral Approach to Early Education," *Educational Technology*, XI (1971), 32–45.

Ulrich, R., Wolf, M., and Bluhm, M. "Operant Conditioning in the Public Schools," *Educational Technology Monographs*, I (1968), 1.

Unikel, I. P., Strain, G. S., and Adams, H. S. "Learning of Lower Socio-economic Status Children as a Function of Social and Tangible Reward," *Development Psychology*, I (1969), 553–55.

Van de Riet, H. "Effects of Praise and Reproof on Paired Associate Learning in Educationally Retarded Children," *Journal of Educational Psychology*, LV, No. 3 (1964), 139–43.

Vriend, T. J. "High-performing Inner-city Adolescents Assist Low-performing Peers in Counseling Groups," *The Personnel and Guidance Journal*, XLVII (1969), 897–904.

Wagner, M. K. "A Case of Public Masturbation Treated by Operant Conditioning," *Journal of Child Psychology and Psychiatry*, IX (1968), 61–65.

———. "Parent Therapists: An Operant Conditioning Method," *Mental Hygiene*, (1968), 452–55.

Wahler, R. G. "Oppositional Children: A Quest for Parental Reinforcement Control," *Journal of Applied Behavior Analysis*, II (1969), 159–70.

———. "Setting Generality: "Some Specific General Effects of Child Behavior Therapy," *Journal of Applied Behavior Analysis*, II (1969), 239–46.

Wahler, R. G., and Erickson, M. "Child Behavior Therapy: A Community Program in Appalachia," *Behavior Research and Therapy*, VII (1969), 71–78.

Wahler, R. G., Winkel, G. H., Peterson, R. F., and Morrison, D. C. "Mothers as Behavior Therapists for Their own Children,"

Behavior Research and Therapy, III (1965), 113–24. (Example 80)

Walker, H. M. "Empirical Assessment of Deviant Behavior in Children," *Psychology in the Schools*, VI (1969), 93–97.

Walker, H. M., and Buckley, N. K. "The Use of Positive Reinforcement in Conditioning Attending Behavior," *Journal of Applied Behavior Analysis*, I (1968), 245–50.

Walls, R. T., and Smith, T. S. "Development of Preference for Delayed Reinforcement in Disadvantaged Children," *Journal of Educational Psychology*, LXI (1970), 118–23.

Walters, R. H. "Delay of Reinforcement Gradients in Children's Learning," *Psychology Science*, I (1964), 307–10.

Walters, R. H., Parke, R. D., and Cane, V. A. "Timing of Punishment and the Observation of Consequences to Others as Determinants of Response Inhibition," *Journal of Experimental Psychology*, II (1965), 10–30.

Walters, R. H., and Willors, D. C. "Imitative Behavior of Disturbed and Nondisturbed Children Following Exposure to Aggressive and Nonaggressive Models," *Child Development*, XXXIX (1968), 79–89.

Ward, M., and Baker, B. "Reinforcement Therapy in the Classroom," *Journal of Applied Behavior Analysis*, I (1968), 343–48.

Wasik, B. H. "The Application of Premack's Generalization on Reinforcement to the Management of Classroom Behavior," *Journal of Experimental Child Psychology*, X (1970), 33–43.

Wasik, B. H., Senn, K., Welch, R., and Cooper, B. R. "Behavior Modification with Culturally Deprived School Children: Two Case Studies," *Journal of Applied Behavior Analysis*, II (1969), 181–94.

Watson, L. S. "Applications of Behavior-shaping Devices to Training Severely and Profoundly Mentally Retarded Children in an Institutional Setting," *Mental Retardation*, VI (1968), 21–33.

Weisberg, P., and Kennedy, D. B. "Maintenance of Children's Behavior by Accidental Schedule of Reinforcement," *Journal of Experimental Child Psychology*, VIII (1969), 222–33.

Werry, J. S., and Quay, H. C. "Observing the Classroom Behavior of Elementary School Children," *Exceptional Children*, XXXV (1969), 461–70.

Werry, J. S., and Wollersheim, J. P. "Behavior Therapy with Children: A Broad Overview," *Annual Progress in Child Psychiatry and Child Development*, eds. S. Chess, and A. Thomas, New York: Brunner-Mazel, 1968, 356–78.

Wetzel, R. J. "Behavior Modification Techniques and the Training of Teacher's Aides," *Psychology in the Schools*, VII (1970), 325–30.

———. "Use of Behavioral Techniques in a Case of Compulsive Stealing," *Journal of Consulting Psychology*, XXX (1966), 367–74.

Whelan, R. J., and Haring, N. G. "Modification and Maintenance of Behavior Through Systematic Application of Consequences," *Exceptional Children*, XXXII (1966), 281–89.

Whitlock, C., and Bushell, D. "Some Effects of 'Back-up' Reinforcers on Reading Behavior," *Journal of Experimental Child Psychology*, V (1967), 50–57.

Williams, C. D. "The Elimination of Tantrum Behavior by Extinction Procedures," *Journal of Abnormal and Social Psychology*, LIX (1959), 269.

Wilde, G. J. S. "Behavior Therapy for Addicted Cigarette Smokers: A Preliminary Investigation," *Behavior Research and Therapy*, II (1964), 107–9.

Witryol, S. L., Lowden, L. M., Fagan, J. F., and Bergen, T. C. "Verbal Versus Material Rewards as a Function of Schedule and Set in Children's Discrimination Preference Choice Behavior," *Journal of Genetic Psychology*, CXIII (1968), 3–25.

Wolf, M. M., Giles, D. K., and Hall, V. R. "Experiments with Token Reinforcement in a Remedial Classroom," *Behavior Research and Therapy*, VI (1968), 51–69.

Wolf, M. M., Risley, T., Johnston, M., Harris, F., and Allen, E. "Application of Operant Conditioning Procedures to the Behavior Problems of an Autistic Child: A Follow-up and Extension," *Behavior Research and Therapy*, V (1967), 103–11.

Wolf, M. M., Risley, T., and Mees, J. "Application of Operant Conditioning Procedures to the Behavior Problems of an Autistic Child." *Behavior Research and Therapy*, I (1964), 305–12.

Wolpe, J. "Psychotherapy: The Nonscientific Heritage and the New Science," *Behavior Research and Therapy*, I (1963), 23–28.

Woody, R. H. "Behavioral Techniques in Community Service: A Psychobehavioral Perspective," *Journal of School Psychology*, VIII (1970), 82–88.

———. "Behavior Therapy and School Psychology," *Journal of School Psychology*, IV (1966), 1–14.

————. "Forward a Rationale for Psychobehavioral Therapy," *Archives of General Psychiatry*, XIX (1968), 199–204.

————. "Psychobehavioral Therapy in the School: Implications for Counselor Education," *Counselor Education and Supervision*, VIII (1968), 253–58.

Zeilberger, J., Sampson, S. E., and Sloane, H. N., Jr., "Modification of a Child's Problem Behavior in the Home with the Mother as Therapist," *Journal of Applied Behavior Analysis*, I (1968), 47–53.

Zimmerman, E., and Zimmerman, J. "The Alteration of Behavior in a Special Classroom Situation," *Journal of Experimental Analysis of Behavior*, V (1962), 59–60.

Zimmerman, E., Zimmerman, J., and Russell, C. D. "Differential Effects of Token Reinforcement on Instruction-following Behavior in Retarded Students Instructed as a Group," *Journal of Applied Behavior Analysis*, II (1969), 101–12.

ADDENDUM

In both practice and research the authors are dedicated to the improvement of education at all levels and in all specialties. Thus, we share some of the same values expressed by teachers in many divergent programs throughout teaching and related professions. Most of the specific techniques and principles found in this book came from teachers—beginning teachers, special education teachers, elementary, secondary, vocational-technical, and college teachers; teachers for gifted, for emotionally disturbed, for physically handicapped, and for children with learning disabilities; art, music, speech and hearing, home economics, and physical education teachers; content area specialists, subject matter specialists, and resource specialists; preschool, child development, and nursery school teachers; social workers, counselors, and school psychologists; more especially *older teachers* whose long-term experiences have too long been ignored or repudiated by those very students who through scholarly denunciation attest to the effectiveness of their past learning.

In a continuing effort to learn of effective and ineffective practices in teaching, the authors sincerely encourage written responses from teachers. We would like information concerning techniques, materials, special projects, and any conceivable procedure used in teaching social and/or academic behaviors. Written responses will be used toward the goal of improving education through research, application, and continuous dissemination. Teachers who share this concern please send responses to:

Madsen & Madsen
Teaching/Discipline
Allyn and Bacon
470 Atlantic Avenue
Boston, Mass. 02210